REAL-TIME SOFTWARE TECHNIQUES

REAL-TIME SOFTWARE TECHNIQUES

Walter S. Heath

VNR VAN NOSTRAND REINHOLD
_____ New York

Library of Congress Catalog Number: 90-33145
ISBN 0-442-00305-6

Printed in the United States of America

Van Nostrand Reinhold
115 Fifth Avenue
New York, New York 10003

Van Nostrand Reinhold International Company Limited
11 New Fetter Lane
London EC4P 4EE, England

Van Nostrand Reinhold
102 Dodds Street
South Melbourne 3205, Victoria Australia

Nelson Canada
1120 Birchmount Road
Scarborough, Ontario M1K 5G4, Canada

16 15 14 13 12 11 10 9 8 7 6 5 4 3 2 1

Library of Congress Cataloging-in-Publication Data

Heath, Walter S., 1940–
    Real-time software techniques/Walter S. Heath.
        p.   cm.
    ISBN 0-442-00305-6
    1. Real-time data processing. 2. Computer software. I. Title.
QA76.54.H43 1991
005.1—dc20   90-33145
                                                 CIP

Contents

TRADEMARKS

Preface

It is interesting to reflect on the reasons why people build and use machines. Without a doubt, there is a continuing appetite for increasingly clever and capable electromechanical devices of all sorts. Although we accept the idea that machines bring benefits to society, many people nevertheless have a lingering ambivalent attitude toward them.

It is clear that machines are a primary source of change. When a new class of machines is accepted by a society, patterns of behavior are often altered in unpredictable ways. Thus political, legal, and financial institutions find that they must constantly redefine the rules of social interaction to accommodate an ever-changing technological environment. It is not surprising that the introduction of a new technology is not always universally applauded, since the attendant social disruption can be painful.

Some people object to the fact that technology seems to have a life of its own. That is, if a new technology is created and a need for it is perceived to exist, products based on it will inevitably be introduced. One could argue that the very existence of a viable market is sufficient indication by society that a product should be produced. But the product may serve the interests of only a small sector of that society and be detrimental to others. Some would encourage more social control over the introduction of new technology. Whether this is compatible with a healthy economy in a competitive and unregulated world is an appropriate subject for debate.

We use machines to aid and extend our physical, sensory, and mental capabilities and to perform the menial and dangerous tasks that affect our lives. Increasingly, these devices are controlled by computers.

Most of us are familiar with the various automatic devices available for use in the home. Although the market for personal home computers never really materialized, many home products now contain computers internally. These range from environmental and security control systems to entertainment and food preparation appliances.

In the office and factory, computers and computer-controlled machines have found many applications. Office computers relieve the burden of repetitive procedures and enhance communication, while machines containing computers are used in the factory to perform automatic manufacture of a variety of products—including other machines.

We use machines to explore regions outside our immediate environment. In some cases we are able to use them to actually transport modern-day explorers to these regions. In others we send unmanned sensors that operate automatically or under remote control. By the use of machines we are able to extend our presence several billion miles into space and to the deepest regions of the ocean.

The military has made a massive commitment to computer-controlled machinery. One example of this predilection is the modern fighter aircraft. This remarkable machine extends human sensory, mental, and physical capabilities in every imaginable dimension. In addition to providing the pilot with the means to fly faster and higher than any living organism, it also applies radar to extend his vision and radio to increase his range of communication. Other instruments assist him in determining his position and aid him in performing his primary mission—which is to deliver weapons on target. Clearly, the fighter aircraft is an example of the ultimate application of computer-controlled machinery to extend and multiply human capabilities.

It may be safely predicted that society's future endeavors will require increasingly sophisticated machines. Although few can predict with any degree of certainty the nature of the machines that will be needed, it seems clear that they will be even more highly automated. Since these machines will be complex, we will need to ensure a continuing supply of qualified people to design and build them.

When computer technology was first applied in machine control applications, most designers were drawn from the ranks of Electrical Engineering. But as a larger share of system functions were moved into the computer and as educational institutions established Computer Science departments, more graduates entered the field with formal training in computer technology. Although each of these disciplines addressed some of the skills needed to design automatic machines, neither prepared the student to cope with the unique hardware and software requirements that characterize this class of systems. It was still necessary for entrants to learn the additional skills either by self-study and experimentation or through apprenticeship to an in-house expert.

At present, although the market for people equipped with the skills to design automated machinery is substantial and growing, it is still unusual to find an academic institution that offers a program designed to fill this need. Employers wishing to market computer-controlled devices must be prepared to offer supplemental training through formal or informal means. But it is difficult to collect and coordinate appropriate instructional material for this purpose.

This book is an attempt to present, in a readable form, some of the specialized knowledge needed by professionals engaged in the design of computer-controlled machinery. Although the book emphasizes software techniques, many aspects of hardware design are also discussed in relation to the software. The book will be useful to people who are currently involved in the design of these systems and find that they need additional background information and to those who wish to prepare themselves or others to enter the field.

Although the concepts discussed may be applied in a variety of hardware contexts, they are presented in this book using specific examples appropriate for the Motorola 680X0 family of microprocessors. The reader should therefore be familiar with the architecture and assembly language for this group of processors. It is also necessary to be reasonably fluent in the C compiler language. Later chapters present advanced concepts using VMEbus computer systems for illustration. Previous exposure to the VMEbus technology would be useful but is not strictly necessary since sufficient background material on this topic is included for purposes of the presentation. Beyond these specific prerequisites the reader should have a general knowledge of the various aspects of computer technology—and a keen interest in knowing how automatic machines are controlled by computers.

PREVIEW OF CHAPTERS

In the following chapters I shall present the design for an executive that satisfies the system software requirements of many real-time programs. This design is offered as an example of a functional executive that incorporates the basic components needed to support real-time, multitask application programs. The executive is complete and may be used as presented. Alternatively, you may wish to "embellish" it with additional features, or you may decide to simply use the concepts that are discussed in a completely different design of your own. In any case, the executive will be used in this book to focus our attention on the important issues and concepts that must be addressed during the course of a real-time system design. It will provide a common basis for relating these subjects and for understanding how the various components of a system work together to achieve the ultimate objective.

To aid the discussion, I shall describe the executive at several conceptual levels. In Chapter 2, the design philosophy that forms the basis for the executive design will be reviewed and then the executive will be examined at the highest functional level, using block diagrams to show component parts and the flow of processor control among them.

Chapters 3 and 4 are dedicated to the detailed analysis of executive components. Since the executive is naturally divided into two distinct sections—task scheduling and data communication—a chapter is devoted to each. In each chapter complete program listings for executive functions are presented and examined. Where necessary, reasons are given for the design choices that were made.

Chapter 5 presents the first of three example application programs. The chapter contains a description of a program that demonstrates basic task scheduling and intertask data communication. The listings for all program application functions are presented and reviewed. These functions may be linked to the functions described in Chapters 3 and 4 to form a complete, working demonstration program. At the end of the chapter, program performance is analyzed by examining logic analyzer plots of program timing. The executive's basic task-to-task switch time measurement results are also given and discussed. Application functions presented in this chapter furnish concrete examples of the types of functions an application writer would need to construct to use the executive in an actual system design.

Hardware interface concepts are discussed in Chapter 6. This chapter reviews the general nature of device interfaces and introduces the concept of the interrupt. The hardware operations that are performed by one processor group in response to an interrupt are examined in detail. With this background in place, we are then in a position to examine and justify the software procedures that are necessary to properly support an interrupt. Since interrupts play such an important role in real-time systems, it was felt that a thorough examination of the subject was justified. The chapter concludes with a review of the various ways real-time systems use the interrupt mechanism to accomplish design objectives.

Chapter 7 contains a description of a second example application program. This example extends the program presented in Chapter 5 by adding a timer task and an interrupt handler. It assumes that a programmable source of timer interrupts is available. Listings for all new functions are presented and discussed. Logic analyzer plots from test runs show program performance. The program gives a specific example of I/O device initialization and interrupt support within the context of a multitask, real-time program.

The executive presented in the first seven chapters is complete and supplies all system software needed for a large class of application programs. But in some systems an additional feature is needed. Chapter 8 introduces the concept of preemptive scheduling. This advanced option extends the capability—and complexity—of the executive. Since this topic has several aspects, a separate chapter is devoted to it. The chapter reviews design requirements, implementation strategy, and several operational considerations, including multiple level preemption and protection of critical regions of code. Program listings showing executive changes that are needed to support preemptive scheduling are included and examined.

Two additional example application programs are presented in Chapter 9. The first extends the program described in Chapter 7 to include preemptive scheduling of the timer task by the timer interrupt handler. Again, the listings for all of the additional application functions required to support preemptive scheduling are presented and discussed. Logic analyzer measurement results from test runs are also shown. A fourth test program that implements multiple level preemptive scheduling is also examined.

In some designs the data processing and sensor servicing demands are so severe that a single-processor computer system is simply not adequate, no matter how efficient its system software is. In these situations, it is reasonable to consider a multiple processor design. With the advent of nonproprietary buses, it has become relatively easy to configure a multiprocessor system that is custom-tailored to the needs of an application. The advantages of concurrent processing may then be realized by distributing application tasks among the processors. This reduces the computational demands imposed on any single processor and multiplies overall system throughput. To support these systems, it is convenient to establish a standard method for interprocessor communication.

In Chapter 10 we address the subject of multiprocessor systems and present a set of queue access functions that may be used to pass buffer pointers between application programs running in separate processors. Since the processors run asynchronously, it is necessary for the functions to use a semaphore to guarantee exclusive access to a queue by a processor. Queues are especially appropriate for handling data communication between multiple processors since they provide natural time-ordered buffering of data. The material is presented within the hardware context of the VMEbus. This popular, nonproprietary bus architecture is viewed from a software writer's perspective and at the functional level.

Much of a software writer's time is devoted to testing, modifying, and retesting application programs. For real-time systems, software is typically developed on a general-purpose computer and then transported to a dedicated computer system that is embedded in the equipment to be controlled. As a result, the software development process involves repeated cycles of (1) software modification on the general-purpose computer, (2) transportation of the modified program to the target embedded system, and (3) testing of the new version in the operational environment of the target system. Since this cycle recurs so often, it is important that the equipment and software provided to support it is as efficient as possible.

Chapter 11 addresses the subject of real-time software development. Special attention is given to the commonly used S-record method for transporting programs from the software development computer to the target-embedded system. Methods for either manually or automatically starting programs are also reviewed. These techniques are developed for both single and multiple processor systems. Loading and starting procedures provide the missing link for programs that are written on a general-purpose computer produced by one manufacturer but are run on target real-time processors provided by another.

After the extensive review of real-time software techniques that is presented in the first 11 chapters, we are prepared in Chapter 12 to draw some meaningful conclusions concerning the characteristics of system hardware that will best support software design requirements. The nature of real-time systems is such that, as a practical matter, it is often not possible to specify the hardware components of a system before the computational requirements of certain parts of the program are known. This is a "chicken-and-egg" problem since some form of hardware system must initially be available to gather the necessary program performance data. To resolve this dilemma, it is important that the hardware chosen at the outset be amenable to change. It may then be reconfigured as processing requirements become better known.

In Chapter 12 we explore various system hardware characteristics that have been found to be especially useful in the design, testing, and operation of real-time systems. Again, these characteristics are discussed within the context of the VMEbus technology.

ACKNOWLEDGMENTS

It is a pleasure to acknowledge the assistance of several people who have given generously of their time and expertise during the preparation of this book. Many helpful suggestions were forthcoming from Tim Bowler, my associate for several years in the design of real-time systems. Seemingly endless editing was also endured by my wife, Marie. In addition to her constructive criticism of the text, Marie also wrote the floppy disk interface software described in Chapter 12. I am also much indebted to the reviewer provided by the publisher for his enlightened analysis of the text and the many helpful suggestions that ensued. The process of preparing actual copy for the book was made more bearable by the generous and good-natured support of the members of the staff at Van Nostrand Reinhold, Inc.

REAL-TIME SOFTWARE TECHNIQUES

1

Getting Started

The category of computer systems that we shall be discussing in this book is often identified by the term "real-time." Perhaps a good way to get this discussion started would be for me to present my definition of this term. Offhand, it would seem that it refers to a type or class of time measurement. But when the term is used to identify a class of computer systems, it takes on additional meaning.

People write simulation programs to model the operation of real physical systems. These programs usually run at speeds either faster or slower than the system being modeled. The programs are said to operate in "simulated time" or "simulated real time." For example, CAD/CAM systems, used to design integrated circuits, often include a program that allows the designer to test the operation of a circuit through simulation. These tests usually run at speeds well below the operational rate of the final circuit. By contrast, meteorologists use computer simulation programs to predict future weather conditions. Obviously, for such systems to be useful, they must run at speeds faster than real time.

In this book we shall be discussing computer systems that operate in concert with real physical systems and are, in fact, an integral part of such equipment. These so-called "embedded" systems monitor equipment performance and control its operation. Since they proceed "in step" with the equipment, they are said to be operating in real time.

It is interesting to note that, historically, real-time systems were being used long before computers were available. A classic example is the fly-ball governor control system used on stationary steam engines in the last century to control the speed of the engine under varying load conditions. This mechanical device sensed changes in the engine's rotational velocity and adjusted the main steam valve to maintain a constant operating speed. This is an example of a feedback control system, a class of applications for real-time systems that is still very important today.

In the 1960s, I participated in the design of some of the first computer implementations of Loran and Omega radio navigation systems. These systems replaced earlier designs that used analog electronic phaselock loop circuits to track the phases of received radio signals. In the computer implementations, the phaselock loop algorithm was implemented in software. In fact, it was possible to implement adaptive (Kalman) filtering algorithms, which improved performance considerably. By that time, computer technology had advanced to the point where specially designed computers were sufficiently small, light, and fast to be adopted as replacements for electronic analog circuits in low data rate systems. As technology has advanced over the intervening years, computers have been incorporated into increasingly higher performance real-time systems.

Today, real-time systems have become ubiquitous in equipment ranging from automobile electronic control systems to deep space probes. Modern commercial airplanes incorporate "fly-by-wire" control systems that use computers to control the hydraulic systems that power the flaps and, thus, replace direct mechanical or hydraulic control systems in previous designs. They also use inertial navigation systems and automatic flight recorders, both of which incorporate real-time technology. Since these systems operate in a "life-threatening" environment, they must operate reliably and accurately. To ensure continuous operation, substantial redundancy is built in.

Industrial applications of real-time techniques are also extensive. Automatic manufacturing systems are a natural application for real-time control and monitoring. Robots use feedback control algorithms to implement dexterity and to automate sequential operations.

It is clear that, as computer technology advances, increasingly sophisticated applications for real-time techniques will be found. As a consequence, it will be important for us to become familiar with the characteristics of these systems and to devise efficient and reliable strategies for designing them. Perhaps a good first step in this process is to examine the operational environment for such systems.

1.1 THE REAL-TIME SYSTEM OPERATIONAL ENVIRONMENT

The term "real-time" is used to describe systems with substantially different performance characteristics. A dominant characteristic that seems to be common to virtually all systems in this class is that the system being described must respond to an external stimulus within some "short" time interval. How short this interval must be depends on the nature of the problem being solved and the characteristics of the equipment being used. At one end of the spectrum are systems that respond at a rate commensurate with human reaction time, which is on the order of a fraction of a second. At the high performance end, systems are now being built with response times well below 1 microsecond. Clearly, a term that is used to classify a group of systems with over six orders of magnitude variation in their performance characteristics is not too precise! But these systems do have certain qualitative properties in common.

Typically, real-time systems must be capable of responding to several external sensors at essentially the same time. The inherently parallel nature of this requirement poses an especially difficult problem for a conventional single instruction stream computer system, which is intrinsically serial in its operation. Evidently some form of serial-to-parallel transformation is called for if a single processor is to be used. The alternative is to use several processors in parallel. We will consider both approaches in this book.

Since input and output (I/O) devices are monitoring and controlling ongoing physical processes in external equipment, the computer system must not be delayed too long in servicing sensor requests or it will fall behind the physical process being monitored. Control parameters fed back to the equipment will then be incorrect for the current state of the process. This requirement points to the need for response time predictability. A real-time computer system must be able to guarantee that it can respond to an external stimulus within a specified maximum time interval. The nature of the equipment environment is such that it is usually not sufficient to guarantee this upper limit on the basis of probabilities. Even a single violation of the limit can often cause catastrophic failure of the system. This is one reason why response time is so important in real-time systems.

If a real-time system must service several external sensors, it must contain several I/O ports. Different sensors present widely varying interface characteristics to the computer and operate asynchronously. In addition, some sensors are more important to system performance than others and may require more of the computer's processing resources. As a result, the computer must order its data processing activities on a priority basis.

When a sensor requires service, it must be possible for the device to interrupt the computer's current processing activity and temporarily transfer control to a separate module of code, called an interrupt handler, that can satisfy the immediate processing needs of the sensor. Depending on system requirements this module may also post a request for additional processing to be performed at a later time and at a lower priority.

High performance real-time systems must often be designed to cope with very demanding data collection and transport rates and large volumes of received data. As a result, it is important for these systems to utilize very efficient techniques for transferring data and data access rights between processing modules. Data should be physically moved as little as possible within the computer. Instead, a mechanism should be implemented that transfers access rights to data that remains stationary in memory. In an ideal design, data should move only twice: once when it enters the system through one port and once when it leaves through another. When data must be moved, high speed transfer techniques (e.g., direct memory access, DMA) may be needed.

Some real-time systems perform little or no data processing operations. Instead, they simply collect and buffer data into large blocks for transport to a mini- or mainframe computer or to a data storage device. Processing is then performed by the larger computer either as the data is received (online) or later, by reading the data from the storage device (offline). In this role, the real-time system serves as a versatile front end processor that is easier to interface to I/O devices and is capable of supporting short system response times and high data collection rates. Data processing is left to the larger back-end computer that can perform analysis at a faster rate.

If the real-time system performs data processing in addition to data collection, it will frequently be required to perform high speed floating point operations. In this case data must often be transferred to and from a floating point coprocessor chip or a separate array processor. This places additional data transport demands on the system.

When real-time computer systems are embedded within larger electrical/mechanical systems, they must often start automatically and run reliably without supervision. Thus, it is important that they be designed to cope with unusual operational events. Specific procedures must be implemented to facilitate automatic recovery after a sensor malfunction or system power failure.

Finally, some real-time systems must provide an operator interface for program initiation and system performance monitoring. This access port often takes the form of a serial line to a computer terminal. Since terminal data rates are likely to be very slow relative to other sensor I/O, these operations are ordinarily performed at low processor priority (or by a separate processor).

In this short introduction we have discussed some of the principle characteristics of real-time systems. We have seen that they include:

- Short sensor response times
- Multiple, asynchronous I/O operations
- Essentially parallel sensor support
- Sensor response time predictability
- Widely varying sensor characteristics
- Sensor servicing priority
- Immediate processor attention (interrupt support)
- High data collection and transport rates
- Large data volumes
- Support for data processing (floating point)
- Automatic recovery from equipment malfunctions
- Operator interface

These requirements obviously put severe demands on the computer system. Indeed, the environment would seem, at least at first glance, to be nothing less than chaotic, with the processor constantly being "yanked" out of one processing operation to start another. What is needed is a formal program architecture that can deal with the demands of the real-time environment and bring order to this potential chaos. This architecture is implemented physically as a layer of software between the application program and the computer hardware. It is typically referred to as the executive or operating system or, more generally, as system software.

1.2 THE ROLE OF SYSTEM SOFTWARE

In general, system software presents the computational resources of the computer to a user or an application program in a form that is useful and convenient for the types of problems the computer system is designed to solve. For example, the system software for a computer designed to provide time-shared access to many users will emphasize short terminal response time at the expense of computational throughput. On the other hand, a machine designed to run large batch programs will use system software that makes the terminal user wait.

Most of us are familiar with the characteristics of one or more operating systems for general-purpose data processing computers. This system software presents the user with an interface to the computer that is relatively easy to use. It provides services that may be accessed either by entering commands at a terminal or by calling service routines from a program. The interface frees the user from having to deal with the operational details and inner workings of the computer and allows him or her to concentrate on using the computer as a tool to solve some unrelated problem. Such environments are said to be "user friendly," although many would dispute this characterization.

Operating systems have played an important role in making the computational resources of computers available to a large group of users who do not necessarily happen to be experts in computer technology. But a significant price is paid, in terms of computational efficiency and throughput, to support these services. It is worthwhile to compare the operational environment of a data processing computer running an operating system with the environment of a real-time system running an executive, as described in the previous section, and to note the differences.

Multiuser, multiprocessing operating systems usually present a virtual address space to application programs. So far as the application is concerned, its addresses start at zero and can extend to values well above the amount of physical memory present in the computer. The operating system allocates pages of physical memory to each user process and translates each program address from its virtual address space to the appropriate physical page address. If a program generates an address for a page that is not in memory, the operating system swaps the page in from disk. For such systems it is evident that a substantial number of logical operations must be carried out for each memory access. By contrast, real-time systems generally run directly in physical memory and consequently do not require these additional address translation steps.

There are other reasons why operating systems use virtual addressing for user processes. One good reason is that it provides a mechanism for protecting user programs from interfering with the operating system and each other. As addresses are translated, they may also be checked to make sure that they reference memory pages allocated to the program. It is important that operating systems do this, since user programs generally are not aware of the presence of other programs in the computer and the allocation of resources to them. Real-time systems, by contrast, are usually designed to support only one application program. The various components of this program are designed to cooperate with each other and to share system resources based on priority. As a result, it is generally not necessary to burden the program with protection mechanisms.

Another important difference between operating systems and real-time executives is in the way they allocate processor time to application programs. An operating system will typically allocate slices of processing time to application processes using some sort of priority/round-robin scheduling algorithm. Each time the allocated time for a process expires (or the process is suspended for some other reason, usually I/O), the entire context (hardware environment, registers, etc.) of the running process must be saved. When the next process to run has been selected, its context must be loaded into the computer before it can proceed. This continual switching of contexts uses computer resources that might otherwise be used to run useful application code.

The way in which scheduling is performed in a computer system has a direct impact on its ability to guarantee sensor response times. In an operating system environment, scheduling decisions are not generally under the direct control of the application software. Instead, they are based on time slice allocation strategies, *a priori* fairness rules, and process-initiated suspension due to I/O device latency. Although the user ordinarily has some control over initial process priority, the scheduling decisions made by the operating system bear little relationship to the specific scheduling needs of the application program. In this environment it is virtually impossible to guarantee sensor response times.

By contrast, a real-time executive is typically designed to give the application program substantial control over scheduling decisions. Here the program module that is scheduled is normally called a task, rather than a process. In most designs a task may run until the task, itself, chooses to suspend. The executive may also be designed so that a high priority task may run immediately when an external device requires service. To accomplish this, it will temporarily suspend any lower priority task the processor might be executing and then allow that task to resume when the high priority task has finished. In this environment, an application task may also disable interrupts below a specific level and thus remove interference from less essential devices during critical processing periods. It is also possible for an application program to change task priorities and add or delete tasks from the list that may be run by the scheduler at any given time. This flexibility is essential if sensor response times are to be guaranteed.

As a result of the fact that many scheduling decisions are made directly by the application program, the task scheduling algorithm for an executive can be much simpler in design and will therefore operate faster than its counterpart in an operating system. This contributes to the system's ability to guarantee sensor response times.

Another difference between operating systems and real-time executives is in the way they handle data I/O. A user application program running under an operating system typically makes a system call to "open" an I/O device and then follows with a call to read from or write to the device. When the program is finished with the device, it makes a system call to "close" it. The operating system processes these system calls by running system level functions that are specially designed to control and access the I/O device. This set of functions is collectively called a driver.

A driver must typically be able to support all of the capabilities of the I/O device so that user programs may operate the device in any of its modes. In addition, either the driver or the operating system must control access to the device by several user programs so that requests are handled sequentially or, at least, without mutual interference. If the I/O device is not capable of responding immediately to the request (due, for example, to the need for mechanical motion of the device), the driver will cause the application program to be suspended so that the computer can do other useful work. When the device is again ready, it will typically cause an interrupt. The driver must then provide interrupt processing support to reschedule the application process to run again. Clearly, a typical device driver is a complex collection of functions!

On the other hand, in a real-time system, I/O is typically handled directly by the application program. No call to the executive is made. Since application software accesses the device's control, status, and data registers directly, the processing overhead associated with system calls to driver functions is eliminated. To be sure, I/O operations similar to those performed by a driver must be implemented. But this code can be much more streamlined and efficient, since these operations can be tailored to the specific needs of the application and can use only the device operating modes required. In addition, since the application writer has direct access to the device interface, it is usually possible to write the program such that device response time may be guaranteed. It was pointed out earlier that this is often difficult, if not impossible, when designing applications to run in an operating system environment. A real-time computer system is therefore able to optimize sensor I/O response time—a primary requisite for real-time applications.

Operating systems typically provide services for passing data between application processes. The mechanism is typically called a mailbox or pipe and is ordinarily implemented by opening a file or common memory region which is accessible, through system calls, by both processes. Data may then be transported from one process to the other. These interprocess communication services are not usually designed to be used in time-critical applications and are therefore often slow.

If a real-time system must be designed to collect and transport large quantities of data at fast rates, intertask communication must be highly optimized. It is especially important to avoid moving data unnecessarily. As we will see in Chapter 4, it is possible to use queues to move data and pointers to data very efficiently. Moving a pointer to a buffer containing data avoids the necessity of moving the data, itself. This saves processor cycles for more useful work.

An operating system often furnishes a host of administrative services designed to account for and to equitably distribute computer resources among several users. These generally fall into the catagories of permissions, quotas, and accounting services. In a real-time system these services are not needed, since application tasks are designed to run cooperatively and at fixed priorities. A resource allocation strategy is chosen early in the design and is built into the program.

Finally, many operating systems are designed to access the system disk on a periodic basis to perform various "housekeeping" tasks. These might include flushing process pages to the disk and updating user accounting information. Since a disk access requires tens of milliseconds, this behavior is unacceptable for high speed real-time systems that must be able to guarantee sensor response times on the order of microseconds.

It is sometimes possible to configure an operating system for real-time operation. This usually includes limiting or eliminating disk operations. For example, the accounting function can be disabled and processes can be locked into memory, so that pages will not be swapped to disk. If this is possible, the system may be able to support applications with modest real-time performance requirements. Other limitations, such as I/O response time and interprocess communication rate, will then become the principle system performance impediments.

Although it is tempting to attempt to build a real-time application program within the seemingly secure and user-friendly environment of an operating system, one must consider the appropriateness and limitations of this environment in relation to the requirements of the application. It is especially important to determine the system's ability to support I/O timing and data throughput requirements at an early stage in the design process. You should also consider carefully the difficulties involved in attempting to debug a real-time program in this environment—especially the I/O interfaces.

In summary, it is evident that the design requirements for an operating system and a real-time executive are significantly different. An operating system must create a protected, user-friendly environment for users who are not necessarily interested in the internal operation of the machine and do not need exceptionally fast service from external sensors. A real-time executive must, by contrast, present an environment that can allocate processor resources to time-critical application programs such that sensor I/O timing requirements may be met. It must also support data collection, transport, and processing operations at sufficiently fast rates. Since the characteristics of the executive have a large impact on the structure and ultimate performance of a real-time application program, it is important that the executive's design blends harmoniously with the needs of the application.

2

The Executive, an Overview

It will be important to have a functional overview of the basic structure and operation of the executive before launching into a study of its individual components. It will then be possible to see the executive as an integrated functional unit consisting of several mutually supporting subunits rather than as a collection of vaguely related parts. This will be helpful when we study executive program listings in the next two chapters.

A good design is one that emphasizes important design objectives and resolves any conflicts between objectives in some optimal fashion. This chapter will begin with a discussion of the design objectives that were considered to be important for a real-time executive. It will also consider design conflicts and present reasons for choosing one approach rather than another. The chapter will then present a high level view of the structure of the executive and introduce its component parts. Executive operation will be discussed at a functional level, emphasizing, in general terms, the purpose of components and the flow of computer control among them. The executive divides naturally into task scheduling and data communication functional areas, so these two areas will be discussed in separate sections. A concluding section will review software development and program structure topics—in preparation for Chapter 3.

2.1 EXECUTIVE DESIGN GOALS

The discussion in the previous chapter indicated that a primary objective for the design of a real-time executive must be to optimize the speed and efficiency of its operation. Clearly, a computer cycle that is wasted by the executive is a double loss to the application, since both a cycle of real time and a cycle of computation are lost. As a consequence, it is important to keep the executive functions small and fast.

If speed and efficiency of operation were the only considerations, the executive should be written completely in assembly language. But it is also very important for the design to be easily understood by the people writing application programs, since application functions must necessarily be tightly coupled to it to get optimum performance. The executive is therefore written in the C language, where possible, and in assembly language only where necessary. Test data presented later will demonstrate that writing the executive in C results in a real-time program environment with very satisfactory performance. Consequently, little price is paid for using a high level language.

Since the executive is small and relatively simple, it is possible for the application software writer to understand its operation in detail and therefore to have a complete conceptual understanding of every component of an entire real-time program, including system software and application functions. This overview is especially important when attempting to debug a system. Often it is necessary to conduct a "thought experiment" in which an operational scenario is postulated that conforms to the observable symptoms and explains errant operation. Having a complete understanding of the executive's operation aids this process considerably.

To get highest performance, it is desirable to be able to couple application functions as tightly as possible to executive services. The most efficient way to do this is to simply link executive functions directly to application functions to form a single runable program module. In an operating system environment this level of coupling is not possible, since system and user functions must be protected from each other. But in a real-time environment all program components are designed to work together. By directly linking executive and application functions, the substantial overhead associated with making system calls to an operating system may be avoided.

The executive to be described consists of a set of functions that may be linked to application functions. With this arrangement the only overhead associated with a system call is the code required to make a standard function call. If desired, executive files may be placed in a development system library so that they may be linked to several application programs.

Most computer hardware makes provision for operation in at least two modes, usually called supervisor mode and user mode. Typically, the operating system runs in supervisor mode and user processes run in user mode. In supervisor mode all capabilities of the hardware are available to the program. User mode prohibits a user process from performing certain operations that could compromise the integrity of the operating system or interfere with the operation of other user processes. In a real-time environment it may usually be assumed that application functions will be designed such that they do not interfere with each other or with the executive. If interference does occur, it will be discovered during system testing. It is therefore unnecessary to execute executive and application functions in different hardware modes.

The executive to be described runs in supervisor mode and also runs application tasks in that mode. As with other design choices, this approach reduces complexity and increases performance, since it eliminates the need to switch modes at each executive/application transition.

Often system software will include utilities to interface to standard I/O devices, such as disks, tapes, printers, and consoles. This executive makes no such provisions. Experience has shown that to get maximum performance, an interface to an I/O device must be custom-tailored to application requirements. A general-purpose interface will often contain code that is unnecessary or inefficient for a particular application. In addition, the need to perform I/O operations occurs naturally within the flow of application functions and should therefore be performed immediately by those functions rather than by means of a detour through the system software. Coupled with this is the fact that so many different I/O devices exist that it would be impractical to consider supplying interfaces to even a small subset of them. Consequently, for the executive to be described here, it is assumed that all I/O interfaces will be part of application code. However, we will discuss the interaction between device interface code and the executive.

Finally, a design objective that usually applies to application software as well as system software in real-time systems has to do with the tradeoff between memory usage and execution time. Often a function may be programmed to optimize one or the other. If a real-time program is concerned mostly with data collection and transport, rather than data processing, program size is likely to be relatively small. If the target processor has memory to spare, it might as well be used. Since real-time systems are often concerned with minimizing execution time, it is usually wise to choose to spend memory to gain speed. The executive design presented here is based on this choice, in most cases, but the impact on executive program size is small. In the area of intertask data communications, the executive gives the user a choice between two sets of queueing functions—one set emphasizes execution speed, the other preserves memory.

To summarize, the goals chosen for this executive design are to:

- Optimize speed and efficiency of operation—but not at the expense of design comprehension.
- Keep executive functions small and fast.
- Couple executive services tightly to application functions.
- Run both executive and application functions in supervisor mode.
- Choose to spend memory to gain speed.

With these goals in mind we are now prepared to begin a discussion of the executive's operation.

2.2 TASK SCHEDULING

We shall begin our study of executive operation by considering its support for application task scheduling. Figure 2.1 is a block diagram of scheduler functions and required data structures, and their relationship to application tasks and interrupt handlers. Executive functions consist of **sched(), run(), sleep(),** and **wake()**. The three important data structures are the task control blocks (TCBs), the executive stack, and the application task stacks. Data flow is indicated by dashed lines; program flow by solid lines. We will start this discussion by becoming familiar with the operational role that each of these program components plays, and the flow of program control and data between them. It will then be

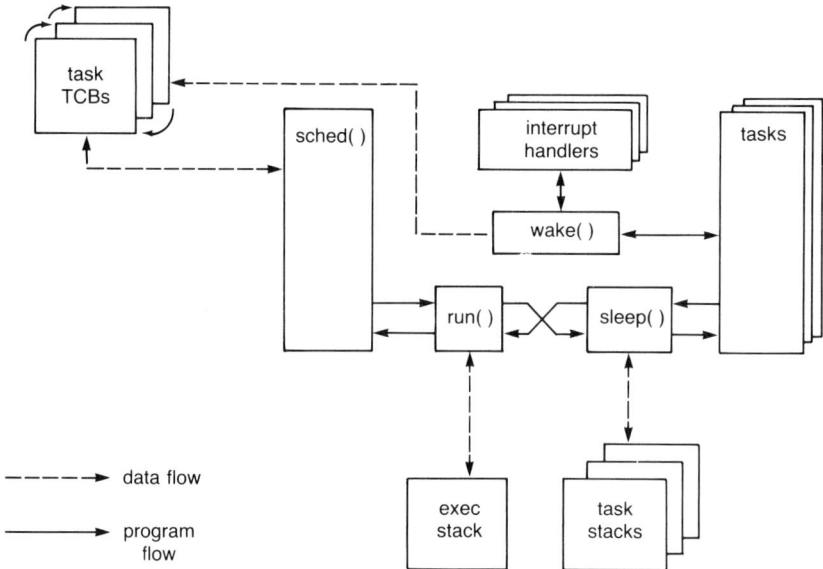

Figure 2.1. Executive Task Scheduling.

appropriate to consider some specific design concepts in greater detail. These will be covered in three subsections.

A task control block (TCB) must be defined for each application task. It is used by the scheduler to determine which task to run next and contains data needed to transfer control to that task. A TCB contains five items, as shown in Figure 2.2: a forward link pointer to the next TCB, a pointer to the start of the task, storage for the task's stack pointer, and two flags used to indicate whether the task has been awakened, that is, scheduled to run.

TCBs are linked in a linked list in task priority order. The last TCB is linked to the first to form a closed loop. When scheduler function **sched()** runs, it scans TCBs starting with the TCB for the highest priority task (at the beginning of the list) and looks for a task that has been awakened. It then runs that task. Note that it scans TCBs in descending task priority order, so that the first task it finds to run is the currently highest priority, awakened task. If no task has been awakened, it will simply follow the linked list, loop back to the start of the list and continue scanning TCBs. This is the normal "idle" mode of the program. It is entered when the real-time system does not need any computer processing support. Eventually, an interrupt will occur and the associated interrupt handler will call function **wake()** to schedule another task to run.

Function **wake()** is very simple. Its single argument is the task identification number (actually the index of the task's TCB in the TCB data structure). It simply increments the status flag in the task's TCB and returns. This function may be called from an interrupt handler or a task. In either case it signals the executive to run the indicated task—when that task is the currently highest priority, awakened task.

Referring again to Figure 2.1, when **sched()** finds a task to run it calls function **run()**. This function is written in assembly language. One reason for this is that it does not return

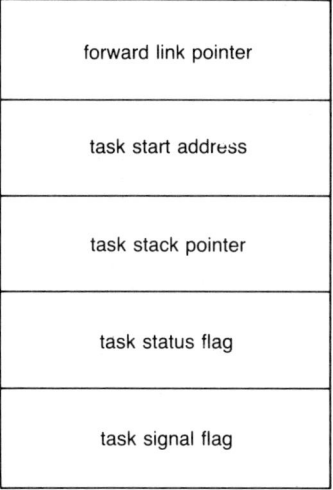

Figure 2.2. Task Control Block (TCB) Structure.

directly to the point in **sched()** from which it was called (C functions must return to their calling points). Instead, it transfers control to a location in **sleep()**. As Figure 2.1 indicates, at some later time, when **sleep()** is called from a task, it will transfer control to **run()** and **run()** will then return to the point in **sched()** from which it was originally called.

An application task consists of an infinite loop with at least one call to **sleep()** within the loop. When control is transferred from **sleep()** to a task, the task proceeds to perform application-specific operations until **sleep()** is again called. Function **sleep()** then transfers control to **run()** and **run()** returns to **sched()**. Since **sched()** is also an infinite loop, it again scans TCBs and eventually selects another task to run.

2.2.1 Executive and Task Stacks

Separate stacks are declared for the executive and for each application task. When the processor runs executive code, it uses the executive's stack; when it runs a task, that task's stack is used.

Figure 2.3 shows a simplified view of the executive that emphasizes stack operations. As indicated earlier, when **sched()** has found a task to run it calls **run()**. Among other operations this function saves the executive's stack pointer (SP) and transfers control to a point in **sleep()**. This function gets the selected task's stack pointer from its TCB and loads it into the processor's SP register before transferring control to the task. The task then proceeds to perform application-specific operations and eventually calls **sleep()** to suspend. Function **sleep()** then saves the task's stack pointer in its TCB and transfers control to a point in **run()**. The **run()** function retrieves the executive's stack pointer value (saved earlier) and places it in the processor's SP register. It then returns control to the scheduler.

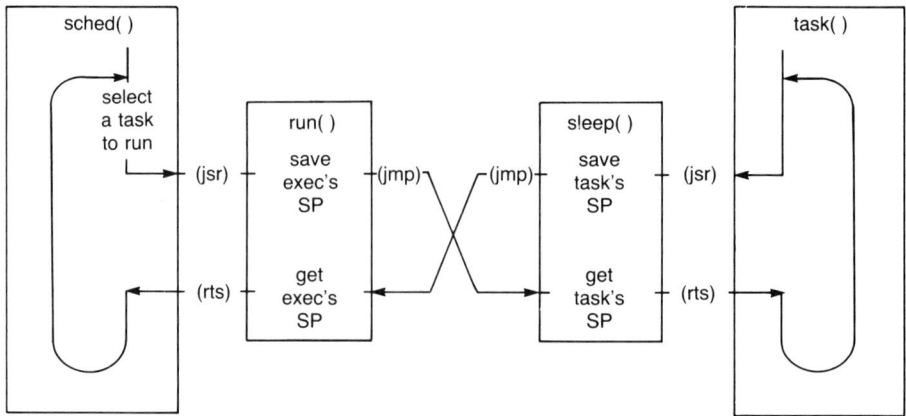

Figure 2.3. Executive Control Transfer Stack Operations.

As a result of these operations, each time the executive or a task is entered, it is operating with the same stack pointer it had when it relinquished control earlier. The reason for using separate stacks will become clear as executive operations are examined in greater detail in the following sections.

2.2.2 Executive Transfer of Control

One reason for using separate stacks for executive operations and tasks is to facilitate the transfer of control between them. Figure 2.3 also illustrates that when function **sched()** calls **run()** and when an application task calls **sleep(),** the compiler uses the "jump-to-subroutine" (**jsr**) assembly language instruction. This instruction first pushes the contents of the processor's program counter onto the currently active stack and then transfers control to the starting address of the called function. The address that is pushed onto the stack in this operation is the location of the next instruction after the subroutine call in the calling function. Thus, the address that the subroutine should return to is preserved on the calling function's stack.

When the subroutine eventually does return, it uses an assembly language "return-from-subroutine" (**rts**) instruction. This instruction pops the return address from the currently active stack and places it in the processor's program counter. By using separate stacks for the executive and each application task, the return addresses for these functions are preserved and are available when control must be transferred back to them either from **run(),** in the case of **sched(),** or from **sleep(),** in the case of a task.

Clearly, to be assured that a proper return address is available for **run()** or **sleep(),** it is necessary that a subroutine call operation precede a subroutine return. This is obviously the case when a normal subroutine is called in a program. But the situation is somewhat different for functions **run()** and **sleep(),** since these subroutines have two entry and two exit points.

Referring again to Figure 2.3, when **sched()** selects a task to run, it calls **run()** to transfer control to it. Function **run()** then transfers to **sleep()**, using a "jump" (**jmp**) instruction, and **sleep()** uses a "return-from-subroutine" (**rts**) instruction to transfer control to the selected task. In this sequence it would appear that **sleep()** returns to its calling function before it is called! Obviously, a proper return address must be available on the task's stack for this operation to be successful. In other words, a call to **sleep()** from the task must precede the return to the task from **sleep().** Moreover, the **sleep()** call must be performed such that the return address is left on the task's stack. That is, it must not be removed by a subsequent "return-from-subroutine" (**rts**) instruction. These requirements define a set of operations that must be performed to initialize each task before it can be scheduled and run within the operational real-time environment.

Figure 2.4 shows the operations that are performed at program startup to initialize each application task. The primary objective of these operations is to place a return address for function **sleep()** on each task's stack. These addresses may then be used to transfer control to the tasks. A secondary objective is to initialize each task's application code.

Executive startup code gets the task's stack pointer from its TCB and places it in the processor's stack pointer register. It then gets the task's starting address (again, from the

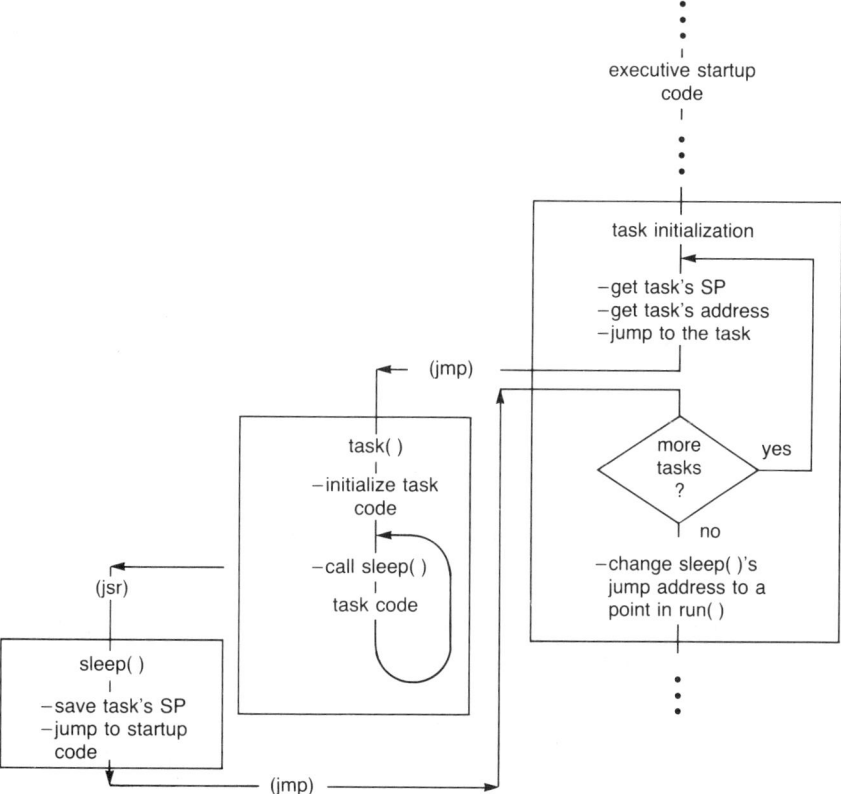

Figure 2.4. Task Initialization.

task's TCB) and jumps to the task. As shown in the figure, a task consists of an infinite loop containing at least one call to **sleep()**. A task may also contain some code outside the loop that initializes task application parameters. These operations are performed only once—during task initialization.

The task call to **sleep()** is performed by a compiler-generated "jump-to-subroutine" (**jsr**) instruction. As indicated earlier, this assembly language instruction pushes the address of the next instruction after the call onto the task's stack. This is the address that is needed to transfer control back to the task under normal program operation.

The **sleep()** function completes task initialization by saving the task's updated stack pointer in its TCB. What remains for **sleep()** is to transfer control back to the executive startup code—without disturbing the return address placed on the task's stack. It does this by performing a direct jump to a specific address in the startup code.

The figure indicates that the startup code performs the same set of operations for each application task and then concludes by changing **sleep()**'s jump address from a point in the startup code to a location in **run()**. In all subsequent calls, **sleep()** will jump to **run()**.

At this point, each task's stack pointer points to an address which is the location of the next instruction after the first call to **sleep()** in that task. As a consequence, when a task is selected by **sched()** and control is transferred to it by means of the "return-from-subroutine" (**rts**) instruction in **sleep(),** the task will be entered at the next instruction after the previous call to **sleep()**. The task then proceeds to perform application-specific operations until another call to **sleep()** is made and control is transferred back to **sched()**.

Note that there is no reason why a task cannot contain more than one call to **sleep()**. The task will always be reentered at the point just after the **sleep()** call that was performed to suspend the task the last time it ran.

2.2.3 Additional Details

Several additional details need to be discussed at this point. First, nothing was said in the above discussion about saving and restoring the context of application tasks when a task switch occurs. Actually, two context parameters are saved and restored. The task's stack pointer is saved in its TCB, as was discussed. But before it is saved, the task's frame pointer is pushed onto its stack. The C compiler uses the frame pointer to allocate space on the stack for local variables and function arguments. Since the compiler sees to it that the context of a calling function is safely saved on the stack before it calls a subroutine (in this case, **sleep()**), all that is needed to save the task's context is to save its frame and stack pointers.

When the task is again run and control is returned through **sleep(),** the task's stack pointer is restored and the frame pointer is popped off the stack before the task is reentered. As far as the task is concerned, its call to **sleep()** operated the same as any other subroutine call. It is "unaware" of the fact that control was transferred to **sched()** via **run()** and that possibly one or more other tasks were executed before it resumed. It is clear that this executive takes advantage of a property of the C compiler to reduce the amount of data that must be saved and restored in a task switch. We will see later that this results in a very fast task-to-task switch time.

Note that the fact that this executive design relies on the C compiler to save and restore function context places some restrictions on the kinds of program optimization that may be applied to executive functions. If a compiler optimizer violates the context save/restore assumption made here, it will be necessary to either disable it for some executive functions or to add statements to **sleep()** and **run()** that explicitly save and restore context.

Another detail that was passed over quickly in the discussion of task initialization is that, as shown in Figure 2.4, if operations need to be performed to initialize the application code in a task, they may be placed before the task's infinite loop. This code will be executed only once—during startup.

Clearly, the application code in a task can have any program structure within the outer loop. This code may also contain several calls to **sleep()**. The only real restriction to the structure of a task is that a call to **sleep()** must always be available at some point in every path—so that control may eventually be transferred back to the scheduler.

It is not strictly necessary to use a linked list mechanism to search through TCBs. Function **sched()** could simply use an index to access data structure entries. This would be faster and simpler. However, the linked list offers a mechanism for efficiently and dynamically changing task priorities and adding or removing tasks from the list by simply reordering list forward pointers. Although no executive services will be presented in this book to support these operations, the code required should be obvious after we have discussed the code for **sched()** in Chapter 3. The linked list mechanism was retained to support application programs that might require this dynamic reordering of the TCB list.

The task scheduler described so far performs nonpreemptive scheduling of application tasks. That is, once a task is given control, it will continue to run until it voluntarily gives control back to the scheduler (calls **sleep()**). An interrupt may cause an interrupt handler to run and the handler may wake a task with possibly higher priority. But that task will not run until the interrupted task relinquishes control. In other words, the currently active task cannot be preempted (suspended) to allow a higher priority task to run.

Preemptive scheduling will be discussed in Chapter 8, and the executive will be extended to support it at that time. The point will also be made that preemptive scheduling has its costs. In addition to adding complexity to the executive, it also places restrictions on the structure of application code and makes debugging more difficult. But in certain applications it is needed and must be used.

Nonpreemptive scheduling is sufficient for a large class of applications. To use it effectively, application tasks must be designed to cooperatively share processing resources. That is, a task must voluntarily suspend periodically to allow the scheduler to check for higher priority tasks that should be run. The executive includes a small function called **pause()** to facilitate this. The function simply rewakes the running task and then calls **sleep()**. If the scheduler finds a higher priority task that has been awakened, it will run that task next. Otherwise the task that called **pause()** will be reselected and allowed to continue. Calls to **pause()** are usually added to a real-time program to improve performance after it has been initially debugged. These calls can be placed at convenient locations in tasks—between coordinated blocks of code.

One advantage of nonpreemptive scheduling is that a task can safely assume that no other task is modifying items in a data structure at the same time it is. As a result, it is unnecessary to implement procedures to lock data structures when they are being updated.

The other major component of the executive is concerned with data communication. Support for these operations will be examined in the next section.

2.3 DATA COMMUNICATION

The second component of the executive consists of a set of functions that facilitate the transfer of data between application tasks and between interrupt handlers and tasks. The functions use queues for this purpose. The relationship between a program's queues and its other components is shown in Figure 2.5. One application function puts data into a queue; another takes it out.

It is also entirely reasonable and practical to simply pass data through common memory variables and data structures. Since the entire real-time program consists of a single linked module, global variables may be defined in one source file and accessed by functions in one or more other files. This mechanism is often useful for passing status and control flags. It does not require any executive support. But when the real-time system must collect and transport sensor data, it is better to use queues, since data is automatically kept in time-ordered sequence. Queues also provide data buffering between program components which must, necessarily, process the data serially. As we will see, queues are very efficient mechanisms for passing data and data access rights between program modules.

Figure 2.6 shows the basic structure of a queue. A data queue is similar to a queue of people waiting, for example, to enter a movie, in that items are added at the queue's tail and removed from its head. But, unlike a queue of people, the data in a data queue is not moved forward each time an item is removed. Instead, two pointers are maintained, one pointing to the next item to be removed from the head and another pointing to the location where the next item may be added at the queue's tail. This is obviously a much more efficient arrangement, since large quantities of data do not have to be copied forward each time an item of data is removed.

As data items are added and removed from a queue, the head and tail pointers move up the data structure. Since a queue can only occupy a finite block of memory, a point is reached where insufficient room exists in the block to store the next item. It is then necessary to "wrap" the pointer around so that it points to an open region at the bottom of the block. Clearly, a situation will eventually arise in which the queue is full. That is, adequate space is no longer available to store the next item of data. Similarly, an application program may attempt to get data from a queue that is empty. In both cases the application program must be informed that the attempted access has failed. Naturally, one would hope to be able to design the program so that queues are either empty or full only occasionally and for short periods of time.

It should be clear from Figure 2.6 that data are stored in time-ordered or first-in–first-out (FIFO) sequence. The queue may therefore be thought of as analogous to a pipe in which fluid (data) enters at one end and emerges later at the other. The fact that queues also serve to buffer data is also evident from the figure. This feature is important in a multitask system where tasks and interrupt handlers must temporarily store data so that they may be processed by a task that will run later. The data can be "queued" to that task and the task can be awakened.

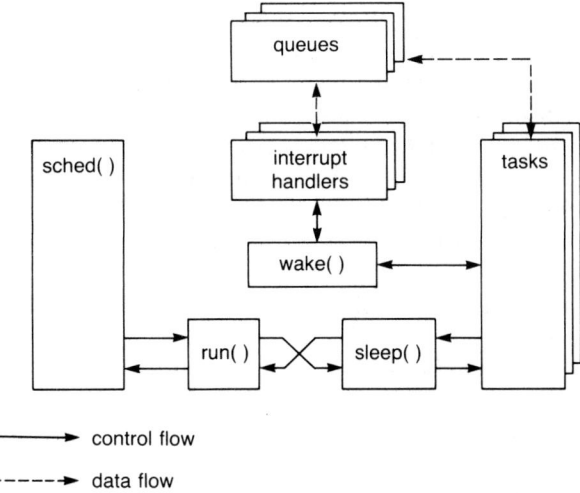

Figure 2.5. Program Data Queues.

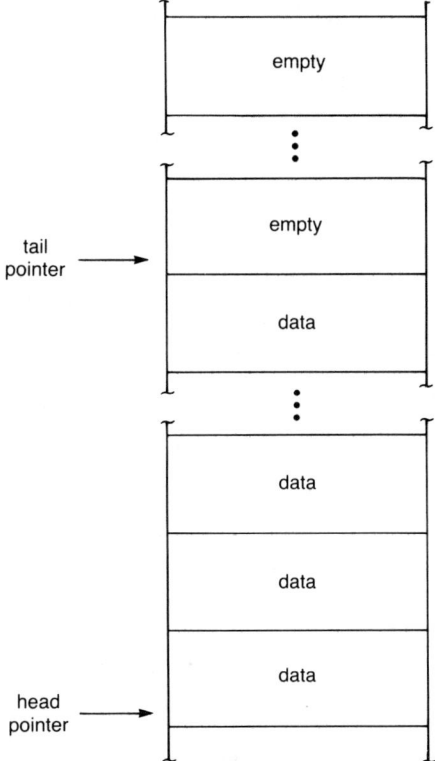

Figure 2.6. Data Queue Structure.

Queues may be designed so that data are stored in fixed or variable length records. The most efficient method, in terms of memory usage, is to use variable length records, since the next data record will start immediately after the data for the previous record. With fixed length records, if a data item is shorter than the record size, the additional space in the record is wasted. But fixed length records are more efficient with respect to execution time, since, if a record is available, it is not necessary to test further to see if sufficient room exists in the queue to store an item.

If the application program is designed so that data are naturally blocked into fixed size records, then record length may be assumed by the application code. But if data items have variable length, it will be necessary to store the length with the data—usually at the beginning of the record.

One type of fixed length queue that is especially useful and efficient is the buffer pointer queue. Figure 2.7 shows its basic structure. The figure shows a queue of pointers to fixed size buffers. Since each queue record contains only a pointer, the queue access operations are simplified.

Figure 2.8 shows the most common arrangement for using pointer queues in an application program. For every communication channel between application functions, a set of two queues is defined: a free list queue and an occupied list queue. The free list queue is loaded with pointers to buffers during program initialization. During normal operation, when a task needs to send data, it gets a pointer to an empty buffer from the free list queue, fills the buffer with data, and puts the pointer into the occupied list queue. Similarly, when a receiving task needs data to process, it gets a pointer to a buffer containing data from the occupied list queue, processes the data, and then puts the pointer to the (now empty) buffer into the free list queue.

Buffer pointer queues are very efficient with respect to execution time, since only a pointer to the data is actually accessed. The data stays stationary in memory. This fact may

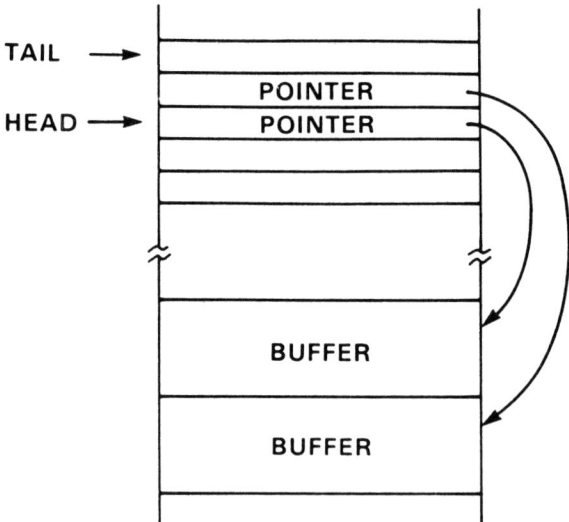

Figure 2.7. Buffer Pointer Queue Structure.

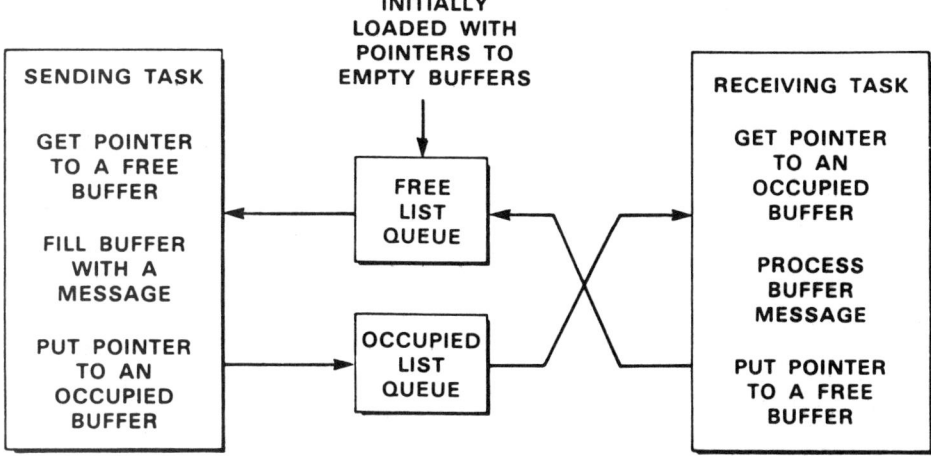

Figure 2.8. Buffer Pointer Queue Usage.

be used to minimize the amount of data movement required in an application design. For example, it is sometimes possible to build a system in which data moves only twice—once when it enters the system from an input port and once when it leaves through an output port. While the data is in the system, only a pointer to it is passed from task to task. For systems that collect and transport large quantities of data, this arrangement can be very efficient.

Note that access time for buffer pointer queues is fixed, since only a pointer is moved. This is in contrast to variable record size queues in which access time is proportional to the amount of the data that is moved into or out of the queue.

Queues are sufficiently important and common in real-time systems that it is worthwhile to provide standard functions to access them. This executive contains two sets of functions—one set for accessing variable record size queues, another for accessing buffer pointer queues. Each set contains a subset pair of primitive functions that manage actual access to the queue and move the data. The remaining functions provide enhanced queue access services and call the primitive functions when they are needed.

A data structure must be defined and initialized for each queue in an application program. As diagrammed in Figure 2.9, each structure contains the head and tail pointers and a pointer to the queue data buffer. It also contains a task ID variable, which will be discussed shortly, and a length variable that specifies the size of the queue data buffer. A queue structure may also contain a "full" flag to distinguish between a full and an empty queue (when the head and tail pointers are equal). Although this flag is not strictly necessary, its use does reduce queue access code complexity in some instances. The primitive queue access functions work with the data in this data structure to access the queue.

For variable record size queues, the defined primitive functions are **putq**() and **getq**(). These functions put and get data to/from a queue, respectively, or return minus one if they fail. As mentioned earlier, **putq**() will fail when insufficient space is available to store data, and **getq**() will fail when the queue is empty. Arguments to these functions specify the

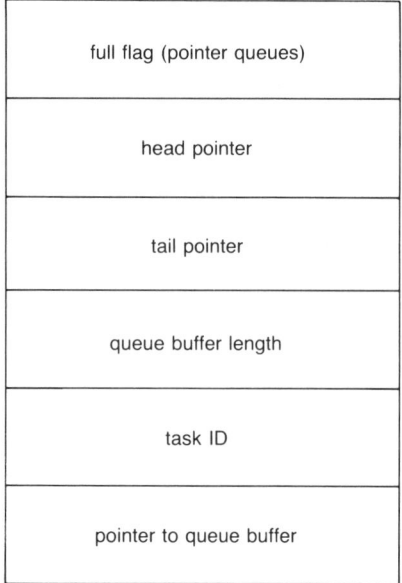

Figure 2.9. Queue Header Structure.

queue to be accessed, the source or destination for the data and, in the case of **putq(),** data size in bytes.

It is useful to automate the operations that must often be performed when a queue access fails. For this purpose two additional functions are also defined for variable record length queues. These functions are **putqwt()** and **getqwt()**. They perform **putq()** or **getq()** operations, respectively, if they can, or wait—that is, suspend the task (call **sleep()**)—if they can't. They also set the task ID variable in the queue header data structure to the ID of the calling task. These functions may be used in an application as follows:

If function **putqwt()** is called by a task to store data in a queue and insufficient room exists, it will set the queue's task ID variable to the ID of the calling task and suspend. Then, when another task runs and uses **getqwt()** to remove data from the same queue, it will check the task ID field and, if a valid ID is present, it will wake that task. When the sending task again runs, it will again attempt to store its data (call **putq()**). If sufficient room is present, it will return successfully; otherwise, it will suspend again. This process will continue until the sending task is successful.

Similarly, if **getqwt()** attempts to get data from a queue and no data are present, it will set the task ID variable in the queue header and suspend the calling task. When the sending task places data in the queue, using **putqwt(),** it will also check the task ID and wake the waiting task.

It should be clear that **putqwt()** and **getqwt()** provide the necessary mechanisms to allow data flow to control program flow. That is, tasks are awakened to run when data are available in their input queues to process. Tasks are also suspended when no room exists in their output queues to store data—and awakened later when room becomes available. These functions therefore expedite the flow of data through the system.

Since there is space in a queue header for only one task ID, a conflict would arise if two tasks called **putqwt()** or **getqwt()** to access the same queue and both found the queue to be full or empty, respectively. Each call would record the ID of the calling task and then suspend the task. But the ID for the second call would overwrite the ID for the first. As a consequence, the first task would never be reawakened.

Clearly, queues and their access functions could be designed to compensate for the task ID conflict phenomenon. But the problem may also be avoided by simply defining a separate queue for each communication path between pairs of tasks. Although this approach requires more memory for queues, the queue access functions would be simpler and thus faster. This is another example of the tradeoff between memory usage and execution speed. As usual, we will choose the latter for time-critical, real-time systems.

The executive contains a similar set of functions for accessing buffer pointer queues. The primitive functions are called **putbp()** and **getbp(),** and the enhanced functions are **putbpwt()** and **getbpwt().** These functions provide functionally the same operations as were described for variable record size queues—except buffer pointer queues are accessed.

When program listings are examined in Chapter 4, it will be clear that the buffer pointer queue functions are more efficient and therefore faster. Note, however, that a separate set of buffers must be defined for each communication path in the application program and that buffers are not allocated from and returned to a central pool, as in some system software designs. Clearly, the tradeoff here was made in favor of speed of operation at the expense of preservation of memory.

In Chapter 10, where we discuss support for multiprocessor systems, an additional set of buffer pointer queue functions will be presented. These functions automate the exchange of buffer pointers between processors that can access common memory over a bus. The functions use a semaphore to lock access to a queue while one processor is performing an operation. Again, the buffer pointer queue proves to be a very efficient mechanism for transferring data between processors.

2.4 SOFTWARE DEVELOPMENT

Perhaps a few words would be appropriate at this point concerning the software development environment that was used to produce and test the software to be described in subsequent chapters. Some thoughts on the structure and content of program listings may also be in order.

Mention was made earlier that the executive is written primarily in the C language. Where necessary, assembly language is used. Programs were prepared on a Sun-3 workstation running the SunOS 3.2 operating system (based on Berkeley UNIX 4.2). The supplied UNIX C compiler and assembler for the Motorola 68020 processor were used. Programs were then linked using the UNIX **1d** linker with the **-T** option to produce a program image that starts at an absolute physical memory address. Executive and application functions were simply linked together to form one runable program image.

Programs were transported to a separate VMEbus single board computer for testing and operation. Testing could then be accomplished by using this computer's PROM monitor/

debugger. The addresses of program functions and global variables were obtained from a memory map produced by UNIX utility **nm.**

More will be said about software development in Chapter 11. Suffice it to say here that the environment just described has been found to be highly efficient for producing real-time programs for 68020-based, VMEbus systems.

There is no technical or design reason why the executive described in this book could not be implemented in some other environment and for a different target processor. In fact, the executive was first developed on a DEC LSI-11 system for a target Z80 processor by using a cross compiler and assembler. It was later ported to the PC/8086 and then the 68000 environments.

The only software changes needed to make the executive work on a different target processor are in the short sections of the program written in assembly language. If the target processor does not support a linear address space for code and data (e.g., the Intel 80X86 series), some additional design changes may be necessary. The functions written in C have been found to port without significant change.

There are probably as many programming styles as there are software writers. Each individual has preferences concerning the level of clarity or obscurity that should be present in the code and the amount of verbal commentary that should accompany it. For this executive to be useful, it is important for users to be able to understand its operation in detail. Consequently, I have made a special effort to present the software in a form that (I hope) can be followed without great difficulty.

Throughout the program listings, I have used variable and function names that are relatively short. This was done to accommodate some software development and testing tools that require the first six or eight characters in a name to be unique.

In the C language parts of the program I have attempted to use standard and commonly known syntax and have avoided the more obscure and less familiar C constructs. I have also used global variables freely. This was done to make debugging easier, since the addresses of global variables are present in the memory map produced by the UNIX **nm** utility.

It can also be noted that I have avoided the use of the **int** data type. The C language defines this type as having the size of a standard word in the target computer. This is usually either 16 or 32 bits for current real-time processors. To be explicit and to improve software portability, I have used **short** (always 16 bits) and **long** (always 32 bits) data types instead. This does not place any restriction on the use of the **int** data type in application functions. It may be used if one wishes.

The assembly language portions of the program use the syntax of the UNIX 68020 assembler. This syntax has its roots in DEC assembly language (the original host for the UNIX operating system) and is not the same as Motorola assembler syntax. But the differences are quite obvious and one becomes accustomed to the UNIX assembler syntax after a short period of exposure.

I have tried to reach a reasonable compromise concerning the amount of verbal commentary included in the listings. It is my personal view that the details of a program's operation are best explained by comments placed immediately with the code, and I shall rely on listing comments to explain detailed operations in the discussions that follow.

Generally speaking, I have included comments at three levels: At the highest level, each file begins with a caption describing, in general terms, the content and purpose of the functions included in the file. Each function also begins with a caption. At the intermediate level I have included line comments that might be described as "paragraph headings." These short statements summarize the operations that will be performed by the code that follows them. Finally, I have placed comments at the ends of individual lines of code where the operation being performed is not obvious or needs explanation. Sometimes the comment is extended to one or more additional lines if space is needed and the point to be made is especially important. It is my hope that the listings found in subsequent chapters are reasonably easy to understand and follow.

Now that we have reviewed the executive at the functional level and have considered software development matters, let us begin our study of the executive software in detail.

3

Task Scheduling Software

We are now prepared to examine the executive task scheduler at the code level. We shall start by reviewing executive data structures and variables and then move on to executive functions. These functions will be discussed in the order in which they actually run when a real-time program is started. Accordingly, we shall proceed from executive initialization, through the scheduling of a task, and then to task suspension and return of control to the executive.

To gain a complete understanding of the operation of the executive, it will be necessary to consider a few operations that are performed by application functions during initialization. To do this, we shall need to look at some files for the example application program that will be discussed in detail later in Chapter 5.

The listings in this and subsequent chapters contain all of the code needed to produce a working version of the executive and example application programs. That is, it should be possible for one to reconstruct the executive and demonstration programs by compiling and linking the code as shown in these listings. The listings contain complete files of program functions and associated data declarations as I have organized them for my personal use.

I have used a simple file naming convention to distinguish between executive and example application files. Files with names that end in a number are for the example application program associated with that number. Files with names that do not end in a number are executive files. For example, files **cxn.c, cxsymb.h,** and **sys.s** are part of the executive; files **cx2.c** and **apsymb2.h** contain code for example application program number 2.

The code for the executive in this and the next chapter will be analyzed in substantial detail, since it is important that executive operation be thoroughly understood. Example application programs in subsequent chapters will be examined in more general terms.

3.1 SCHEDULER DATA STRUCTURES AND VARIABLES

The executive task scheduler code is presented in Figures 3.1, 3.2, and 3.3. These figures show files **cxn.c, cxsymb.h,** and **sys.s,** respectively. File **cxn.c** contains the C language functions and variables for a nonpreemptive version of the scheduler (a preemptive version, in file **cx.c,** will be discussed in Chapter 8). File **cxsymb.h** is an include file that contains a definition for the structure of a task control block (TCB). The third file, **sys.s,** contains the assembly language components of the task scheduler. Let us begin by becoming familiar with the variables defined at the beginning of file **cxn.c.**

> **ntsks:** This variable contains the number of tasks defined in the application program. As we will see, it is set by the program's **main()** function and remains fixed thereafter.
>
> **tidx:** This is the index into the task control block structure, to be discussed next.

```
/*
 * The  information  in  these  files  is  subject  to  change  without  notice.
 * Permission to make  backup  copies  for  personal use is  hereby  granted.
 * Programs may also be  modified to  suit  user needs,  provided  that  the
 * copyright  notice is included in the final listings and reference is made
 * to the fact that modification privileges were granted by the author.
 *
 * The distribution or use of all or part of the source code in a commercial
 * product or service  offered for sale  is not  authorized and  constitutes
 * a violation of  the  program's  copyright  protection.  Binary  (machine
 * executable) application programs that are  produced from source code that
 * uses all or part of CX/68K may be sold without obtaining a license.
 *
 * These programs are not covered by a warranty, either expressed or inplied.
 * The author will not assume responsibility for any damages (including con-
 * sequential)  caused  by  reliance on the  materials  presented, including
 * but not limited to typographical errors or arithmetic errors.
 *
 *          CX/68K  Executive, Version 1.0  (4/10/86)
 *
 *     (c)  1984  Walter S. Heath, all rights reserved.
 *
 *               A  Real-time  System  Executive
 *                          for
 *                   680X0  Computers
 *
 *     FILE CXN.C   - Nonpreemptive Version
```

Figure 3.1. Executive Kernel C Functions.

```c
 *
 *                      Kernel Program and Scheduler.  Function cx() is
 *                      called from the application main() function.
 *      REVISED:
 *              8/8/88
 */

#include "cxsymb.h"                 /*CX/68K executive symbols          */

short ntsks                         ;/*number of tasks defined          */
short tidx                          ;/*task index                       */
extern struct tcbdef tcb[]          ;/*task control blocks (TCBs)       */
long cxsp                           ;/*cx()'s SP-save longword          */
short cxsr                          ;/*cx()'s SR-save word              */
short *rtnadr                       ;/*sleep()'s return address         */
short *runadr                       ;/*run()'s re-entry address         */
short *tskaddr                      ;/*task's address                   */
long *spaddr                        ;/*task's SP location in its TCB    */
extern long cxst[]                  ;/*cx()'s stack                     */
long *cspadr                        ;/*cx()'s stack-start addr.         */

/*---cx()
 *      This is the CX/68K kernel function.  It initializes vectors, Task
 *      Control Blocks (TCBs), each application task and the TCB link
 *      list.  It then performs application-specific initializations
 *      and calls the task scheduler, sched().
 */

cx()
{
/*Switch to supervisor mode, disable levels 1 - 6 interrupts and
 *initialize cx()'s stack pointer.
 */
cspadr = &cxst[255]                 ;/*get stack's start address        */
swcx()                              ;/*call assembly lang. function     */

/* Note: Before this point the program is using the calling environment's
 *       stack.  Your debugger may get confused if you set breakpoints
 *       before this point.
 */

/*
 *Initialize I/O device and trap vectors.
 */
initvec()                                   ;

/*
 *Initialize task TCBs.
 */
initcb()                                    ;
```

(Continued on next page.)

```
/*
 *Initialize each task.
 */
for(tidx = 0; tidx <= ntsks - 1; tidx++){
      tskaddr = tcb[tidx].tskadr ;/*get task's start address          */
      spaddr = &tcb[tidx].tsksp  ;/*get task's SP location in its TCB  */
      tcb[tidx].tsksta = 1       ;/*initialize task wake flags         */
      tcb[tidx].tsksig = 0       ;
      tskinit()                  ;/*Call assembly language task        */
                                  /*initialization function.           */
}
rtnadr = runadr                  ;/*Change sleep()'s return addr       */
                                  /*so it returns to run().            */
/*
 *Initialize TCB link list.
 */
for(tidx = 0; tidx <= ntsks - 2; tidx++)
      tcb[tidx].tsklnk = tidx + 1  ;

tcb[tidx].tsklnk = 0             ;/*close the loop                     */

/*
 *Initialize queue headers and semaphore structures.
 */
qinit()                          ;

/*
 *Perform application-specific initialization operations.
 */
apinit()                         ;

sched()                          ;/*call the scheduler                */
                                  /*( sched() never returns )          */
}                                 /*end of cx() function               */

/*
 *---sched()
 *    This is the task scheduler.  Beginning at the start of the TCB
 *    link list (highest priority), it searches for a TCB with its
 *    status flag set.  It then runs the corresponding task.
 */

sched()
{
for( ; ; ){                       /*begin infinite loop                */
                                  /*loop looking for a task            */

      for(tidx = 0; tcb[tidx].tsksta == 0; tidx = tcb[tidx].tsklnk ) ;
```

Figure 3.1. (*continued*) Executive Kernel C Functions.

```
                              /*A task was found to run.           */
        spaddr = &tcb[tidx].tsksp  ;/*get its SP location in its TCB   */

        run()                      ;/*run it                           */

}                              /*end of infinite loop
}                              /*end of sched() function          */

/*
 *---sleep()
 *    This function is called by a task to suspend its operation and
 *    transfer control back to the scheduler.
 */

sleep()
{

asm(" movw    sr,_cxsr      ")   ;/*save sr (save interrupt level)    */
asm(" orw     #0x0700,sr    ")   ;/*disable interrupts                */

if(tcb[tidx].tsksig)             /*If current task should be         */
                                 /*rerun, leave last wake.           */
     --tcb[tidx].tsksig          ;/*remove a task re-wake signal      */
else                             /*If current task should not be     */
     --tcb[tidx].tsksta          ;/*rerun, remove a task wake.        */

sleepa()                         ;/*call assembly lang. sleepa()      */

asm(" movw    _cxsr,sr      ")   ;/*restore sr (restore interrupt     */
                                 /*level)                            */

}

/*
 *---wake()
 *    This function is called by a task or an interrupt handler to wake
 *    (that is, schedule) a task to run.
 */

wake(tcbidx)
short tcbidx                     ;/*ID (TCB index) of task to run     */
{
++tcb[tcbidx].tsksta             ;/*wake it                           */
}                                /*end of wake() function            */
```

(Continued on next page.)

```
/*
 *---pause()
 *    This function is called by a task to suspend its operation temp-
 *    orarily to allow the scheduler to run higher priority tasks if
 *    any have been awakened.  The calling task is left awakened (by
 *    sleep()) so that it will resume operation after the pause.
 */

pause()
{
++tcb[tidx].tsksig          ;/*Signal sleep() to leave the      */
                            /*current task awakened.            */
sleep()                         ;/*then suspend                 */
}                           /*end of pause() function           */

                            /*end of CXN.C file                 */
```

Figure 3.1. (*continued*) Executive Kernel C Functions.

```
        /*
         *    CX/68K  Executive, Version 1.0   (4/10/86)
         *
         *    (c)  1984  Walter S. Heath, all rights reserved.
         *
         *    FILE CXSYMB.H
         *
         *    CX.C Kernel Symbol Definitions.
         */

        struct tcbdef {                      /*TCB structure        */
                short tsklnk            ;/*forward link pointer     */
                short *tskadr           ;/*start address            */
                long tsksp              ;/*stack pointer            */
                short tsksta            ;/*status flag              */
                short tsksig            ;/*signal flag              */
                short dummy             ;/*Dummy to make 16 byte struct. */
                                         /*(so compiler won't multiply   */
                                         /*to compute tidx in sched()).  */
        }                               ;

                            /*end of CXSYMB.H file               */
```

Figure 3.2. Task Control Block Data Structure.

```
|*****************************************************************
|*
|*      CX/68K Executive, Version 1.0     (4/10/86)
|*
|*      (c)  1984  Walter S. Heath, all rights reserved.
|*
|*      FILE SYS.S
|*
|*      Assembly language components of the  executive.
|*
|*      REVISED:
|*           8/8/88
|*****************************************************************


        .data

        .comm  _cxsp,4
        .comm  _cxsr,2
        .comm  _rtnadr,4
        .comm  _tskaddr,4
        .comm  _spaddr,4
        .comm  _cspadr,4
|*
|*---swcx
|*    This function is called by cx().  It switches the processor to
|*    supervisor state, disables levels 1 - 6 interrupts, gets _run's
|*    re-entry address and sets the cx() program's stack pointer to
|*    point to its stack.
|*
        .text
        .globl _swcx


_swcx:
        movl   sp@+,a0              |pop return address off current stack
        movl   #_trapm,0x80         |set trap0's vector to _trapm
        trap   #0                   |do a trap0 to get to supervisor
|*                                   state
LABM:   movw   #0x2700,sr           |disable levels 1 - 6 interrupts
        movl   #RUNADR,_runadr      |get _run's re-entry point addr.
        movl   _cspadr,sp           |set cx()'s stack pointer
        movl   a0,sp@-                  |push return address on new stack
        rts                         |return to cx()
```

Figure 3.3. Executive Kernel Assembly Language Functions. (*Continued on next page.*)

```
|*
|*---trapm
|*      This function is the trap #0 handler used by _swcx (above) to
|*      switch to supervisor state.  The trap #0 operation switches state.
|*
        .text
        .globl _trapm

_trapm:
        jmp LABM
```

```
|*
|*---run
|*      This function is called by sched() and performs the actual transfer of
|*      control to a task via an entry point in _sleepa.  It also receives
|*      control back from _sleepa.
|*
        .text
        .globl _run

_run:
        movw    sr,_cxsr                |save sr (save interrupt level)
        orw     #0x0700,sr              |disable interrupts
        movl    a6,sp@-                 |push a6 (a6 is C frame ptr)

        movl    sp,_cxsp                |save cx()'s SP
        jmp     SLPADR                  |jump to SLPADR

|*                                      re-entry point from _sleepa
RUNADR:
        movl    _cxsp,sp                |restore cx()'s SP

        movl    sp@+,a6                 |pop a6
        movw    _cxsr,sr                |restore sr (restore interrupt
                                        |level)
        rts                             |return to sched()
```

Figure 3.3. (*continued*) Executive Kernel Assembly Language Functions.

```
|*
|*---sleepa
|*      This function is called by sleep() and performs the actual transfer of
|*      control back to the scheduler via an entry point in _run.  It also
|*      receives control back from _run when a task is run.
|*
        .text
        .globl _sleepa

_sleepa:
        moveml #0x0082,sp@-          |push a0,a6 (a6 is C frame ptr)

        movl   _spaddr,a0            |store task's SP in its TCB
        movl   sp,a0@
        movl   _rtnadr,a0            |jump to _rtnadr
        jmp    a0@

|*                                   re-entry point from _run
SLPADR:
        movl   _spaddr,a0            |get task's SP from its TCB
        movl   a0@,sp

        moveml sp@+,#0x4100          |pop a0,a6
        rts                          |return to a task

|*
|*—tskinit
|*      This function is called by cx() as part of the task-initialization
|*      process.  It transfers control to the beginning of a task.  It then
|*      receives control back from the task's first call to sleep().
|*
        .text
        .globl _tskinit

_tskinit:
        movw   sr,sp@-               |push SR
        moveml #0x0082,sp@-          |push a0,a6 (a6 is C frame ptr)
        movl   #STRADR,_rtnadr       |store STRADR address in _rtnadr
        movl   sp,_cxsp              |save cx()'s SP
        movl   _spaddr,a0            |get address of task's SP in its TCB
        movl   a0@,sp                |get task's SP from its TCB
        movl   _tskaddr,a0           |get task's start address
        jmp    a0@                   |jump to task start
```

(Continued on next page.)

```
|*                              re-entry point from _sleepa
STRADR:
      movl   _cxsp,sp           |restore cx()'s SP
      moveml sp@+,#0x4100        |pop a0,a6
      movw   sp@+,sr            |pop SR

      rts                       |return to cx()
|*
|*                              end of SYS.S file
|*
```

Figure 3.3. (*continued*) Executive Kernel Assembly Language Functions.

tcb[]: This is an array of task control blocks. The statement declaring this array is an external reference to the data structure, which is defined elsewhere (in the application code). Each TCB is declared to have structure type **tcbdef.** Include file **cxsymb.h,** shown in Figure 3.2, contains a definition of this structure. We will examine it shortly.

cxsp and cxsr: The executive must save and restore its stack pointer register (SP) and status register (SR). These variables provide the necessary storage locations.

rtnadr: As discussed in Chapter 2, function **sleep()** returns to function **tskinit()** during task initialization and to **run()** thereafter. The proper return address is maintained in this variable.

runadr: The address in **run()** that **sleep()** transfers to is placed in this variable during initialization.

tskaddr: This variable is used to pass a task's starting address to assembly language task initialization function **tskinit().**

spaddr: This is used to pass the address of the stack pointer storage location in a selected task's TCB to assembly language functions **tskinit()** and **sleepa().**

cxst[]: This is the executive's stack. It is actually defined in an application file and externally referenced in this file.

cspadr: This variable is used to pass the address of the start of the executive's stack to assembly language startup function **swcx().**

The structure of a task control block is defined in file **cxsymb.h,** shown in Figure 3.2. We will review the individual data items in that structure.

tsklnk: In Chapter 2 we discussed the fact that TCBs are linked in a linked list. This variable is initialized to the index of the next TCB in the list. The scheduler uses this pointer to find the next entry in the list.

tskadr: This variable is initialized to the starting address of the application task assigned to the TCB. It is used by **tskinit()** when it initializes the task by running it from its start to its first call to **sleep().**

tsksp: When a task suspends, **sleep()** saves the task's stack pointer in **tsksp;** when it is again run, **sleep()** restores its pointer from this variable.

tsksta, tsksig: These status and signal flags are used to indicate to the scheduler that a task has been awakened and should be run.

dummy: A dummy (unused) variable is added to the **tcbdef** structure to make it a power of two bytes long. The C compiler will then use a shift instruction rather than a multiply when computing the **tcb[]** array index. The shift instruction takes much less execution time.

Some of the variables described are referenced by file **sys.s** in Figure 3.3. The **.comm** statements in this file establish external references to variables actually declared in **cxn.c.**

3.2 SCHEDULER FUNCTIONS

Like any other C program, a real-time program using this executive starts with a **main()** function. I have chosen to make this an application program function so that some application-dependent variables may be declared and initialized in it and in case an application design requires some non-real-time processing at startup. As a result, it will be necessary to look at an example application file to get this discussion of the task scheduler software underway.

Figure 5.6 in Chapter 5 shows file **cx2.c.** It contains the **main()** function for example program 2. For this example the operations performed in **main()** are simple. Variable **ntsks** is set to the number of application tasks defined and the executive kernel function, **cx()**, is called. The number-of-tasks value, **NTSKS**, is declared in include file **apsymb2.h.** Its actual value is not important for the present discussion. This file also declares the executive's stack, **cxst[].** The declaration is placed in this application file so that its size may be adjusted to fit the needs of an application without having to alter the executive's kernel file.

Kernel function **cx()** is in file **cxn.c,** Figure 3.1. This function initializes the executive and application functions and finally calls task scheduler function **sched()**.

The **cx()** function must perform some initial startup operations, including a switch to the executive's stack. Up to this point the program uses the stack provided by the computer's PROM monitor. Since the amount of space on this stack is usually quite limited, it is important to switch to a stack space that is of known size. The program gets the starting address of the stack array **cxst[]** and puts it into variable **cspadr.** Note that this is the address of the last entry in the array—stacks advance from high to low addresses as data is pushed onto them. It then calls assembly language function **swcx()**.

The stack array is declared in file **cx2.c** to have only 256 longword entries. This size is adequate for the example application programs presented in this book, but may not be large enough for other applications. Generally speaking, the amount of stack space needed depends on the depth of subroutine call nesting present in the program and the number and priority levels of interrupts defined in the system. Interrupt handlers and subroutine calls push data onto the stack when they are entered and pop data off when they exit. Stack space is also needed for C language variables declared to be of type automatic.

Since real-time programs operate asynchronously, it is difficult—if not impossible—to predict the amount of space needed on a stack before the program is run. A good way to handle this situation is to initially define a stack space that is substantially larger than the program can be expected to need. After the program has been debugged, the amount actually used may be determined by filling the stack space with a known value before running the program and then checking to see how much was changed after the program is stopped. An adequate safety margin may then be added to this value. In an actual design, this procedure should also be followed for the application task stacks as well.

Function **swcx()** is in file **sys.s,** Figure 3.3. The first operation performed is to pop the function's return address off the stack and into address register **a0.** Since the function will switch stacks, it will be necessary to push this value back onto the new stack before the function can return. The next operation is a bit of a trick to make sure the processor is running in supervisor mode (it may have been left in user mode by the previously run program). The program puts the address of trap handler **_trapm** into the processor's trap number zero vector location and then performs a trap-zero operation. When a trap is performed, the processor automatically switches to supervisor mode. The trap handler function **_trapm** simply jumps to the next statement in **_swcx()**, labeled **LABM.** This curious use of a system **trap** instruction is necessitated by the fact that the trap operation is the only way that a program running in user mode can switch to supervisor mode.

The **swcx()** function performs some additional startup operations. It disables interrupts and then loads variable **_runadr** with address **RUNADR,** the entry point in function **run()** that is needed later by function **sleep()**. The processor's stack pointer register is then loaded with the address of the executive's stack. It gets this address from variable **_cspadr.** The proper stack address was loaded into this variable by **cx()** before **swcx()** was called. After the previously saved return address is pushed onto the new stack, the function returns to **cx()**. At this point, interrupts have been disabled, the program is definitely running in supervisor mode, and it is using the executive's stack.

Function **cx()** proceeds to call application function **initvec()**. This function initializes processor interrupt and trap registers. We will return to the subject of interrupts, traps, and their software handlers in Chapters 6 and 7. At that point we will review the kinds of operations that this function might perform.

The next important step performed by **cx()** is to initialize the task control blocks. Again, we will need to refer to an application program file to see an example of function **initcb().**

Figure 5.8 in Chapter 5 shows application file **api2.c** for example program 2. Function **initcb()** in this file contains code to initialize TCBs for three application tasks—named **consol()**, **keybd()**, and **idle()**. We will be studying these tasks in greater detail in Chapter 5. For present purposes it is sufficient to see that the starting addresses for each task and each task's stack are loaded into TCB variables **tskadr** and **tsksp,** respectively.

It is important to note that the initialization operations performed in **initcb()** determine task priority. Since the task scheduler scans TCBs starting at the first entry in the **tcb[]** array, the task assigned to this entry has highest priority. Tasks assigned to **tcb[]** entries below the first have progressively lower scheduling priorities. In the case shown in Figure 5.8, task **consol()** has highest priority, followed by **keybd()** and then by **idle()**.

After preparing TCBs, function **cx()** must initialize each application task. Recall from our discussion in Chapter 2 that it is necessary to run each task from its start to the point where it first calls **sleep()**. This is done so that **sleep()**'s return address will be left on the task's stack for later use and also to perform any task application initialization operations. Function **cx()** performs these operations by calling assembly language function **tskinit()** repetitively—once for each task. As the listing shows, the address of the task is placed in variable **tskaddr** and the address of the selected task's SP storage location in its TCB is placed in **spaddr** before each call. These are used by **tskinit()**. In addition, the flags used to control task scheduling must also be initialized.

Assembly language function **tskinit()** is shown in file **sys.s,** Figure 3.3. In Section 2.2 we noted that **sleep()** transfers control to a point in **tskinit()** during task initialization and to a point in **run()** thereafter. The address that it transfers to is maintained in variable **_rtnadr.** Accordingly, **tskinit()**, after initially saving some registers, places internal address **STRADR** in **_rtnadr.** Function **sleep()** will then transfer to this address during task initialization. The **tskinit()** function then saves the executive's stack pointer in **_cxsp** and moves the task's stack pointer from the location pointed to by **_spaddr** to the processor's SP register. Finally, it gets the task's starting address from **_tskaddr** and jumps to that location. The task then runs and eventually calls **sleep().**

The **sleep()** function will be examined in detail in the next section. At this point it is sufficient to note that it calls assembly language function **sleepa()** and **sleepa()** transfers to the location currently pointed to by **_rtnadr.** Since this variable was loaded with address **STRADR** earlier in **tskinit()**, it will return to this location during task initialization. The **tskinit()** function then continues from **STRADR.** It first restores the executive's stack pointer from **_cxsp** and then pops other saved registers from this stack. It then returns to kernel function **cx().** After all tasks have been initialized in this fashion, the **cx()** function switches the address that **sleepa()** transfers to from **STRADR** in **tskinit()** to address **RUNADR** in **run().** In all future calls, **sleepa()** will transfer control to this location.

One final TCB initialization operation is required. The forward link pointers must be set. The **cx()** listing shows a program loop that does this. Note that a forward pointer is simply the index of the next TCB. Note also that the linked list loop is closed by setting the forward link pointer for the last TCB to the index of the first.

Two more application initialization functions are called before the scheduler is started. The first initializes application data queue headers; the second performs any other initialization operations the application may require. As we will see later, this may include calling **wake()** to schedule the first task to run. Examples of these functions will be presented in subsequent chapters.

The executive's task scheduler is function **sched().** It is called by **cx()** and never returns. The function is shown in Figure 3.1. Its operation and the operation of functions **run()** and **sleep()** will be examined next.

3.2.1 Functions sched(), run(), and sleep()

Function **sched()** contains two program loops. The outer loop is infinite. That is, it never terminates. The inner loop scans TCBs looking for a task that has been awakened. This condition is indicated by the task's status flag, **tsksta,** having a nonzero value. As long as TCB status flags are found to be zero, this single instruction loop will continue to search.

When a nonzero status flag is found, the TCB polling loop is exited and **sched()** continues. The function then puts the address of the selected task's stack pointer in variable **spaddr** and calls assembly language function **run()**. Note that when **run()** returns, after the selected task has run, the outer infinite loop in **sched()** transfers control back to the inner TCB polling loop and the scheduler resumes scanning for another task to run, starting with the highest priority task.

Function **run()** is shown in file **sys.s,** Figure 3.3. It starts by saving the executive's status register in **_cxsr,** disabling interrupts, and saving the executive's context by saving the C program's frame pointer on its stack and then saving its stack pointer in **_cxsp.** It then jumps to entry point **SLPADR** in **sleepa()**.

The assembly language part of **sleep()**, called **sleepa()**, is also shown in Figure 3.3. The first operation performed in **sleepa()** (after address **SLPADR**) is to get the task's stack pointer from its TCB, using the stack pointer's address in **_spaddr.** It then pops the context of **sleepa()**'s calling function—the C language **sleep()** function—from the task's stack and returns to **sleep()**. Note that this context was pushed onto the task's stack during task initialization—when **sleep()** was called for each task.

The C language **sleep()** function is shown in Figure 3.1. When **sleepa()** returns, the only operation performed by **sleep()** is to restore the status register value in **_cxsr** (note the use of inline assembly code to do this). Variable **_cxsr** was last loaded at the beginning of **run()**—just before interrupts were disabled. So, it contains **sched()**'s last status register value. The important field in the register at this point is the interrupt priority level. As a consequence of this operation, the processor's interrupt priority level is restored to the value present when **sched()** was running.

When **sleep()** returns, it pops a return address from the selected task's stack. This is the address pushed onto the stack by the last task call to **sleep()**. This may have been the call that was made during task initialization, as was described earlier, or it may have been from a call to **sleep()** during normal operation. In any case, control is transferred to the next instruction after the last call to **sleep()** in the chosen task.

At this point the application task runs. After performing application-specific operations, it must call **sleep()** again. When **sleep()** is entered, it first saves the task's status register—to preserve the task interrupt level—and then disables interrupts. Function **sleep()** then performs some operations involving the task status and signal flags. We will come back to these when we discuss the **wake()** and **pause()** functions in the next section. Assembly language function **sleepa()** is then called.

On entering **sleepa()**, as shown in Figure 3.3, the context of the calling **sleep()** function is saved and the task's stack pointer is stored in its TCB. The function then jumps to the address present in **_rtnadr.** In reviewing the **cx()** kernel function earlier, it was pointed out that **_rtnadr** was loaded with address **RUNADR** in **run()** after the tasks had been initialized. So **sleepa()** jumps to this point in **run()**.

Before returning to **sched()**, **run()** must restore the executive's stack pointer from **_cxsp** and then restore the context of the **sched()** function. It also loads the status register with the value in **_cxsr.** This variable was loaded with the value of the task's status register when **sleep()** was called from the task. Thus, the interrupt priority level that was present when the task was running is restored just before **sched()** is reentered. Function **run()** can now return to **sched()** by simply popping the return address off the executive's stack, since this address was left there when **run()** was originally called from **sched()**.

We have now completed the trip from the task scheduler, through **run()** and **sleep()** into an application task, and then back through **sleep()** and **run()** to the scheduler again. As was pointed out earlier, the scheduler simply loops back and starts scanning for another awakened task. The only part of the code that was bypassed concerned the manipulation of the task status and signal flags by **sleep()**. We will return to this subject as part of our study of the **wake()** and **pause()** functions.

It should be noted that to save the calling function's context, it was only necessary to save the contents of the frame and stack pointer registers (and register **a0,** in the case of **_sleepa**). But some compilers reserve other registers for code generation. If these registers must be preserved across function calls, their contents must also be saved during a context switch. This, of course, will increase the time it takes to suspend one task and start another.

3.2.2 Functions wake() and pause()

Function **wake()** is called from a task or an interrupt handler to wake a task—that is, schedule it to be run. As shown in Figure 3.1, this function simply increments the task's status flag, **_tsksta,** in its TCB. Since **sched()** tests this flag to see if the task should be run, this operation effectively wakes the task. Whenever the flag is nonzero, **sched()** will run the task. Clearly, at some point the flag must be decremented to cancel the wakeup. This is done in **sleep()**. It should also be evident that by incrementing and decrementing the signal flag (instead of just setting and clearing it), several wakeups of the task may be "queued" at the same time. This is useful in certain application situations.

In addition to **wake(),** the **pause()** function may be used to reschedule a task. Recall from Chapter 2 that **pause()** is used to allow a task to suspend itself temporarily to let the scheduler check to see if a higher priority task should be run. Function **pause()** signals **sleep()** to wake its calling task and then calls **sleep()** to suspend. The **pause()** function is also shown in Figure 3.1. It signals **sleep()** to wake the running task by incrementing the task's signal flag, **_tsksig.**

We are now prepared to return to **sleep()** and discuss its manipulations of the task status and signal flags. The function tests the signal flag for nonzero. If this condition is true, it simply decrements the signal flag—but leaves the status flag alone. That is, it leaves the previous wake pending. This effectively wakes the task again.

On the other hand, if the signal flag is not set (**pause()** was not called), it decrements the task's status flag. This removes the current task wakeup. In other words, the signal flag is used by **pause()** to signal **sleep()** to leave the task in the waked condition when control is returned to the scheduler. The task will then be run again (resumed) when it becomes the currently highest priority, awakened task.

In Chapter 8 we will see that **pause()** has an additional role to play in supporting preemptive scheduling. The reason the task signal flag is incremented and decremented (rather than just set and cleared) will become evident at that time.

This completes our discussion of the executive task scheduler code. Before leaving this subject, it should be observed that interrupts are disabled during **run()**/**sleep()** transitions, and that the interrupt level going into the transition is restored coming out. The level is held in variable **_cxsr** during the transition. It is important that interrupts are enabled while

sched() is running, since, if no tasks are currently scheduled, the only way to get one awakened is for an interrupt handler to call **wake()**. Viewed from a system perspective, if the computer is idle (spinning in the scheduler, looking for an awakened task), it must be possible for an external sensor to cause an interrupt and schedule a task to run.

Another important observation concerns the executive's support for multiple wakeups of a task. This is needed, for example, when an interrupt occurs while a task is running and the interrupt handler wakes the interrupted task. In this case it is important that the task be scheduled to run again, since it may be necessary for the task to process data input by the interrupt handler. But if the interrupt occurs early in the task the input data may get processed immediately by the task when the handler returns. In this case the extra wakeup is not necessary. The task must therefore be programmed so that if no data is present for it to process, it will call **sleep()** and return control to the scheduler.

4

Data Communication Software

In Chapter 2 we discussed the functional operation of queues and their role in moving data between application tasks and interrupt handlers. In this chapter we will be concerned with the detailed operation of the executive functions needed to support these queues.

We discussed two types of queues in Chapter 2. For variable record size queues, the actual message data is stored in the queue. For brevity, we will refer to these as message queues in this and subsequent chapters. Buffer pointer queues store only a pointer to the message data in the queue. The actual data is placed in a separate buffer.

We will examine the code for each type of queue separately in this chapter, starting with message queues. For each queue type we will first describe the queue data structure and its initialization, and then proceed to investigate the operation of the queue access functions. The chapter will be concluded with a discussion of reentrancy as it relates to queues and their access functions.

In actual real-time programs, queues are defined and initialized by application code. To study these operations, we will therefore need to refer to a figure in Chapter 7 that shows these operations for the example application program described in that chapter.

As was the case for the task scheduler code in Chapter 3, the code in this chapter is organized into files of logically related functions and data declarations. All of the code that is needed to support queue access is present in these files. It should therefore be possible to implement these operations by duplicating these files as shown.

Since the queue access functions are part of the executive and thus play a central role in a real-time program, it is important that their operation is fully understood by application software writers. Consequently, we will examine them in considerable detail in the sections that follow. Let us begin by investigating the message queue header structure and its initialization.

4.1 THE MESSAGE
QUEUE HEADER

Figure 4.1 shows include file **qsymb.h.** This file contains the definition of a message queue header data structure. It consists of head and tail pointers, the queue length, a task ID field, and a pointer to the actual message queue buffer. A data structure of this type must be declared for each application queue.

Message queues for example program CX3 are declared in file **ques3.c,** shown in Figure 7.3. Three queues are declared: **contim, timcon,** and **rtctim.** The associated message buffers are **ctbuf[], tcbuf[],** and **rtbuf[],** respectively. These queues are initialized when executive kernel function **cx()** calls application function **qinit().** Figure 7.3 also shows this function for the CX3 example program. The code at the end of the function initializes all fields of the queue header data structure for the three queues.

Note that the head and tail pointers are actually byte indexes into the associated queue buffer. As such, they are not memory pointers in the sense that the C language defines pointers. They may be thought of as pointers relative to the start of the queue buffer array. Note also that the task ID fields are set to minus one. This value is used to indicate that no task is waiting for data or space in the queue. A positive number in this field is interpreted as the task ID of a waiting task.

Pointer field **pbuf** is initialized to point to the first address in the queue's associated buffer array, and the queue's **lngth** field is set to equal the length, in bytes, of this array. The fields in these queue headers will be manipulated by the queue access primitive functions to be discussed in the next section.

```
/*
 *      CX/68K Executive, Version 1.0   (4/10/86)
 *
 *      (c)    1984  Walter S. Heath, all rights reserved.
 *
 *      FILE QSYMB.H
 *
 *      Queue data structure declaration.
 */

struct que {                        /*queue header structure       */
      short head                ;/*head pointer                    */
      short tail                ;/*tail pointer                    */
      short lngth               ;/*queue length in bytes           */
      char task                 ;/*suspended task's ID             */
      char *pbuf                ;/*pointer to actual queue buf.    */
}                               ;

                                  /*end of QSYMB.H file            */
```

Figure 4.1. Message Queue Header Declaration.

4.2 MESSAGE QUEUE ACCESS FUNCTIONS

The message queue primitive functions are present in file **quea.c,** shown in Figure 4.2. Note that file **qsymb.h** is included in this file to define queue header structure **que.** The two primitive functions are **putq()** and **getq().** We will examine these functions in the next two sections.

```
/*
 *      CX/68K   Executive, Version 1.0   (4/10/86)
 *
 *      (c) 1984  Walter S. Heath, all rights reserved.
 *
 *      FILE QUEA.C
 *
 *      This file contains the basic queue access functions getq() and
 *      putq(). They provide direct access to the queues.  Other functions
 *      use them to provide enhanced services.  For example, functions
 *      getqwt() and putqwt() in file QUEAE.C call getq() and putq(),
 *      respectively.  All queue access functions are reentrant.
 */
#include "qsymb.h"

/*
 *---putq(source,dest,count) - "put msg in queue"
 *      This function moves 'count' bytes from address 'source' to queue
 *      'dest'. If 'count' is zero, the function returns the current
 *      status of the queue. WARNING: the maximum value allowed for
 *      'count' is 255.
 *Outputs:
 *      putq() returns:
 *              0 - if queue was initially empty
 *              1 - if queue is partially occupied
 *              -1 - if not enough room exists (transfer failed)
 */

putq(source,dest,count)
char *source                        ;
struct que *dest                    ;
unsigned short count                ;
{
short trytail                       ;/*trial tail            */
short newtail                       ;/*new tail              */
```

Figure 4.2. Primitive Message Queue Access Functions. (*Continued on next page.*)

```
short entsize                  ;/*entry size                          */
short sindex                   ;/*'source' index                      */
short rtnval                   ;/*returned value                       */
rtnval = 1                     ;/*Initially set return value to         */
                                /*indicate partially occupied.         */
if(dest->head == dest->tail)    /*If queue was initially empty,         */
      rtnval = 0               ;/*set return value to zero.             */

if(count == 0)                  /*If requested count is zero,           */
      return(rtnval)           ;/*return queue status.                  */

trytail = dest->tail + count + 1 ;/*compute trial tail                 */

/*If entry would overwrite a current entry, return transfer failed (-1).*/

if(dest->tail < dest->head && trytail >= dest->head)
      return(-1)               ;

if(trytail >= dest->lngth){      /*If trytail is longer than            */
                                /*queue, entry must be wrapped.        */
      newtail = trytail - dest->lngth ;/*wrapped new tail              */

      if(newtail < dest->head){  /*If room exists, store entry.         */
            dest->pbuf[dest->tail++] = count ;/*store count      first */

            entsize = dest->lngth - dest->tail ;/*Number to store at   */
                              /*queue end.                        */
            if(entsize != 0)     /*If some exist, store them.          */
                  mvbyt(source,&dest->pbuf[dest->tail],entsize) ;

            sindex = entsize    ;/*Index of next byte in source.        */

                                /*Now store rest at queue start.       */
            entsize = count - entsize ;/*Number to store at queue       */
                              /*start.                            */
            if(entsize != 0)     /*If some exist, store them.          */
                  mvbyt(&source[sindex],&dest->pbuf[0],entsize) ;

            dest->tail = newtail;/*set new tail pointer                 */
      }
      else{                      /*If not enough room exists,           */
```

Figure 4.2. (*continued*) Primitive Message Queue Access Functions.

```
          return(-1)              ;/*return transfer failed (-1).          */
       }
}
else{                            /*If no queue wrap necessary,             */
                                 /*store bytes consecutively.              */

      dest->pbuf[dest->tail++] = count ;/*Store count,                     */
                                 /*then store data.                        */
      mvbyt(source,&dest->pbuf[dest->tail],count) ;

      dest->tail = trytail       ;/*set new tail pointer                   */
}
return(rtnval)                   ;/*Return (transfer successful).          */
}                                 /*end of putq()                          */

/*
 *---mvbyt(source,dest,bytc)
 *      This function moves 'bytc' bytes from the location pointed to by
 *      'source' to the location pointed to by 'dest'. If the application
 *      requires exceptionally fast response time this operation may be
 *      performed more efficiently in assembly language.
 */

mvbyt(source,dest,bytc)
char *source                      ;
char *dest                        ;
short bytc                        ;
{
short ibyt                       ;/*byte index                            */
if(bytc <= 0) return             ;/*If 'bytc' negative, return.            */
for( ibyt = 0; ibyt < bytc; ibyt++){
      *dest++ = *source++        ;
}
}                                 /*end of mvbyt()                         */

/*
 * ---getq(source,dest) - "get msg from queue"
 *      This function moves bytes from queue 'source' to address 'dest'.
 *      If no entry exists in 'source' it returns -1. If an entry exists,
 *      it returns the number of bytes in the entry.
 */
```

(Continued on next page.)

```
getq(source,dest)
struct que *source              ;
char    *dest                   ;
{
short entsize                   ;/*entry size                          */
unsigned short count            ;/*Number of bytes in entry            */
                                 /*(excluding count, itself).          */
short dindex                    ;/*destination index                  */

if(source->head == source->tail)  /*If buffer is empty,                */
      return(-1)                ;/*return -1.                          */

count = source->pbuf[source->head++]    ;/*get byte count first        */

if(source->head == source->lngth) /*If new head should be wrapped,     */
      source->head = 0          ;/*wrap it.                            */

if(source->head + count > source->lngth){ /*If entry was wrapped, remove */
                                /*bytes at queue end first.            */

      entsize = source->lngth - source->head ;/*number to remove       */
      mvbyt(&source->pbuf[source->head],dest,entsize) ;/*remove them    */

      dindex = entsize          ;/*Get index of next open byte         */
                                 /*in dest.                            */
                                 /*Now remove rest at queue start.     */
      entsize = count - entsize ;/*number to remove                    */
      mvbyt(&source->pbuf[0],&dest[dindex],entsize) ;/*remove them      */

      source->head = entsize            ;/*set new head pointer         */
}
else{                                /*Entry was not wrapped, so        */
                                     /*remove 'count' bytes.            */
      mvbyt(&source->pbuf[source->head],dest,count) ;

      source->head = source->head + count ;/*set new head pointer       */
      if(source->head == source->lngth) /*If head should be wrapped,    */
            source->head = 0    ;/*wrap it.                            */
}
return(count)                   ;/*Return (transfer successful).        */
}                                /*end of getq()                        */

                                 /*end of QUEA.C file                   */
```

Figure 4.2. (*continued*) Primitive Message Queue Access Functions.

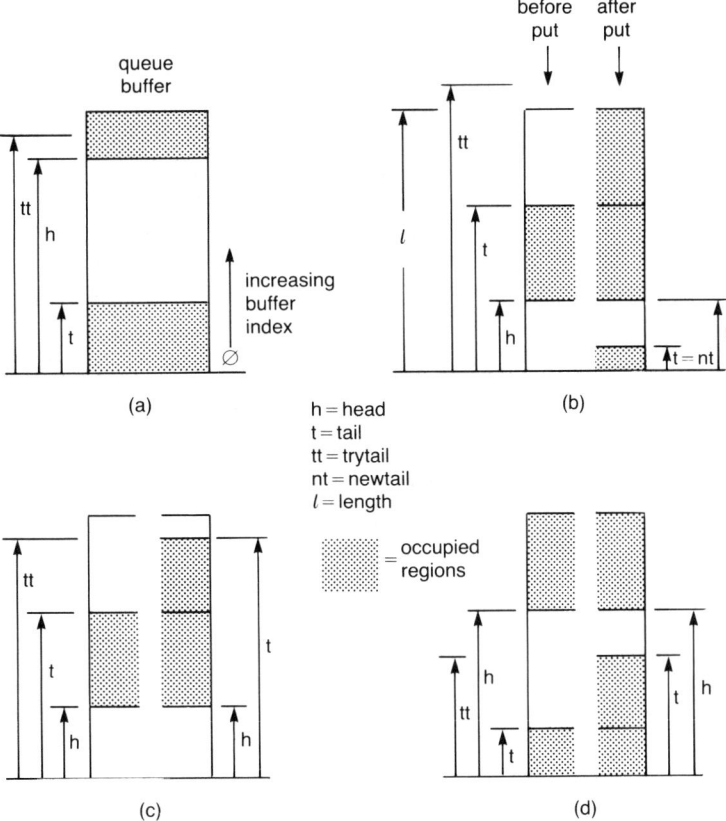

Figure 4.3a–d. Message Queue Put Situations.

4.2.1 The putq()
Primitive Function

The **putq()** function puts a message pointed to by argument **source** into the queue pointed to by **dest.** The size of the message in bytes is specified by argument **count.** For example, a call to this function might be:

$$putq(\&timmsg, \&contim, 1) \;;$$

In this case, a single byte message in variable **timmsg** is placed in queue **contim.**

To study the operation of the **putq()**, function it will be helpful to have some diagrams that show the various situations that can arise in a queue data buffer. Figure 4.3 contains an appropriate set. We will refer to these diagrams as the code is examined.

The first code in **putq()** declares some variables used by the function. Since they are declared within the scope of **putq()**, they are identified as automatic variables by the C compiler. This means that when **putq()** is called, space is allocated on the processor's stack for them. They are referenced by means of offsets from the program's stack frame pointer. The important point here is that space is allocated on the calling function's stack for a new set of these variables each time the **putq()** function is called. We will discuss the importance of this when we consider the subject of reentrancy at the end of this chapter.

The first executable code in **putq()** initializes variable **rtnval.** This value will be returned to the calling function if the function is successful in placing a message in the queue. The queue is empty when its head and tail pointers are the same. In this case, **rtnval** is set to zero. Otherwise it is left set to one, to indicate that the queue contains at least one message.

Note that the queue's head and tail pointers are referenced by means of pointer **dest,** which is declared in the function's argument list to be a pointer to a structure of type **que.** This is the structure of a queue header, as defined in include file **qsymb.h.** All variables in the queue's header will be referenced in this way.

The next code in **putq()** tests the function's **count** argument for zero and returns with return value **rtnval** if it is. This feature may be used to determine the condition of the queue (i.e., empty or partially occupied). It may also be used when **putq()** is called with a variable for the **count** argument and this variable can be zero. In this case the function performs properly—no message is stored.

It is necessary to compute a trail new tail pointer to determine if sufficient room exists in the queue buffer to store the message. Variable **trytail** consists of the current tail pointer plus the size of the new message and one more byte. The additional byte is used to store message size with the message.

A test is made immediately to determine if one condition exists in the queue that would indicate that insufficient space is available. An additional test will be made later. The condition for the test is shown if Figure 4.3a. The diagram shows a situation in which the head pointer is greater than the tail pointer and **trytail** is greater than the head pointer. Under these conditions the message will not fit in the queue and the function returns minus one.

Function **putq()** must next determine whether the new queue entry will need to be "wrapped"—that is, whether part of the message will be stored at the end of the queue buffer and the remainder at the beginning. This situation is shown in Figure 4.3b. Here the left side of the diagram shows conditions before the message is stored and the right side shows the buffer after storage. The diagram demonstrates that if **trytail** is greater or equal to the length of the buffer, the message will have to be wrapped.

To wrap a message in a queue the function must compute a new tail pointer, **newtail.** This is simply equal to **trytail** minus the length of the buffer. Then another test must be made to determine whether sufficient room exists in the queue to store the message. If room exists, the function may proceed to store the message.

As mentioned briefly earlier, when a message is stored in a queue it is preceded by a byte containing the message size. Since only one byte is allocated for this purpose, a message may not be larger than 255 bytes (for larger messages, buffer pointer queues may be used). Note that it is the software writer's responsibility to limit messages to this size—the function does not test for a violation of this limit.

To wrap a message in a queue, it is necessary to store part of it at the end and the remainder at the beginning of the queue buffer. Function **putq**() computes the number of bytes to store at the end and proceeds to move the computed number from the message source to the queue buffer. But a condition may arise in which only one open byte remains at the end of the queue. In that case, after the message byte count is stored, no more room exists at the end to store message bytes. The function tests for this condition before the message byte transfer begins.

Message bytes are moved by subfunction **mvbyt**(), which is also shown in Figure 4.2. This function simply moves the requested number of bytes from address **source** to address **dest.** The function is used by both **putq**() and **getq**(). If the application program requires exceptionally fast message transfers, this function may be replaced by an optimized assembly language version.

After the end of the queue's buffer has been filled, **putq**() must move the remaining message bytes to the region at the start of the buffer. The operations are similar to those described for the move operation at the buffer end. After the move, the queue's tail pointer may be updated to the value in **newtail.**

If it is not necessary to wrap the message in the queue buffer, it may be stored in consecutive memory locations starting at the current tail pointer location. Two subcases exist. Figure 4.3c shows the case in which the tail pointer is greater or equal to the head pointer and Figure 4.3d shows the alternate possibility.

For the first subcase, room exists in the buffer, since the program has already verified that **trytail** is less than the length of the buffer. So the message may be stored. For the second subcase, room also exists, since the tail pointer is less than the head pointer and **trytail** is also less than the head pointer. This is precisely the complement of the test that was made at the beginning of **putq**() for insufficient queue space (shown in Figure 4.3a). Once the message has been moved into the queue buffer, the queue's tail pointer may be updated and the function returns with return value **rtnval.**

Before leaving this discussion of **putq**(), it is worthwhile to observe that a queue buffer is never allowed to fill to the point where the head and tail pointers are equal. The code always leaves one byte open for the tail pointer to point to. The condition of head and tail pointer equality is reserved to indicate that the queue is empty.

4.2.2 The getq()
Primitive Function

The **getq**() function, also shown in Figure 4.2, gets a message from the queue pointed to by argument **source** and moves it to the location pointed to by **dest.** The function returns the number of bytes in the message—or minus one if no message is present in the queue. An example call is:

$$retval = getq(\&contim, \&tskmsg) ;$$

where an attempt is made to get a message from queue **contim** and place it in variable **tskmsg.** The size of the message (or minus one) will be placed in variable **retval.** Some diagrams showing the contents of the buffer queue in various situations are shown in Figure 4.4. We will refer to these in the analysis that follows.

As in the case of **putq(),** function **getq()** begins by defining some variables that are used internally by the function. These are C language automatic variables, and space will be allocated for them on the calling function's stack each time the function is called.

Function **getq()** makes an immediate test to see if the queue is empty, and returns minus one if it is. The empty condition is indicated by the condition of head and tail pointer equality, as shown in Figure 4.4a.

The function then gets the size of the next message in the queue. Since messages are removed from the queue's head, it uses the head pointer. This pointer is also incremented past the message size byte in the buffer as part of this operation. Note that references to entries in the queue's header structure are made using pointer **source,** which is declared in the function's argument list to be a pointer to a structure of type **que.** Since the queue's head pointer was advanced in getting message size, it is necessary to see if it now points outside the buffer, and therefore needs to be wrapped. It is set to zero if it does.

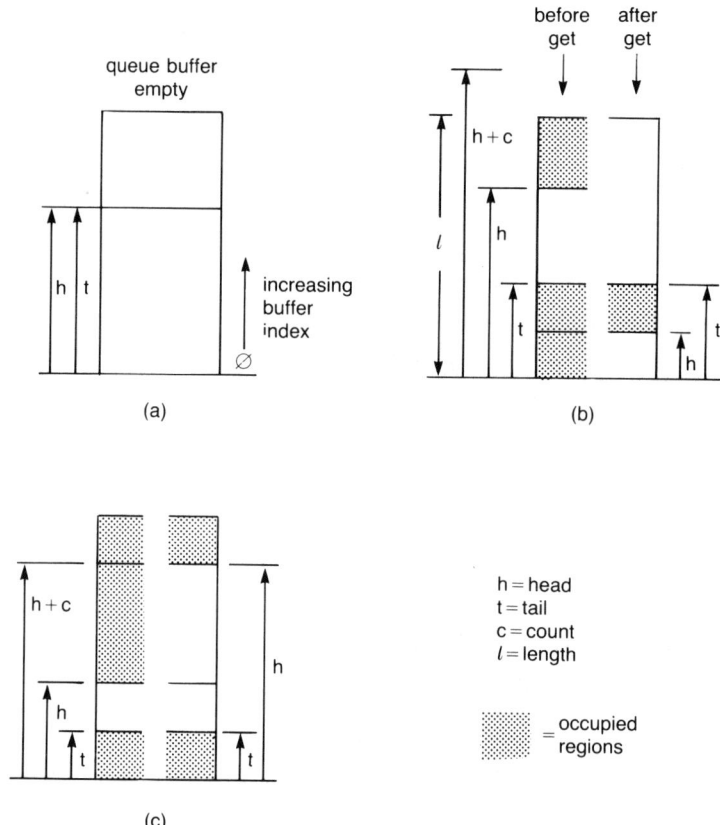

Figure 4.4a–c. Message Queue Get Situations.

It is possible that the message, itself, was wrapped when it was stored in the queue. The function must test for this condition. The situation is shown in Figure 4.4b. If the head pointer plus the length of the message exceeds the length of the buffer, the message is wrapped. In this case the function must remove part of the message from the end of the buffer and the remainder from the buffer's beginning.

To remove message bytes at the buffer's end, **getq()** first computes the number of bytes present and then uses subfunction **mvbyt()** to perform the actual byte transfer. The index of the next open byte location in the destination is then computed for use in the next step.

The remainder of the message is removed from the beginning of the buffer by first computing the number of bytes remaining in the buffer and then using **mvbyt()** again to make the actual byte transfer. Once all bytes have been removed, the queue's head pointer is advanced to point to the start of the next message in the queue.

If the message is not wrapped in the queue, it may be removed in a single operation. This situation is shown in Figure 4.4c. In this case function **mvbyt()** is called just once and the head pointer is then advanced. Since the pointer must point to the next byte after the message just removed, it is possible that this new pointer value points outside the queue's buffer. So it must be tested and wrapped, if necessary. The function then returns to the calling function with the size of the removed message as its return value.

It is evident that functions **putq()** and **getq()** are efficient in their use of memory, since all bytes (save one) of the queue buffer are used to store message data. The functions could have been made simpler if we had decided to simply abandon the space at the end of the buffer when a message would not fit there and store the entire message at the buffer's start. If messages are always short, this might be a worthwhile approach, but, for large messages, this choice would result in a substantial waste of buffer space and a reduction in the number of messages that could be held in the buffer at any given time. The decision to wrap messages causes the functions to be more complex and, as a result, increases their execution time. The benefit is that buffer space is preserved.

It should also be evident that function execution time is proportional to the size of the message and is also dependent upon the situation in the queue. If the message must be wrapped or unwrapped, execution time will be longer. This can be important if timing is critical in an application program.

When we discuss buffer pointer queues in a later section of this chapter, it will be apparent that the alternate set of tradeoffs are implemented. That is, the queue access functions are simpler and therefore faster, their execution times are independent of message size, but they use memory more liberally.

4.2.3 Extended Functions
putqwt() and getqwt()

Certain queue access procedures are performed so often that it is reasonable to write special functions to perform them. These functions, called extended functions, provide enhanced services in addition to calling **putq()** and **getq()** to perform actual queue data transfers. A set of two such functions is shown in Figure 4.5. The role that these functions can play in a program was discussed in Section 2.3. Briefly, they perform a queue access operation if possible, or wait—that is, suspend the calling task—if they cannot. In addition,

```
/*
 *      CX/68K   Executive, Version 1.0   (4/10/86)
 *
 *      (c) 1984  Walter S. Heath, all rights reserved.
 *
 *      FILE QUEAE.C
 *
 *      This file contains extended queue access functions that allow
 *      data flow to control the task execution sequence. If an output
 *      queue is full, putqwt() will suspend its calling task until
 *      room is made available in the queue. Similarly, if an input
 *      queue is empty, getqwt() will suspend its calling task until
 *      an entry is placed in the queue.
 */

#include "qsymb.h"

/*
 *---putqwt(source,dest,stask,count) - "put msg in queue or wait"
 *      This function moves 'count' bytes from the location pointed to
 *      by 'source' to queue 'dest' - if enough room exists in the queue.
 *      If not enough room exists, the calling task's number 'stask' is
 *      stored in the queue's header and the task suspends.  getqwt() will
 *      then wake the task when it removes an entry from the queue.
 *      Similarly, if the queue is empty when putqwt() is called and the
 *      header's task byte contains a value, putqwt() will wake that task.
 *      The task byte was loaded by a getqwt() call when the queue was
 *      empty.
 */

putqwt(source,dest,stask,count)
char *source                    ;
struct que *dest                ;
short stask                     ;
unsigned char count             ;
{
short status                    ;/*queue status:
                                        = 0 , queue was empty
                                        = 1 , queue part loaded
                                        = -1, queue was full        */
```

Figure 4.5. Extended Message Queue Functions.

```
/*
 *Call putq() to determine condition of queue. If it is empty and the
 *'task' byte in the header is not -1 (not empty), wake the task. putq()
 *also stores the message.
 */
do{
    if((status = putq(source,dest,count)) == 0 && dest->task != -1){
        wake(dest->task)            ;/*wake the waiting task              */
        dest->task = -1             ;/*clear the waiting task number      */
    }
    else if(status == -1){           /*If not enough room, suspend        */
        dest->task = stask          ;/*store calling task's number        */
        sleep()                     ;/*suspend this task                  */
    }
}
while(status == -1)                 ;
return                              ;
}                                    /*end of putqwt()                   */


/*
 *---getqwt(source,dest,stask) - "get msg from queue or wait"
 *      This function moves an entry from queue 'source' to the location
 *      pointed to by 'dest' - if the queue is not empty. If the queue
 *      is empty it stores the calling task's number 'stask' in the
 *      queue's header and suspends the task. putqwt() will then wake the
 *      task when it stores an entry in the queue. Similarly, if the
 *      queue is full and the queue header's task byte contains a task
 *      number, getqwt() will wake that task. The task byte was loaded
 *      by putqwt() when it tried to put an entry in the queue.
 */

getqwt(source,dest,stask)
struct que *source              ;
char *dest                      ;
short stask                     ;
{
short status                        ;/*queue status:
                                       = byte count if entry found
                                       = -1 if buffer was empty          */
```

(Continued on next page.)

```
/*
 *Call getq() to determine the condition of the queue. If the 'task'
 *byte in the header is not -1 (not empty), wake the task. getq() also
 *gets the entry.
 */
do{
    if((status = getq(source,dest)) != -1 && source->task != -1){
        wake(source->task)           ;/*wake the waiting task           */
        source->task = -1            ;/*clear the waiting task number */
    }
    else if(status == -1){            /*If buffer empty, suspend.       */
        source->task = stask         ;/*store calling task's number     */
        sleep()                      ;/*suspend calling task            */
    }
}while(status == -1)                  ;

return(status)                        ;/*end of getqwt()                 */
}

                                       /*end of QUEAE.C file             */
```

Figure 4.5. (*continued*) Extended Message Queue Functions.

if they detect that another task is waiting for the completion of their queue operation, they wake that task after the operation is completed. We will review the code required to implement these functions in this section.

Function **putqwt()** puts a message pointed to by **source** into the queue pointed to by **dest**—or waits if insufficient room exists. The task ID of the calling task is specified by **stask** and message size, by argument **count**. An example of the use of this function is:

putqwt(idlbuf,&idlkey,IDLEID, numchrs) ;

where **idlbuf** is the name of an array containing a message of **numchrs** characters, **idlkey** is the target queue, and **IDLEID** (a symbolic name for a constant) is the task ID of the calling task.

Referring to Figure 4.5, the function calls **putq()** to attempt to store the message. If it is successful and the queue was previously empty, it then checks to see if a task was waiting for the stored message. This is indicated by the presence of a valid task ID number in the queue's header **task** variable. If a task is waiting, it wakes it and resets the task ID field in the header.

On the other hand, if **putq()** is not able to store the message, the function puts the calling task's ID in the queue's header and calls executive function **sleep()** to suspend the task. As we will see shortly, function **getqwt()** is designed to wake the suspended task when it removes a message from the queue.

The **putqwt()** function will repeat its operations until its **putq()** call is successful. It may be necessary for it to repeat the call several times before sufficient room becomes available to store the message.

Figure 4.5 also shows function **getqwt()**. This function is the complement of **putqwt()**. It gets a message from the queue pointed to by **source** and puts it in memory starting at the location pointed to by **dest**. Again, the ID of the calling task is specified by **stask**. An example call is:

numchrs = getqwt(&idlkey,keybuf,KEYBID) ;

In this call **idlkey** is the queue name, **keybuf** is the destination array, and **KEYBID** is the symbolic ID number of the calling task. The function returns the size of the message received.

As the figure indicates, the operation of this function is very similar to that of **putqwt()**. Differences are that this function calls **getq()**, rather than **putq()**, and the roles of pointers **source** and **dest** are interchanged.

Functions **putqwt()** and **getqwt()** are usually used together to set up a communication path between two tasks. When no data is present in the queue, **getqwt()**, in the destination task, waits until **putqwt()**, in the source task, provides a message and wakes it. Similarly, when **putqwt()**, in the source task, is unable to deposit a message in the queue, it waits until **getqwt()** removes a message and wakes it. In this way, data flow controls the scheduling of the tasks. In other words, data flow controls program flow.

Note that these functions may be used to implement task synchronization and rendezvous operations. In these applications the content of the message that is sent is not usually important. Instead, the fact that a message is present or absent will determine whether a task will continue or suspend. Thus, tasks may coordinate their operations by passing "signal" messages to each other using these functions.

This completes our discussion of message queues. The alternative type of queue supported by the executive is the buffer pointer queue. We will examine these queues and the functions needed to access them in the next several sections.

4.3 THE BUFFER POINTER QUEUE HEADER

The definition of a buffer pointer queue header structure is presented in include file **pqsymb.h,** shown in Figure 4.6. The structure is similar to the message queue header structure described in Section 4.1. It contains head and tail pointers, the length of the queue array, a task ID field, and a pointer to a queue array. This structure also contains an additional flag to indicate the queue-full condition. For buffer pointer queues the head and tail pointers are equal when the queue is either full or empty. As a result, it is necessary to maintain this flag to distinguish between the two cases. This contrasts with the message queue case, where head and tail equality is used to uniquely define the queue-empty condition.

As with message queues, queue entries are removed from the head and are added at the tail of a buffer pointer queue. Except for the case where a queue is full, the tail pointer always points to the next available empty entry and the head points to the next entry to be

```
/*
 *      CX/68K Executive, Version 1.0      (4/10/86)
 *
 *      (c)  1984  Walter S. Heath, all rights rreserved.
 *
 *      FILE PQSYMB.H
 *
 *      Pointer queue data structure declaration.
 */

struct pque{                         /*buffer pointer queue header   */
        char full           ;/*queue-full flag                       */
        short head          ;/*queue head position (index)           */
        short tail          ;/*queue tail position (index)           */
        short lngth         ;/*queue length (# of entries)           */
        char task           ;/*waiting task ID                       */
        long *pbuf          ;/*pointer to array of ptrs              */
}                            ;

                                     /*end of PQSYMB.H file          */
```

Figure 4.6. Buffer Pointer Queue Header Declaration.

removed. Note that pointer **pbuf** is defined differently for the pointer queue. It points to an array of pointers, rather than to a message buffer.

Buffer pointer queues for example program CX3 are declared in file **ques3.c,** shown in Figure 7.3. The four queues are **fidlkey, oidlkey, okeycon,** and **oconidl.** Their corresponding pointer arrays are **fikbuf[], oikbuf[], okcbuf[],** and **ocibuf[],** respectively. They are initialized when the executive kernel function **cx**() calls function **qinit**(), also shown in the figure. The queue header entries are initialized to values similar to the values for corresponding entries in the program's message queue headers. This is evident in the figure. The **full** variables are set to zero to indicate that the queues are not initially full. Again, the **head** and **tail** pointers are really indexes into the pointer array, rather than actual memory addresses.

Variables in the headers are used by buffer pointer primitive functions to access the pointer arrays. These functions will be examined in detail in the next section.

4.4 BUFFER POINTER QUEUE ACCESS FUNCTIONS

Buffer pointer queue functions are present in file **bptr.c,** shown in Figure 4.7. File **pqsymb.h,** discussed in the previous section, is included in this file to provide the definition of pointer queue header structure **pque.** Primitive functions for accessing buffer pointer

```
/*
 *      CX/68K Executive, Version 1.0   (4/10/86)
 *
 *      (c)  1984  Walter S. Heath, all rights reserved.
 *
 *      FILE BPTR.C  Buffer Pointer Queue Access Functions.
 *                   All functions are reentrant.
 */

#include "pqsymb.h"

/*
 *---putbp(pointer,dest)  "Put a buffer pointer"
 *      This function puts pointer 'pointer' at the tail of the queue
 *      pointed to by 'dest'.  If the queue is full, it returns -1.
 *      Otherwise the function returns zero.
 */

putbp(pointer,dest)
char *pointer                   ;
struct pque *dest               ;
{
short trytail                   ;/*trial tail                             */
/*
 *If the pointer queue is full, return -1.
 */
if(dest->full == 1)
        return(-1)              ;

trytail = dest->tail + 1        ;/*compute a trial tail pointer           */

if(trytail == dest->lngth)       /*If pointer should be wrapped,          */
        trytail = 0             ;/*wrap it.                               */

if(trytail == dest->head){       /*If the queue is full,                  */
            dest->full = 1      ;/*indicate queue is full.                */
}
/*
 *Room exists: update tail pointer and store 'pointer' in queue; return
 *zero.
 */
dest->pbuf[dest->tail] = (long)pointer;
dest->tail = trytail            ;
```

Figure 4.7. Buffer Pointer Queue Functions. (*Continued on next page.*)

```
return(0)                        ;
}                                /*end of function putbp()              */

/*
 *---getbp(source)  "Get a buffer pointer"
 *     This function gets a buffer pointer from the queue pointed to by
 *     'source'.  If no pointers are present, it returns -1.  Otherwise
 *     the function returns the pointer.
 */

char *getbp(source)
struct pque *source              ;
{
char *pointer                    ;/*buffer pointer value returned       */
/*
 *If the pointer queue is empty, return -1.
 */
if(source->head == source->tail && source->full == 0)
      return((char *)-1)         ;
/*
 *Remove a pointer from the queue; advance head pointer; wrap it if
 *necessary.
 */
pointer = (char *)source->pbuf[source->head++] ;
source->full = 0                 ;/*indicate queue is not full          */

if(source->head == source->lngth) /*If pointer should be wrapped,       */
      source->head = 0           ;/*wrap it.                            */
/*
 *Return the pointer.
 */
return(pointer)                  ;
}                                /*end of getbp() function             */


/*
 *---putbpwt(pointer,dest,stask)  "Put buffer ptr or wait if full"
 *     This function puts buffer pointer 'pointer' in queue `dest`—if
 *     enough room exists in the queue.  If not enough room exists, the
 *     calling task's number 'stask' is stored in the queue's header and
 *     the task suspends.  getbpwt() will then wake the task when it
 *     removes an entry from the queue.  Similarly, if the header's 'task'
 *     byte contains a task number, putbpwt() will wake that task.  The
 *     task byte was loaded by a getbpwt() call when the queue was empty.
 */
```

Figure 4.7. (*continued*) Buffer Pointer Queue Functions.

```
putbpwt(pointer,dest,stask)
char *pointer                    ;
struct pque *dest                ;
short stask                      ;
{
short retval                     ;/*putbp() value returned              */
do{
/*
 *Check for successful transfer first.
 */
        if((retval = putbp(pointer,dest)) == 0){ /*If putbp() successful  */
                if(dest->task != -1) {/*if a task is waiting,            */
                        wake(dest->task);/*wake it and                   */
                dest->task = -1    ;/*clear waiting task number.          */
                }
                return             ;
        }
/*
 *If queue is full, suspend.
 */
        if(retval == -1){          /*If queue is full,                   */
                dest->task = stask ;/*store calling task's number        */
                sleep()                  ;/*and suspend this task.        */
        }
}while(retval == -1)               ;/*repeat while queue is full          */
}                                  /*end of putbpwt()                    */



/*
 *---getbpwt(source,stask)   "Get buffer ptr or wait if empty"
 *     This function returns a buffer pointer from queue 'source'—if
 *     the queue is not empty.  If the queue is empty the calling task's
 *     number 'stask` is stored in the queue's header and the task
 *     syspends. putbpwt() will then wake the task when it places an
 *     entry in the queue.  Similarly, if the header's 'task' byte
 *     contains a task number, getbpwt() will wake the task.  The 'task'
 *     byte was loaded by a putbpwt() call when the queue was full.
 */

char *getbpwt(source,stask)
struct pque *source              ;
short stask                      ;
{
char *retval                     ;/*getbp() value returned              */
```

(Continued on next page.)

```
do{
/*
 *Check for successful transfer first.
 */
      if((retval = (char *)getbp(source)) != (char *)-1){
                            /*If getbp() successful,             */
            if(source->task != -1){   /*if a task is waiting,    */
                  wake(source->task);/*wake it and               */
                  source->task = -1 ;/*clear waiting task number. */
            }
            return(retval)             ;/*return the pointer      */
      }
/*
 *If queue is empty, suspend.
 */
      if(retval == (char *)-1){   /*If queue is empty,           */
            source->task = stask;/*store calling task's number   */
            sleep()                    ;/*and suspend the task.   */
      }
}while(retval == (char *)-1)            ;/*repeat while queue is empty  */
}                                 /*end of getbpwt()             */

                                  /*end of BPTR.C file           */
```

Figure 4.7. (*continued*) Buffer Pointer Queue Functions.

queues are **getbp()** and **putbp().** These functions will be reviewed in the next two sections.

The way in which buffer pointer queues are used in an application program was examined in detail in Section 2.3. Before beginning our study of the buffer pointer primitive functions, it will be useful to briefly review that subject again.

An application task sends data to another task by removing a pointer to an empty buffer from a free list queue, filling the buffer with data, and then depositing the buffer pointer in an occupied list queue. It calls **getbp()** to remove the pointer to the free buffer and **putbp()** to store the pointer to the occupied buffer. Recall that the free buffer pointer queue must initially be filled with pointers to free buffers by application code.

The receiving task gets a pointer to a buffer containing data from an occupied list queue, processes the data in some fashion, and then deposits the pointer to a now-empty buffer in the free list queue, where it is then again available for reuse by the sending task. Each communication path between tasks therefore requires two queues—a free list queue and an occupied list queue.

Variations are possible in the way pointer queues are used. For example, it is possible for a task to simply pass a pointer to an occupied buffer on to another task, and that task could pass it on again, etc. But at some point the pointer must be returned to the originating free list queue, thus closing the loop. This procedure is used in the application programs to be described in later chapters.

We are now ready to begin our study of the buffer pointer queue primitive functions.

4.4.1 The putbp()
Primitive Function

As shown in Figure 4.7, the **putbp()** function puts a pointer to a buffer specified by argument **pointer** into the queue located by pointer **dest.** An example use of this function is:

retval = putbp(idlbuf,&fidlkey) ;

Here the address of array **idlbuf[]** is placed in pointer queue **fidlkey** and the function returns a value to variable **retval.**

The **putbp()** function declares variable **trytail.** It is used to compute a trail tail pointer. Since this variable is declared within the scope of the function, it is recognized by the C compiler to be of type automatic. Thus the compiler will allocate new space for it on the calling program's stack each time the function is called.

The function first tests to see if the queue is full. This is indicated by queue header variable **full** being set to one. In this case the function returns immediately with return value minus one.

Note that queue header variables are referenced by means of pointer **dest,** which is declared in the function argument list to be a pointer to a structure of type **pque.** All variables in the queue header are referenced in this way.

If the queue is not full, the function computes trial tail pointer, **trytail.** Since the queue array only holds pointers, and pointers are fixed-size entries, the new trail tail is simply the index of the next entry after the current tail entry. A test must then be made to see if the trial tail pointer points outside the array and therefore should be wrapped. If necessary it is wrapped by setting it equal to zero—the index of the first entry in the queue's array.

With a valid new tail pointer, the function next tests to see if the queue will be full when the new entry is added. This condition will exist if the new tail and the current head pointers are equal. In this case the **full** flag should be set.

At this point the buffer pointer can finally be loaded into the queue's buffer array at the location pointed to by the current tail pointer. The tail pointer is then updated to its new value and the function returns with return value zero, indicating that the function was successful.

4.4.2 The getbp()
Primitive Function

The **getbp()** function, shown in Figure 4.7, gets a pointer from the queue pointed to by argument **source.** The function returns the pointer—or minus one, if it fails. An example call is:

idlptr = getbp(&fidlkey) ;

The statement calls **getbp()** to attempt to get a pointer from queue **fidlkey** and place it in pointer variable **idlptr.** Typically, the returned value is tested to see if the operation was successful.

The function begins by declaring internal variable **pointer.** The C compiler will treat this as an automatic variable and, as a consequence, will allocate new space for it on the currently active stack each time the function is called.

A check is made immediately to see if the queue is empty. This condition exists when the queue's head and tail pointers are equal and its **full** flag is zero. When this condition exists, the function returns with return value minus one. Otherwise, it proceeds to remove a pointer.

Buffer pointers are removed from the queue's head. When a pointer is removed, the head pointer is advanced by one queue array entry. Since an entry was removed, the **full** flag can then be cleared (whether the queue was previously full or not).

Since the queue's head pointer was advanced, it is then necessary to check and see if it should be wrapped. A pointer is wrapped by setting it to zero, so that it points to the first entry in the queue's array. The function then returns with the removed pointer as its return value.

Before leaving the subject of buffer pointer queue primitive functions, we will summarize the characteristics of this type of queue and compare them to the properties of message queues. This will be helpful when it becomes necessary to make a choice between message queues and buffer pointer queues in an application program design.

It is clear from the listings that the buffer pointer queue primitive functions are simpler than the primitive functions for message queues. As a consequence, they execute faster. It is also evident that, in most cases, less actual data are moved to or from a pointer queue, since only a pointer is moved. In addition, since the size of the data is fixed, function execution time is not dependent on message size. Execution time will be shortest when the function fails, and longest when a queue pointer must be wrapped.

On the other hand, what is not evident from the listings is the use of memory by the actual data buffers. When the buffers are declared in the application program, their size must be large enough to hold the largest data block expected by the application. For smaller blocks, the extra space is wasted.

In most real-time applications, speed of operation is the primary consideration, rather than preservation of memory. If memory is available, it might as well be used. Under these circumstances it makes sense to use buffer pointer queues. But if memory space is limited and an execution time margin is anticipated, the better choice might well be message queues.

4.4.3 Extended Functions
putbpwt() and getbpwt()

File **bptr.c,** in Figure 4.7, also contains extended functions **putbpwt()** and **getbpwt().** These functions provide the same enhanced services for buffer pointer queues as functions **putqwt()** and **getgwt()** do for message queues. That is, they attempt to perform a queue operation and suspend the calling task if they cannot. If they are successful, they also check to see if a task is waiting, and wake it if one is. Again, these functions provide a mechanism that allows data flow to control program flow. These functions are especially useful for systems that are primarily concerned with the collection and transport of large quantities of data.

The **putbpwt()** and **getbpwt()** functions are very similar in design to their message queue counterparts; thus it will not be necessary to go through an explanation of their operation again at this point. It will be sufficient to present examples of their use in an application program.

In Chapter 5 we will be discussing an example program that uses these functions. A pointer is passed from a task called **idle()** to a task called **keybd()** using statement

$$\textbf{putbpwt(idleptr,\&oidlkey,IDLEID) ;}$$

Variable **idleptr** contains the pointer to be sent. It is placed in queue **oidlkey.** The task ID that will be placed in the queue's header if the operation fails is specified by symbolic constant **IDLEID.** The **keybd()** task contains the following statement to receive the pointer

$$\textbf{keyptr = getbpwt(\&oidlkey,KEYBID) ;}$$

The statement calls **getbp()** to get the pointer from queue **oidlkey** and delivers it to variable **keyptr.** Symbolic constant **KEYBID** specifies the task ID of the receiving **keybd()** task.

It is often the case that an application program will need additional or different functions to satisfy its particular data transport requirements. For example, it is possible that a task might need to know how many buffer pointers are present in a queue or might need to access them in last-in–first-out (LIFO) order. The functions required in these and other situations should be similar in structure to the ones discussed in this section.

Buffer pointer queues may be used to reduce the need to transfer large quantities of data from point to point in a program. For example, a design might consist of a central dispatcher task that receives a pointer to data collected from a device-input task and then "clones" the pointer. It might then send the copies of the pointer to several satellite tasks. These tasks could then access and process the received data and then return the pointers to the dispatcher. When the dispatcher has collected all cloned pointers, it would then return the original pointer to the device-input task. In this way all satellite tasks are given access to the data without having to move it from its original buffer. This a very efficient arrangement.

4.5 QUEUE FUNCTION REENTRANCY

The queue access functions that have been described in this chapter are intended to be used freely by application program tasks and interrupt handlers. But real-time programs run asynchronously, so it is likely that a task or interrupt handler will be interrupted when it is in the process of executing one of these functions. The code that runs as a result of the interruption may call the very same queue access function that was executing when the interruption occurred. As a result, the function is reentered, and if it is not properly designed, this reentry will cause data values computed by the original function execution to be overwritten and lost by the second execution. This may be avoided if the queue access functions are designed to cope with reentrancy.

To be reentrant, a function must create a new set of internal working variables each time it runs. This is usually accomplished by creating space for them on the stack. Each time the function is reentered, a new stack frame is created to hold these variables. As a result, the function works with a separate set of internal variables each time it is reentered. When an instance of function execution is completed, its corresponding stack frame is recovered.

It is also necessary for the interrupting program to save the processor's context (i.e., its registers and flags), since the interrupted function may have data stored in these locations. This context must be restored when the interrupted program resumes. But this is a necessary requirement for any interrupting program and does not impose any additional restrictions on the design of a function to support reentrancy.

It so happens that it is relatively easy to write functions in the C language to support reentrancy. All that is required is to make sure that all internally used variables are declared to be of type automatic. This is accomplished implicitly by placing their declaration statements within the scope of the function. Most C compilers will then create code that will allocate space for them on the program's stack when the function runs. When variables are referenced by statements within the function, the compiler uses offsets from the function's stack frame pointer to access them. This stack space is deallocated by compiler-generated code when the function exits.

When queue access functions were examined in the earlier sections of this chapter, emphasis was placed on the fact that all internally used variables in these functions are declared to be of type automatic. Consequently, the functions are reentrant. But the queue header data structures that these functions access present a different reentrancy problem.

4.6 QUEUE HEADER REENTRANCY

It is also possible for a queue header data structure to be reentered. Consider a case in which a task is performing a **putq()** operation and an interrupt occurs. If the interrupt handler also calls **putq()** to access the same queue, a situation will exist in which two program components are attempting to use the queue's tail pointer to store different entries. Depending on where the interrupt occurs in the task call to **putq(),** a conflict may result. Clearly, a similar conflict will arise with respect to the use of the queue's head pointer if the two program components call **getq().** The same is true if a buffer pointer queue primitive function (**putbp()** or **getbp()**) is called. In each case, the queue header data structure is reentered by the second call before the first call has completed.

There are at least three possible ways to handle the header reentrancy problem: One may disable interrupts during queue accesses, use a semaphore to restrict access to the queue, or restrict the way in which the queue access functions are used. We would like to avoid having to disable interrupts, since this approach has adverse system response time implications. The use of a semaphore will be explored in Chapter 10. In that chapter we will examine a special set of queue access functions that may be used to support communication between multiple processors. Although the semaphore technique works well for that application, it may lead to system deadlock if it is applied improperly in a single processor system. The third option is usually most appropriate for systems that use a single processor. We will explore that option in greater detail.

On reconsideration, the queue header reentry scenario described above is not likely to occur in an actual application. Typically, one program component puts entries into a queue and another removes them. Thus, if we can be assured that the functions will perform properly in this operational mode and we are willing to restrict their use in this fashion, we may avoid the queue header reentrancy problem.

Detailed examination of the code for the primitive queue access functions reveals that since head and tail pointers are updated only after data has been transferred, the functions cannot malfunction by removing an entry that is not there or by overwriting an entry that is. At most, the functions will occasionally indicate that insufficient room exists to store an entry when, in fact, space is available. This is not a serious problem since functions must always have a strategy for dealing with the queue-full condition. Queue buffer size may also be expanded.

Thus, we may be assured that the functions will perform properly if their use is restricted such that only one program component puts entries into a queue and only one removes them. Again, this is not a serious restriction since it is relatively easy to establish a separate queue for each communication path in an application program.

It should be noted that even if one of the program components is an interrupt handler and the other is a task, no problem will arise as long as one component puts data into the queue and the other gets data from it. We will see in Chapter 6 that an interrupt handler must run to completion before the processor will accept another interrupt at the same level. Thus, the queue access operation performed by the handler cannot be reentered. On the other hand, the queue operation performed by the task could be interrupted and the interrupt handler could reenter the queue. But if we have observed the restriction that program components must perform only complementary operations on a queue, no conflict will arise, since the two components will be accessing opposite ends of the queue. We have already observed that the queue access functions have been written to avoid any conflict in this situation.

Although this discussion of reentrancy addresses only issues concerning queue access functions and queue headers, it is important to realize that the same restrictions apply to any function or data structure that is shared by several components of an application program that performs operations asynchronously. For example, if functions to format data for an operator's terminal screen are called from interrupted and interrupting program components, they must also be reentrant. The same is true for the compiler's C and math library functions.

The requirements for reentrancy are somewhat relaxed if the real-time program uses a nonpreemptive task scheduler. In this environment a task will continue execution until it voluntarily suspends—or until an interrupt occurs. As long as a shared function is not called by an interrupt handler, a task may call it and be assured that it will run to completion without being reentered. As a consequence, it is not necessary for the function to be reentrant in this special situation. A similar statement may be made for a shared data structure.

5

Example Application Program CX2

In the first four chapters of this book we studied the operation of a real-time executive both in general terms, at the functional level, and, in detail, at the program listing level. The material presented is consistent and complete; all of the code required to construct a real-time environment for an application program was presented and discussed. At this point it would be possible for one to create a real-time program that uses nonpreemptive task scheduling without further reference to this book. But more can be learned about this executive and about real-time programming in general by studying specific example programs that demonstrate the executive's capabilities and the way executive and application functions interact.

In this chapter we will examine the first of three example application programs to be presented in this book. This first program will demonstrate priority scheduling of multiple application tasks and data communication between tasks using buffer pointer queues.

In Chapter 7, we will extend the program presented in this chapter to include support for interrupts and message queues, and in Chapter 9 we will extend it still further to demonstrate preemptive scheduling. All of the application software needed to construct the first application program is presented in this chapter. Chapters 7 and 9 include all of the software required to modify the program presented in this chapter to demonstrate the additional features. Each chapter will conclude with a section describing program operation and will present the results of performance measurements obtained by monitoring program operation with a logic analyzer.

With the material presented in these chapters it should be possible to reconstruct the example programs, run them on a target real-time computer system, and verify the operation and performance results reported here. It is recommended that this be done if one plans to use the executive, since it will increase familiarity with it and with real-time programming techniques. The example programs also provide a means to test a new version of the executive.

5.1 THE CX2 PROGRAM, A FUNCTIONAL DESCRIPTION

Figure 5.1 shows a block diagram for program CX2. This relatively simple program consists of three tasks and four buffer pointer queues. The tasks are named **idle()**, **keybd()**, and **consol()**. These names are arbitrary and are not intended to indicate the function performed by each task.

A naming convention has been adopted for buffer pointer queues. The name for a queue that holds pointers to free (empty) buffers begins with the letter "f"; a queue that holds pointers to occupied buffers starts with an "o." In addition, the next three letters in the name identify the source task; the last three, the destination task for the communication path being supported. Thus, name **oidlkey** specifies a queue that holds pointers to occupied buffers for the communication path between the **idle()** and **keybd()** tasks.

In a typical application program, each communication path is supported by both free and occupied pointer queues. This was discussed in Section 2.3. But, to simplify this demonstration program, it was decided to simply pass one pointer along from one task to the next. So the program gets a pointer from free pointer queue **fidlkey**, fills the associated buffer with a message, and then passes the buffer pointer from task to task and finally returns it to queue **fidlkey**.

The **idle()** task is the first to run. It is awakened during program initiation. This task contains the interface to the operator. Figure 5.2 shows the display generated by this task.

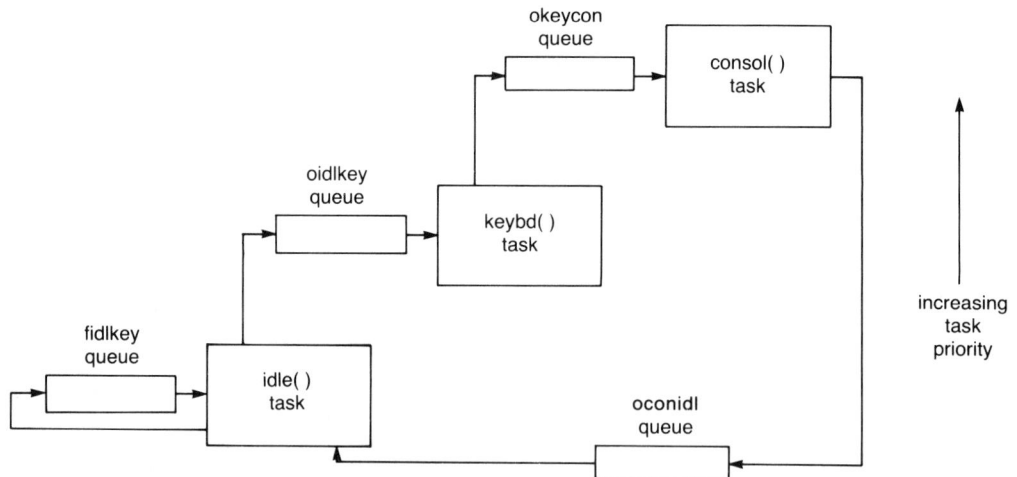

Figure 5.1. CX2 Application Program Flow Diagram.

```
CX/68K  Executive, Version 1.0 (4/10/86)

(c) 1984 Walter S. Heath
    All rights reserved

This program demonstrates the task scheduling and
queue access capabilities of CX/68K.

This text is coming from the idle() task. The message you
enter below will be sent via queue 'idlkey' to the keybd()
task.  Keybd() will pass it on via queue 'keycon' to task
consol().  Consol() will send it back to the idle() task
via queue 'conidl'.

You will also be asked to enter the number of cycles this
loop will be repeated.

To exit the program type <CR> at any prompt.


Enter up to 8 characters:
ASDFGHJK

Enter number of repeat cycles (1 to 500000):
123456

I'm running . . .

ASDFGHJK

Enter up to 8 characters:
```

Figure 5.2. CX2 Application Program Console Display.

As the text indicates, the task prompts the operator to enter a string of up to eight characters (an arbitrary limit). A second prompt requests the number of repeat cycles.

The character string that is entered by the operator is loaded into a buffer pointed to by a pointer previously removed from queue **fidlkey**. After the operator enters the repeat count, the pointer to the message buffer is sent to the **keybd()** task and that task is awakened. The **idle()** task then suspends (calls **sleep()**). When the **keybd()** task is run by the scheduler, it inputs the buffer pointer from queue **oidlkey** and outputs it to queue **okeycon.** It then wakes task **consol()** and suspends. Task **consol()** performs a similar operation. It passes the message buffer pointer from queue **okeycon** to queue **oconidl** and wakes **idle().** This constitutes a program cycle.

The cycle is repeated the number of times requested by the operator before the message text is redisplayed on the console and the operator is again prompted to enter a new message. The buffer pointer is also returned to queue **fidlkey** in the process.

It is evident that the program demonstrates task scheduling and message passing by means of buffer pointer queues. In operation it also gives the operator a feel for the executive's speed. Finally, as we will see in Section 5.7, it provides a test program that we can use to measure task-to-task switch time and other performance parameters using a logic analyzer.

Before we begin our study of the code required to implement the CX2 program, we will review some simple support functions needed to manage operator console I/O.

5.2 CONSOLE I/O
SUPPORT FUNCTIONS

When example program CX2 is run on a target single board computer (SBC), it must access the operator's console via the board's serial port. Most SBCs contain a monitor/debugger program in a PROM that is used to start and test programs. Typically, the monitor will provide a means for application programs to access the operator's console via a **trap** instruction. Various operations may be requested by manipulating parameters passed to the monitor through registers and/or the stack. The example programs in this book use this method to access the operator's console.

If the PROM monitor on the SBC that one plans to use does not provide console access via a **trap** instruction (or by some other means), you can still access the console by simply reinitializing the board's serial port and taking control of it. To do this, one will need a description of the software interface to the SBC's serial port chip and the locations of its registers in the board's memory map. The interface description may be obtained from the chip's data sheet; the chip's memory addresses should be specified in the SBC's manual. If the SBC does not have a serial port, one can use a port on a separate card and access it over the bus.

Note that the code to access the operator's console is the only part of the CX2 program that may need to be altered to run the program on a target SBC. The remaining code should run as shown using any 680X0 processor with appropriate memory.

The console I/O functions are contained in two files. The actual interface to the PROM monitor is handled in assembly language. File **apio2.s,** in Figure 5.3, shows this code. Higher level functions, written in C, are presented in file **conio.c,** shown in Figure 5.4. We will review the assembly language code first.

5.2.1 Console I/O Assembly
Language Code

Three primitive interface functions are shown in Figure 5.3: **_putch, _getlin,** and **_getout.** They provide output, input, and exit interfaces to the SBC's PROM monitor, respectively.

Function **_putch** outputs the ASCII character in global **long** variable **_outchr** to the console. For the SBC supported by this code, it is necessary to load the character onto the stack and to indicate that this is an output operation by placing a four in register **d0.** The **trap #15** instruction then initiates the operation in the PROM monitor.

The **_getlin** function operates similarly. It gets a line of ASCII characters entered at the terminal. In this case the monitor requires the program to place a pointer to a destination buffer on the stack and to load an eight into the **d0** register.

```
|***********************************************************************
|*      CX/68K Executive, Version 1.0   (4/10/86)
|*
|*      (c)  1984  Walter S. Heath, all rights reserved.
|*
|*      FILE   APIO2.S
|*
|*      This file contains functions to interface to the single board
|*      computer's monitor.
|*
|*      REVISED:
|*              8/8/88
|***********************************************************************

        .data
        .comm   _outchr,4
        .comm   _inbuf,40
|*
|*---putch
|*      This function sends a character to the console CRT
|*
        .text
        .globl _putch

_putch:
        moveml #0x0004,sp@-          |save a5

        lea     _outchr,a5          |get address of _outchr
        movl    #4,d0               |set putchar() routine #
        movl    a5@,sp@-            |load character to send
        trap    #15                 |enter monitor

        moveml sp@+,#0x2000         |restore a5
        rts
|*
|*---getlin
|*      This function gets a line of characters entered via the console
|*      keyboard
|*
        .text
        .globl _getlin

_getlin:
        moveml #0x0004,sp@-          |save a5
```

Figure 5.3. CX2 Monitor Interface Functions. (*Continued on next page.*)

```
        lea     _inbuf,a5           |get buffer-start address
        movl    #8,d0               |set getline() routine #
        movl    a5,sp@-             |load buffer pointer
        trap    #15                 |enter monitor
                                    |character count returned in d0
        moveml  sp@+,#0x2000        |restore a5
        rts
|*
|*---getout
|*      This function provides re-entry to the monitor
|*
        .text
        .globl  _getout

_getout:
        movl    #0x07c,a5           |get level 7 (ABORT) vector addr
        jmp     a5@                 |jump to ABORT handler
|*
|*                                  end of APIO2.S file
|*
```

Figure 5.3. (*continued*) CX2 Monitor Interface Functions.

For convenience, a simple function is included to provide a means to exit the program (alternatively, the operator could toggle the SBC's RESET or ABORT switch). The **_getout** function simply gets the address of the monitor's level 7 (ABORT) interrupt handler from its vector location and jumps to that address.

5.2.2 Console I/O C Code

The functions in file **conio.c,** shown in Figure 5.4, provide just enough enhanced console I/O support to satisfy the needs of the example application programs discussed in this book. They call the PROM monitor interface functions in file **apio2.s** to perform the actual I/O operations. Since the PROM monitor uses the polling technique to access the serial port, they are generally not appropriate for use in time-critical applications. For these systems the console interface is normally implemented using interrupts, so that higher priority real-time operations are not delayed by these relatively slow transfers.

Function **conout()** outputs a string of characters pointed to it by its first argument. The number of characters output is specified by its second argument. The function is simply a program loop that places a character to be output in global **long** variable **outchr** and calls assembly language function **putch().** When the requested number of characters have been output, it sends a final carriage return character and returns.

Console input function **conin()** returns characters to an input buffer pointed to by the function's first argument. It loads up to the number of characters specified by the second argument into this buffer and returns the number loaded. If the operator enters more than

```
/*
 *     CX/68K Executive, Version 1.0 (4/10/86)
 *
 *     (c) 1984  Walter S. Heath, all rights reserved.
 *
 *     FILE CONIO.C
 *
 *             Console Input/Output Functions.
 *
 *     These functions provide restricted console I/O services. They
 *     call assembly language functions _putch, _getlin and _getout
 *     to interface to a single board computer's PROM monitor.
 *
 *     REVISED:
 *           8/8/88
 */
extern long outchr                 ;
extern char inbuf[]                ;

/*
 *---conout(addro,numo)
 *     This function outputs 'numo' characters starting at address
 *     'addro' to the console.
 */
conout(addro,numo)
char *addro                        ;
char numo                          ;
{
char chrout                        ;/*output character                  */
char ctrout                        ;/*output loop counter               */

for( ctrout = 0; ctrout < numo; ctrout++ ){
      chrout = *addro++            ;/*get a char to output              */
      outchr = chrout              ;/*store it for putch()              */
      putch()                      ;/*output it                         */
}
outchr = 0x0D                      ;/*output a CR                       */
putch()                            ;
}                                   /*end of conout()                   */
```

Figure 5.4. Console I/O Functions. (*Continued on next page.*)

```
/*
 *---conin(addri,numi)
 *      This function returns up to 'numi' characters in a buffer pointed
 *      to by 'addri'.  If more than 'numi' characters are entered only
 *      the count is returned.
 */
conin(addri,numi)
char *addri                     ;
short numi                      ;
{
short numin                     ;/*number of characters entered    */
short i                         ;/*working index                   */

numin = getlin()                ;/*get a line of input chars       */
if(numin == 0)                   /*If a <CR> was entered,          */
      getout()                  ;/*exit to VME monitor.            */

if(numin <= numi){               /*If within # requested,          */
      for(i = 0; i < numin; i++)  /*copy to requested buffer.       */
            *addri++ = inbuf[i] ;
}
return(numin)                   ;
}                                /*end of conin()                  */
```

```
/*
 *---numin()
 *      This function inputs a number string from the console and
 *      converts it from ASCII to binary for output. It returns -1
 *      if a non-numeric ASCII character was entered or if more than
 *      six numbers were entered.
 */
numin()
{
unsigned long numbr             ;/*return number accumulator       */
char num                        ;/*ASCII number char               */
short numi                      ;/*number of characters input      */
short i                         ;/*loop counter                    */
numbr = 0                       ;/*clear accumulator               */
if((numi = getlin()) > 6)        /*get a line of input chars       */
      return(-1)                ;/*If more than 6, return -1.      */
```

Figure 5.4. (*continued*) Console I/O Functions.

```
if(numi == 0)                        /*If a <CR> was entered,    */
      getout()                       ;/*exit to VME monitor.      */

for( i = 0; i < numi; i++){
      num = inbuf[i]              ;/*get next char               */
      if(num < '0' || num > '9')  /*If a non-numeric char,      */
            return(-1)            ;/*return.                     */

numbr = (numbr * 10) + (num & 0X0F) ;/*accumulate number       */
}
return(numbr)                       ;/*return number entered    */
}                                    /*end of numin()           */

                                     /*end of CONIO.C file      */
```

Figure 5.4. (*continued*) Console I/O Functions.

the specified number, it simply returns the number entered without loading any into the buffer (to prevent buffer overflow).

Function **conin()** calls assembly language function **getlin()** to access the PROM monitor. This function puts the input string in global array **inbuf[]**. The characters in **inbuf[]** are then copied to the buffer specified by **conin()**'s first argument. If the operator simply enters a carriage return (no message characters are entered), the function calls assembly language function **getout()** to terminate the program.

An additional function is provided to input and convert ASCII numeric strings. Function **numin()** calls **getlin()** to get the string, converts each character to its binary numeric equivalent, and accumulates the result. The integer value thus generated is returned. If the number of characters received is greater than six or if a nonnumeric character is entered, it returns a minus one. This function also checks to see if the operator simply entered a carriage return and calls **getout()** in this case to terminate the program.

These functions pass data to and from the assembly language I/O functions using global memory locations. A more conventional method would be to pass them as function arguments. But the assembly language functions would then have to access them on the stack. Since various C compilers manage data on the stack differently, the code to accomplish this would be compiler dependent. The global variable method, although less elegant, avoids this problem and makes the functions more portable.

5.3 PROGRAM QUEUES

As we saw in Section 5.1, the CX2 program uses four buffer pointer queues. These queues must be declared and initialized before they can be used. The operations are performed by the code in file **ques2.c,** shown in Figure 5.5.

```
/*
 *      CX/68K Executive, Version 1.0      (4/10/86)
 *
 *      (c)  1984  Walter S. Heath, all rights reserved.
 *
 *      FILE QUES2.C Application Queues and Queue Initialization
 *                    Function.
 */

#include "pqsymb.h"

/*
 *Declare the pointer queue lengths.
 */

#define FIKLNGTH     10                 /*free lists                              */

#define OIKLNGTH     10                 /*occupied lists                          */
#define OKCLNGTH     10
#define OCILNGTH     10

/*
 *Buffer pointer queue declarations.
 */
struct pque fidlkey             ;/*idlkey queue free list header          */
long fikbuf[FIKLNGTH]           ;/*idlkey queue free list buffer          */

struct pque oidlkey             ;/*idlkey occupied list header            */
long oikbuf[OIKLNGTH]           ;/*idlkey occupied list buffer            */

struct pque okeycon             ;
long okcbuf[OKCLNGTH]           ;

struct pque oconidl             ;
long ocibuf[OCILNGTH]           ;
```

Figure 5.5. CX2 Program Queues.

```
/*
 *---qinit()
 *            This function initializes the application queues
 */

qinit()
{
/*
 *Initialize the buffer pointer queues.
 */

fidlkey.full = 0                    ;/*queue-fill flags        */
oidlkey.full = 0                    ;
okeycon.full = 0                    ;
oconidl.full = 0                    ;

fidlkey.head = 0                    ;/*head pointers           */
oidlkey.head = 0                    ;
okeycon.head = 0                    ;
oconidl.head = 0                    ;

fidlkey.tail = 0                    ;/*tail pointers           */
oidlkey.tail = 0                    ;
okeycon.tail = 0                    ;
oconidl.tail = 0                    ;

fidlkey.lngth = FIKLNGTH            ;/*queue lengths           */
oidlkey.lngth = OIKLNGTH            ;
okeycon.lngth = OKCLNGTH            ;
oconidl.lngth = OCILNGTH            ;

fidlkey.task = -1                   ;/*source task numbers     */
oidlkey.task = -1                   ;
okeycon.task = -1                   ;
oconidl.task = -1                   ;

fidlkey.pbuf = fikbuf               ;/*pointers to queues      */
oidlkey.pbuf = oikbuf               ;
okeycon.pbuf = okcbuf               ;
oconidl.pbuf = ocibuf               ;

}                                    /*end of qinit() function */

                                     /*end of QUES2.C file      */
```

Figure 5.5. (*continued*) CX2 Program Queues.

The first part of the file contains queue declarations. Note that this file includes file **pqsymb.h,** which contains the definition of the buffer pointer queue header structure, **pque,** used in the declarations. The **pqsymb.h** file was discussed earlier in Section 4.3 and is shown in Figure 4.6.

The lengths of the buffer pointer queue arrays are defined first. They are set to ten, which is more than sufficient for our purposes. In an actual real-time application program, the number of pointer locations in the queue's arrays should normally equal the number of buffers allocated. This number will depend on the amount of data buffering required to compensate for differences in the rates at which data is produced by the source and consumed by the destination. If the data are produced in bursts and at a rate that is greater than they can be consumed, a large number of buffers will be needed to temporarily store them. Obviously, the average rate of data consumption must be greater than or at least equal to the rate of production to keep the queues from "backing up" (filling).

Each queue declaration consists of a header declaration and a declaration for the queue's pointer array. The arrays must be of type **long,** since they will hold 32 bit pointers.

Executive kernel function **cx()** calls function **qinit()** to initialize the queue headers. This function, for the CX2 program, is also shown in Figure 5.5. We discussed the operations required to initialize buffer pointer queue headers in Section 4.3.

One additional queue initialization operation is required. The addresses of data buffers must be loaded into the free pointer queue arrays. For the CX2 program this operation is performed in the **idle()** task. In more complex programs it could be done in **qinit().**

5.4 PROGRAM INITIALIZATION FUNCTIONS

In this section we will examine several functions that are needed to get the CX2 program initialized and running. One function calls the executive's kernel; the others are called by the kernel. These operations were also discussed in Chapter 3.

5.4.1 The main() Function

In Section 3.2 we saw that the executive's kernel, **cx(),** is called from the program's **main()** function, which is the first function to run in the program and is present in an application file. For the CX2 program this file is **cx2.c.** It is shown in Figure 5.6.

The **cx2.c** file includes file **apsymb2.h,** shown in Figure 5.7. This file defines several symbolic constants needed by the program. The first, **NTSKS,** is the number of application tasks in the program. The remaining three are the task IDs for these tasks. The values correspond to the indexes for the associated TCBs in the TCB data structure. As such, they also indicate task priority, with zero being highest.

File **cx2.c** also contains a declaration for the executive's stack, **cxst[].** We mentioned in Section 3.2 that the stack is declared here—in an application file—so that its size could be adjusted to meet application requirements without having to modify an executive file.

The **main()** function in file **cx2.c** simply initializes variable **ntsks,** needed by the kernel, and then calls the kernel function, **cx().** This function never returns.

```
/*
 *      CX/68K  Executive,  Version 1.0   (4/10/86)
 *
 *      (c)  1984  Walter S. Heath, all rights reserved.
 *
 *      FILE CX2.C   Main function for runable demonstration program.
 */
#include "apsymb2.h"

extern short ntsks                  ;/*number of tasks defined         */
long cxst[256]                      ;/*cx()'s stack                    */

main()
{
/*
 *Initialize some application-dependent variables
 */
ntsks = NTSKS                       ;

/*
 *Call the CX/68K kernel
 */
cx()                                ;

}                                   /*end of main()                    */

                                    /*end of CX2.C file                */
```

Figure 5.6. CX2 Main Program.

```
/*
 *      CX/68K  Executive,  Version 1.0   (4/10/86)
 *
 *      (c)  1984  Walter S. Heath, all rights reserved.
 *
 *      FILE APSYMB2.H
 *
 *      Application Symbol Definitions for Demonstration Program CX2.
 */

#define NTSKS            3       /*number of defined tasks          */

#define CONSID           0       /*task ID numbers                  */
#define KEYBID           1
#define IDLEID           2

                                 /*end of APSYMB2.H file            */
```

Figure 5.7. CX2 Application Symbols.

5.4.2 The Vector
Initialization Function

The executive kernel calls application function **initvec()** to initialize any interrupt or trap vectors needed by the application (see Figure 3.1). For the CX2 program this function is present in file **api2.c,** shown in Figure 5.8. Since this program does not use interrupts or traps, the function is null. However, it must be defined so that the kernel function call can be satisfied. We will demonstrate the use of this function in example application program CX3, described in Chapter 7.

5.4.3 The TCB
Initialization Function

The executive kernel must also initialize the program's task control blocks (TCBs). These operations are accomplished by function **initcb()**. For the CX2 program this function is also present in file **api2.c,** Figure 5.8. The operations performed here were discussed in Section 2.3. Briefly, TCB structure entries for the task starting address and stack pointer are initialized for each task in the program. Note that the operations performed in this function (along with the declarations in file **apsymb2.h,** Figure 5.7) determine task priority. For the CX2 program, task priority was arbitrarily assigned, with **consol()** highest and **idle()** lowest.

```
/*
 *      CX/68K  Executive, Version 1.0  (4/10/86)
 *
 *      (c)  1984  Walter S. Heath, all rights reserved.
 *
 *      FILE API2.C  Application Initailization Functions and
 *                   Application Data Structures
 *      REVISED:
 *               8/8/88
 */
#include "cxsymb.h"
#include "apsymb2.h"

struct tcbdef tcb[NTSKS]        ;/*task control blocks              */

long const[256]                 ;/*consol()'s stack                */
long keyst[256]                 ;/*keybd()'s stack                 */
long idlst[256]                 ;/*idle()'s stack                  */

short consol()                  ;/*declare tasks (for initcb())    */
short keybd()                   ;
short idle()                    ;
```

Figure 5.8. CX2 Initialization Functions.

```
/*
 *---initvec()
 *      This function performs interrupt and trap vector initailization.
 *      Since program CX2 does not use interrupts, it is a null function
 *      for this demonstration program.
 */
initvec()
{
}                                          /*end of initvec()              */


/*
 *---initcb()
 *      This function initializes Task Control Blocks (TCBs).
 */
initcb()
{
tcb[0].tskadr = (short *)consol       ;/*task start addresses          */
tcb[1].tskadr = (short *)keybd        ;
tcb[NTSKS - 1].tskadr = (short *)idle  ;

tcb[0].tsksp = (long)&const[255]      ;/*task stack pointers           */
tcb[1].tsksp = (long)&keyst[255]      ;
tcb[NTSKS - 1].tsksp = (long)&idlst[255];
}                                          /*end of initcb()               */


/*
 *---apinit()
 *      This function is called by the cx() function. It performs applica-
 *      tion-specific initialization operations. In this demonstration
 *      program the idle() task is awakened and interrupts are enabled.
 *      However, you may perform any other start-up initialization
 *      operations here.
 */
apinit()
{
wake(IDLEID)                              ;/*wake the idle() task          */
asm(" andw   #0xf8ff,sr    ")             ;/*enable interrupts             */
}                                          /*end of apinit()               */


                                           /*end of API2.C file            */
```

Figure 5.8. (*continued*) CX2 Initialization Functions.

5.4.4 The Application
Initialization Function

The kernel calls one last initialization function to perform any additional application program operations that may be needed before the task scheduler is started and real-time operation commences. This function, called **apinit(),** is also included in file **api2.c,** Figure 5.8. It simply wakes the **idle()** task and enables interrupts (actually unnecessary for this program, since interrupts are not used). When the scheduler runs, it will start the **idle()** task.

Note that if no task is awakened at this point, the scheduler will just "spin" in the TCBs looking for a task to run. For a task to be started, it would be necessary for an interrupt handler to wake it.

5.5 THE APPLICATION
TASKS

We are now prepared to look at the structure of the application tasks for the CX2 program. The three tasks are shown in file **tasks2.c,** Figure 5.9. Note that, since the tasks for this example program are small, they were all included in a single file. In an actual application program tasks are usually much larger and each is located in one or several separate files. If a task is awakened by an interrupt handler, it is a good idea to include the C language part of the handler in the file containing the main function for that task.

Figure 5.9 contains data declarations and functions for tasks **idle()**, **keybd()**, and **consol()**. The **idle()** task is the most complex, since it contains code to support the operator interface. To get a feel for the basic structure of a task and the use of buffer pointer queue functions, we will look at the simpler **keybd()** and **consol()** task functions first and return to the **idle()** task later.

The **keybd()** and **consol()** tasks each consist of an infinite loop that encloses a call to **sleep()** and the task application code. When the task is initialized, it is run from its beginning to its first call to **sleep().** In this operation the program enters the infinite loop. Thereafter, whenever the task is run by the scheduler, it operates within the loop. Loop entry and exit is accomplished through the **sleep()** function.

The task application code for functions **keybd()** and **consol()** consists of the input of a buffer pointer from one queue and the output of that same pointer to another queue. The task that is to receive the pointer and is to run next is also awakened.

Extended functions **getbpwt()** and **putbpwt()** are used to access the queues. We could have used the simpler **getbp()** and **putbp()** primitive functions, since, as a result of the program design, we are assured that a pointer will always be available in the input queue and that room will exist in the output queue. The extended functions were chosen simply to demonstrate their use in a program. Note that the task ID of the calling task is specified as the last argument and that the address of the queue is specified by prepending the queue name with the "&" character (a C language syntax convention).

```
/*
 *      CX/68K Executive, Version 1.0   (4/10/86)
 *
 *      (c) 1984  Walter S. Heath, all rights reserved.
 *
 *      FILE TASKS2.C  Tasks for Demonstration Program CX2.
 *
 *      REVISED:
 *              8/8/88
 */
#include "apsymb2.h"
#include "pqsymb.h"

extern struct pque fidlkey      ;/*buffer pointer queues             */
extern struct pque oidlkey      ;
extern struct pque okeycon      ;
extern struct pque oconidl      ;

char *getbpwt()                 ;/*declare returned value            */

char dsp                        ;/*display control flag              */
long cycles                     ;/*execution cycles counter          */

char *dsp0 = "\n\n\n\n" ;
char *dsp1 = "CX/68K  Executive, Version 1.0 (4/10/86)\n\n" ;
char *dsp2 = "(c)  1984  Walter S. Heath\n" ;
char *dsp3 = "     All rights reserved\n\n" ;
char *dsp4 = "This program demonstrates the task scheduling and\n" ;
char *dsp5 = "queue access capabilities of CX/68K.\n\n" ;
char *dsp6 = "This text is coming from the idle() task. The message you\n" ;
char *dsp7 = "enter below will be sent via queue 'idlkey' to the keybd()\n" ;
char *dsp8 = "task.  Keybd() will pass it on via queue 'keycon' to task\n" ;
char *dsp9 = "consol().  Consol() will send it back to the idle() task\n" ;
char *dsp10 = "via queue 'conidl'.\n\n" ;
char *dsp11 = "You will also be asked to enter the number of cycles this\n" ;
char *dsp12 = "loop will be repeated.\n\n" ;
char *dsp13 = "To exit the program type <CR> at any prompt.\n\n";

char *msg1 = "Enter up to 8 characters:\n" ;/*prompt message        */
char *msg2 = "\n"                  ;/*line space message           */
char *msg3 = "Enter number of repeat cycles (1 to 500000):\n" ;
char *msg4 = "I'm running . . .\n"        ;
```

Figure 5.9. CX2 Application Tasks. (*Continued on next page.*)

```
char idlbuf[10]                        ;/*pointer queue buffer        */

short inchrs                           ;/*number of char's input      */

char *idleptr                          ;/*idle() task msg pointer      */
char *keybptr                          ;/*keybd() task msg pointer     */
char *consptr                          ;/*consol() task msg pointer    */


/*
 *---idle()
 *      This function is the lowest priority task.  For purposes of
 *      demonstrating the scheduler it contains a consol interface.
 *      The name is arbitrary.
 */

idle()
{
dsp = 0                                ;
cycles = -1                            ;

for( ; ; ){                            /*Start infinite loop . . .    */
sleep()                                ;

if(dsp == 0){                          /*Display full screen,         */
      dsp = 1                          ;/*first time only.            */
      conout(dsp0,4)                   ;
      conout(dsp1,42)                  ;
      conout(dsp2,27)                  ;
      conout(dsp3,26)                  ;
      conout(dsp4,50)                  ;
      conout(dsp5,38)                  ;
      conout(dsp6,58)                  ;
      conout(dsp7,59)                  ;
      conout(dsp8,58)                  ;
      conout(dsp9,57)                  ;
      conout(dsp10,21)                 ;
      conout(dsp11,58)                 ;
      conout(dsp12,24)                 ;
      conout(dsp13,46)                 ;

                                       /*Put pointer to data buffer   */
      putbpwt(idlbuf,&fidlkey,IDLEID)  ;/* idlbuf[] in free queue.    */
}
```

Figure 5.9. (*continued*) CX2 Application Tasks.

```
if(cycles > 0){                         /*If cycles are running,        */
     idleptr = getbpwt(&oconidl,IDLEID); /*just pull pointer in.        */
}
else{                                    /*Else, prompt operator for input */

     if(cycles == 0){                    /*If previous run just finished, */
          idleptr = getbpwt(&oconidl,IDLEID);/*get buffer pointer.       */
          conout(msg2,1)              ;
          conout(idleptr + 1,*idleptr);/*display msg in buffer           */
          conout(msg2,1)              ;
                                        /*return pointer to free list    */
          putbpwt(idleptr,&fidlkey,IDLEID) ;
     }
                                        /*Get msg from operator to send. */

     idleptr = getbpwt(&fidlkey,IDLEID) ;/*get pointer to free buffer*/
     do{
          conout(msg2,1)              ;
          conout(msg1,26)             ;/*prompt for message              */
          inchrs=conin(idleptr + 1,9) ;/*input entered char's            */
          *idleptr = inchrs           ;/*store # of chars in 1st byte    */

     }while(inchrs > 8 )              ;/*repeat for error input          */

     do{                               /*Get cycles to run.              */
          conout(msg2,1)              ;
          conout(msg3,45)             ;/*prompt for cycles               */
          cycles = numin()            ;/*input cycles                    */

     }while(cycles < 1 || cycles > 500000) ;/*repeat for error input     */

     conout(msg2,1)                   ;
     conout(msg4,18)                  ;/*show "I'm running . . ."        */
}
putbpwt(idleptr,&oidlkey,IDLEID)        ;/*output msg ptr to keybd()      */
cycles--                                ;
wake(KEYBID)                            ;/*wake the keybd() task          */

}                                       /* . . . end infinite loop.       */
}                                       /*end of idle() task              */
```

(Continued on next page.)

```
/*
 *---keybd()
 *      This function is the keyboard task (arbitrarily named). It
 *      receives a message pointer from the idle() task and sends it to
 *      the consol() task.  It then wakes consol().
 */

keybd()
{
for( ; ; ){                           /*Start infinite loop . . .         */
sleep()                         ;

keybptr = getbpwt(&oidlkey,KEYBID);/*get msg ptr from idle()              */
putbpwt(keybptr,&okeycon,KEYBID)  ;/*send it to consol() task             */
wake(CONSID)                      ;/*wake the consol() task  */

}                                     /* . . . end infinite loop.         */
}                                     /*end of keybd() task               */

/*
 *---consol()
 *      This function is the console task (arbitrarily named).  It
 *      receives a message pointer from the keybd() task and sends it to
 *      the idle() task.  It then wakes idle().
 */

consol()
{
for( ; ; ){                           /*Start infinite loop . . .         */
sleep()                         ;

consptr = getbpwt(&okeycon,CONSID) ;/*get msg ptr from keybd()            */
putbpwt(consptr,&oconidl,CONSID)   ;/*send it to idle() task              */
wake(IDLEID)                       ;/*wake idle() to start over           */

}                                     /* . . . end infinite loop.         */
}                                     /*end of consol() task              */

                                      /*end of TASKS2.C file              */
```

Figure 5.9 (*continued*) CX2 Application Tasks.

The **idle()** task has essentially the same structure as the **keybd()** and **consol()** tasks. It consists of an infinite outer loop enclosing a call to **sleep()** and the main body of the task. The function also uses **getbpwt()** to remove a pointer from queue **oconidl** and **putbpwt()** to put a pointer into queue **oidlkey.** It calls **wake()** to schedule **keybd(),** the next task in the loop.

At the very beginning of the task, before the infinite loop is entered, some task control variables are initialized. When task initialization was discussed in Section 2.2, the point was made that application code parameters could be initialized in this fashion.

The code after the call to **sleep()** displays text on the operator's console. It also calls **putbpwt()** to preload a pointer to the program's only data buffer, **idlbuf[],** into free pointer queue **fidlkey.** In an actual application program this operation might be replaced by a loop that puts pointers to several buffers into the queue. Again, the **putbp()** function is entirely adequate for these operations. Free queue initialization might also be more conveniently performed in function **qinit(),** as was suggested earlier in Section 5.3.

The next code in **idle()** checks to see if the real-time program is already running. That is, if counter **cycles** is greater than zero, the operator has already entered a message and the number of times the loop should be repeated. In this case the program simply gets a pointer from the **oconidl** queue, puts it in the **oidlkey** queue, and wakes the **keybd()** task.

If the real-time program is not already running, the program first checks to see if a run just finished (**cycles** is zero). In this case it gets the pointer to the message, displays the message on the console, and returns the pointer to the free queue **fidlkey.** In displaying the message, the program gets message size from the first byte in the buffer. When we discuss operator prompts in the next paragraph, we will see that message size is stored there when the message is received from the console. The program then proceeds to the code that prompts the operator for a message.

To get the program started (when **cycles** is minus one) and to rerun it (when **cycles** is zero) the program first gets a pointer to the free buffer from the **fidlkey** queue and then prompts the operator for a message to place in it. When the message is loaded into the buffer the first byte in the buffer is bypassed. This byte is later loaded with the size of the message.

Once the message is loaded, the operator is prompted for the number of times the message buffer pointer should be passed around the loop of tasks. This value is placed in variable **cycles.** The program then outputs a string to the console to indicate that the real-time program has started and then proceeds to send the buffer pointer to the **keybd()** task and wake it. The **idle()** task then loops back (via the infinite loop) and calls **sleep()** to suspend itself.

Note that each time the **idle()** task runs in the real-time mode, variable **cycles** is decremented. When it reaches zero, the program reenters the non-real-time mode and again prompts the operator.

This completes our review of the code for example program CX2. In the next section we will see how these functions may be linked to the executive functions to form a runable program.

5.6 PUTTING THE CX2 PROGRAM TOGETHER

The commands presented in this section are appropriate for building a real-time program under the SunOS operating system on a Sun-3 workstation. This version of UNIX is based on the Berkeley BSD 4.2 UNIX root. Commands for building it under another flavor of UNIX or some other operating system may use different syntax, but the steps required will be essentially the same.

The C language files for the executive and example program may be compiled using command

cc -c filename.c

The **-c** option will cause linkable object file **filename.o** to be produced. The C optimizer may also be used as follows:

cc -c -O filename.c

It is recommended that one not use it in the beginning, since the program will have to be debugged at the assembly code level and it is easier to understand the nonoptimized code produced by the compiler.

The **-R** compiler option is also of interest. If one is producing a program that will be burned into a PROM, this option causes initialized variables (data) to be placed in the text (code) segment of the program, rather than the data segment. The text segment may then be burned into the PROM. Note that these variables will then be read-only.

Assembly language files may be assembled using

as -o filename.o filename.s

The **-o** option indicates that the name of the linkable object file follows. Actually, it is also possible to assemble a file using the compile command

cc -c filename.s

The file must end in **.s** to be recognized as an assembly language file.

The CX2 program may be linked to produce runable program file cx2 using the following command:

ld -x -T 1000 -o cx2 cx2.o tasks2.o ques2.o api2.o\
apio2.o conio.o sys.o bptr.o cxn.o -lc

The **-x** option preserves global variables (including function names) in the program's symbol table. Option **-T 1000** specifies that the program will be linked such that its text segment starts at physical memory address 1000 hex. By default, the program's data segment is placed immediately after the text segment (it may be placed elsewhere by using another option). Obviously, you may change the starting address to match the mapping of memory on your target computer. The **-o cx2** option indicates that the name of the runable program file is to be **cx2** (not **a.out,** the UNIX default). Finally, the **-lc** option at the end of the command line specifies that the linker should try to resolve any unresolved references by linking program modules from the C library.

It is also convenient to place executive functions in a library (using the **ar** utility) and then link them to application files from there. Using this approach, the linker command becomes

**ld -x -T 1000 -o cx2 cx2.o tasks2.o ques2.o api2.o\
apio2.o conio.o -lcx -lc**

where the **-lcx** option specifies that library **libcx.a** should be searched for executive references.

Once the program has been compiled, assembled, and linked, it is ready to be loaded into the target computer and run. Several options exist for transporting programs from a development system to a target processor. The subject is discussed in Chapter 11.

Programs may be debugged in the target processor using its PROM monitor/debugger. Since the program is tested at the assembly language level, it is necessary to have a memory map containing the addresses of global variables and function start addresses. In the UNIX environment this may be produced from the program module using command

nm -g cx2 > cx2.map

which produces a list of symbols in alphabetical order and their corresponding memory addresses. To get a list in ascending memory address order, use

nm -ng cx2 > cx2.map

File **cx2.map** may be printed in triple columns using

pr -3 cx2.map | lpr

With this map it is possible to use the PROM monitor to set breakpoints, run the program to them, and look at data in registers, global variables, and data structures.

The PROM monitor usually includes a disassembler. This feature converts assembled binary instructions back into their equivalent assembly language source code statements and displays them on the console. With experience, one soon becomes proficient at recognizing the assembly language constructs generated by the C compiler.

Debugging a C program at the assembly language level may seem primitive to software writers who are accustomed to using a high level language debugger in an operating system environment. Unfortunately, since the timing of real-time programs is critical, it is usually difficult to use a high level debugger. To be useful, the debugger must be designed to run the program at full speed and be able to cope with interrupts and multitasking.

An important tool for diagnosing both hardware and software problems as well as for monitoring the performance of properly operating systems is the logic analyzer. It may be used to view timing relationships between events in a system. In the next section we will evaluate the performance of the CX2 program by analyzing plots of timing measurements made using this instrument.

5.7 CX2 PROGRAM PERFORMANCE EVALUATION

It is important to measure the performance of an executive to determine whether its operation will excessively monopolize processor execution time in an actual application program. Performance metrics will also be valuable for comparing the operation of alternative system software environments. The CX2 program may be used to make one such measurement—the task-switch time. Other measurements will be made using the example programs presented in Chapters 7 and 9.

The task-switch time is the amount of time it takes the executive to suspend one task and start another. It is the interval between a call to **sleep()** in one task and the return from **sleep()** in another. It includes the time to run functions **sleep()**, **sched()**, and **run().**

If the processor used to run CX2 has an accessible parallel port, we can measure the task-switch time interval by adding statements to the CX2 program to set and clear bits in the port and then monitor these changes with a logic analyzer. In the remainder of this section we will identify the program changes that are needed to "instrument" CX2 and then review the results from test runs using this measurement technique.

5.7.1 Performance Test Setup

Before a parallel port can be used, it must be initialized. For the target processor board used in these measurements the port is supported by a Motorola 68230 Parallel Interface and Timer (PIT) chip, which is mapped into the processor's address space starting at address ff0e0000 hex. The chip provides three eight bit ports. We will use port C only.

The code required to initialize port C is very simple. The port's data direction register is set to make it an output port and all bits are initially set high. The instructions are

```
asm(" movb #0xff,0xff0e0004 ") ;/*set port C for output */
asm(" movb #0xff,0xff0e000c ") ;/*set port C to all 1's */
```

It is recommended that these instructions be added to the **apinit()** function in file **api2.c,** shown in Figure 5.8. They may be placed anywhere in this function.

The next step is to place statements in each task. A port C bit will be dedicated to each task. It will be set high when the task is entered (when **sleep()** returns) and cleared when it is suspended (when **sleep()** is called). Figure 5.10 shows the additions to the **tasks2.c** file that are required to set and clear bits in the **keybd()** and **consol()** tasks. Note that a bit is set or cleared by ORing or ANDing an appropriate mask and the port C output data register.

```
/*
 *---keybd()
 *     This function is the keyboard task (arbitrarily named). It
 *     receives a message pointer from the idle() task and sends it to
 *     the consol() task.  It then wakes consol().
 */

keybd()
{
for( ; ; ){                         /*Start infinite loop . . .        */
sleep()                                 ;

asm(" orb    #0x04,0xff0e000c ");/*set PIT port C, bit 2              */

keybptr = getbpwt(&oidlkey,KEYBID) ;/*get msg ptr from idle()        */
putbpwt(keybptr,&okeycon,KEYBID)  ;/*send it on to consol() task      */
wake(CONSID)                        ;/*wake the consol() task         */

asm(" andb   #0xfb,0xff0e000c ");/*clear PIT port C, bit 2            */

}                                   /* . . . end infinite loop.       */
}                                   /*end of keybd()                  */
/*
 *---consol()
 *     This function is the console task (arbitrarily named).  It
 *     receives a message pointer from the keybd() task and sends it to
 *     the idle() task.  It then wakes idle().
 */

consol()
{
for( ; ; ){                         /*Start infinite loop . . .        */
sleep()                                 ;

asm(" orb    #0x10,0xff0e000c ");/*set PIT port C, bit 4   */

consptr = getbpwt(&okeycon,CONSID);/*get msg ptr from keybd()         */
putbpwt(consptr,&oconidl,CONSID)  ;/*send it to idle task             */
wake(IDLEID)                        ;/*wake idle() to start over       */

asm(" andb   #0xef,0xff0e000c ");/*clear PIT port C, bit 4 */

}                                   /* . . . end infinite loop.       */
}                                   /*end of consol()                 */

                                    /*end of TASKS2.C file            */
```

Figure 5.10. File tasks2.c Modifications for Performance Tests.

The **keybd()** and **consol()** tasks use bits 2 and 4, respectively. A similar set of statements is added to the **idle()** task to control bit zero. They are

> **asm(" orb #0x01,0xff0e000c ") ;/*set PIT port C, bit 0 */**
> **asm(" andb #0xfe,0xff0e000c ") ;/*clear PIT port C, bit 0 */**

As in **keybd()** and **consol(),** the first instruction should be added just after the call to **sleep();** the second just before the end of the infinite loop.

One additional set of statements was added to the program to measure the amount of time the program spends in the scheduler. Port C bit 7 is set in the **sched()** function (file **cxn.c,** Figure 3.1) just after the call to **run()** using statement

> **asm(" orb #0x80,0xff0e000c ") ;/*set PIT port C, bit 7 */**

It is then cleared just before the call to **run()** with

> **asm(" andb #0x7f,0xff0e000c ") ;/*clear PIT port C, bit 7 */**

The bit will therefore be set when the processor is running code in **sched().**

At this point the logic analyzer may be connected to the appropriate pins and the tests may be run. We will look at test results in the next section.

5.7.2 Performance Test Results

Any executive timing measurements will obviously depend on the type of processor being used, its clock rate, and the speed of the memory accessed by the processor. For the test results discussed in this book, the processor was a Motorola 68020 running at 16.67 MHz. The DRAM memory chips had an access time of 120 nsec (two processor wait states required). Executive and application C programs were compiled using the Sun-3 C compiler without optimization. Better performance can be expected by using the optimizer. The nonoptimized results are shown here so that you may compare the performance of your version of the program (presumably compiled and debugged without the optimizer invoked) or compare results using the Sun C compiler to a version prepared using another compiler.

Figure 5.11a shows the first plot of CX2 program performance. It was obtained using a Hewlett Packard 1630D logic analyzer and associated screen printer. The figure shows plots of the signals from pins of the port C parallel port. Tasks are shown in ascending order of scheduling priority. A plot line is high when the processor is executing code within the named program module. Note that the sampling period is 5 μsec for this run.

The task scheduling activity of the CX2 program is clearly visible from this plot. After passing a message buffer pointer to the **keybd()** task, **idle()** wakes **keybd()** and suspends. Then **keybd()** runs and passes the pointer to **consol().** Finally, **consol()** runs and passes the pointer back to **idle().** The sequence is then repeated.

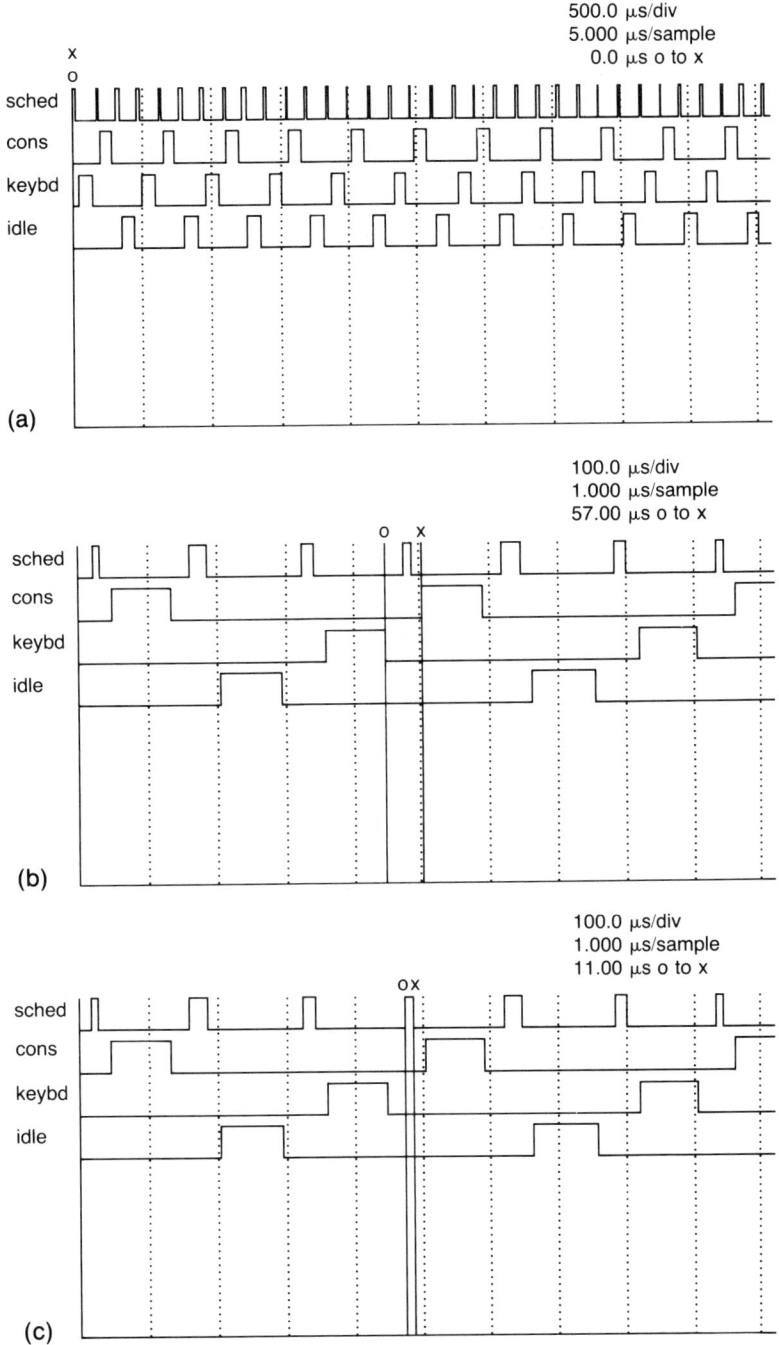

Figure 5.11a–g. CX2 Performance Test Results. (*Continued on next page.*)

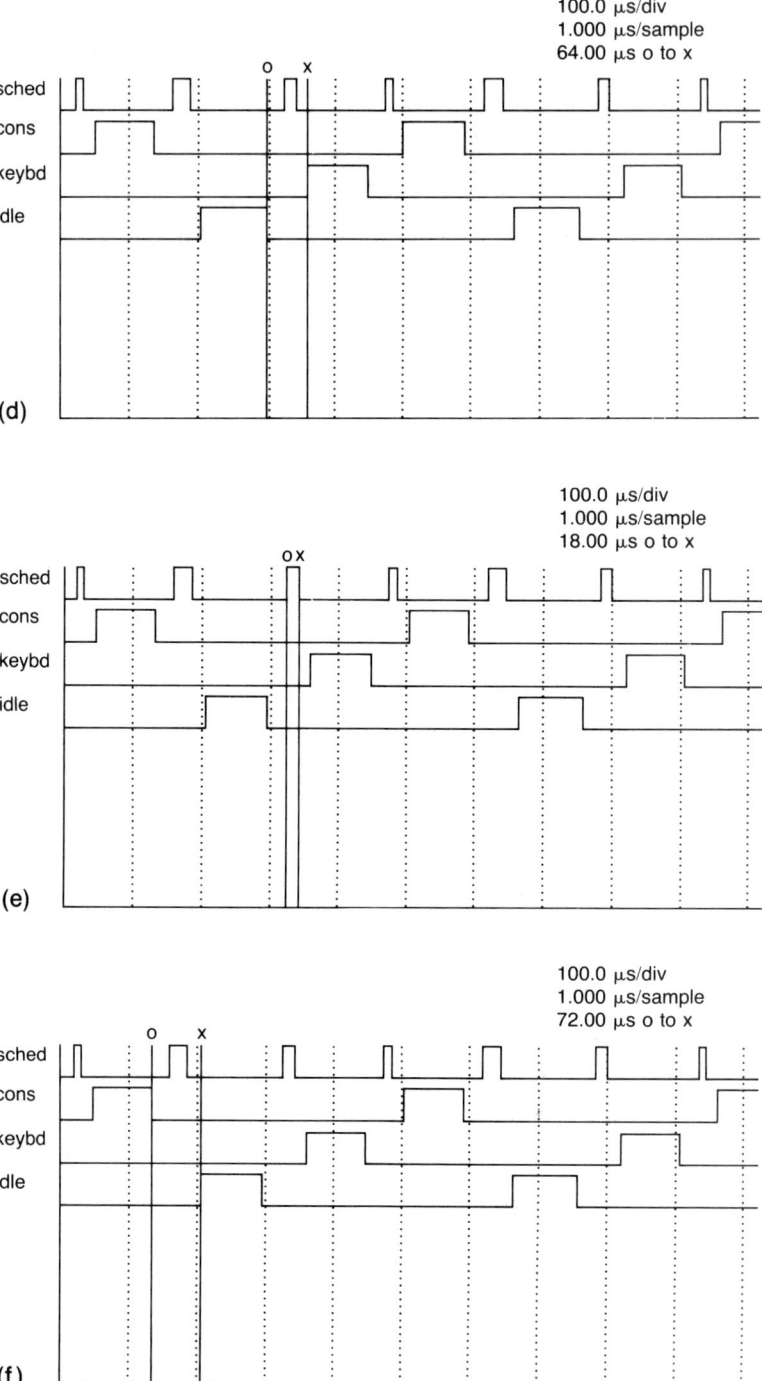

Figure 5.11a–g. (*continued*) CX2 Performance Test Results.

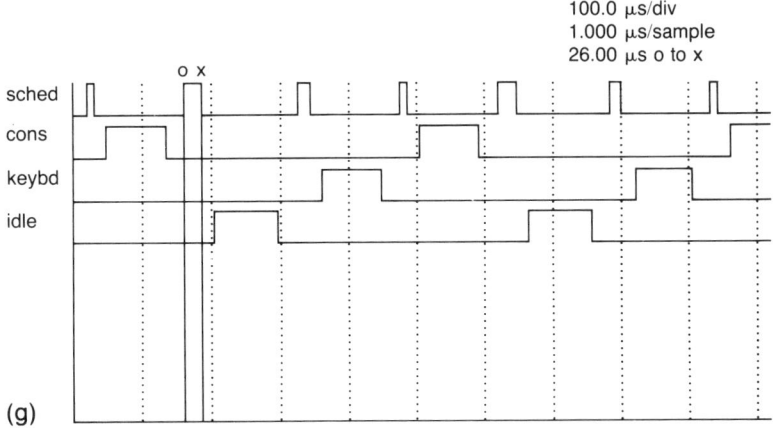

Figure 5.11a–g. (*continued*) CX2 Performance Test Results.

Note that the amount of time the processor spends in **sched**() depends on the scheduling priority of the task that is run next. This is a result of the fact that the scheduler must scan more task control blocks for lower priority tasks before finding one to run. So it is clear that task-switch time depends on the priority of the task to be run next.

Figure 5.11b shows a measurement of task-switch time when the task that is run has highest priority. Since the scheduler finds a task to run when it looks at the first TCB in the linked list, this task-switch time is the shortest possible. The figure indicates that this time is 57 μsec, at a measurement resolution of 1 μsec—the plot sample period. This is a good number to compare with published results for other real-time executives (running on comparable equipment). The comparison is generally favorable to this executive and indicates that writing the executive in C has not resulted in a significant performance penalty.

It is also interesting to measure **sched**()'s execution time. Figure 5.11c shows that it is 11 μsec when the highest priority task is selected to run next. Note that the difference between the task-switch time and the **sched**() execution time is the cumulative time the processor spends in **run**() and **sleep**().

Figures 5.11d and 5.11e show the same two measurements when the task selected to be run next has next-to-highest priority. In this case the task-switch time is 64 μsec and **sched**() execution time is 18 μsec. These times are 7 μsec slower than the previous results, indicating that the scheduler takes about 7 or 8 μsec to access and test a TCB. This result is confirmed by the third measurement set, shown in Figures 5.11f and 5.11g. The plots show timing measurements for scheduling the third-highest-priority task. Execution times are about 8 μsec longer than those for the previous case.

It is clear from these measurements that task-switch time will not consume excessive amounts of the computer's processing bandwidth for application programs with a moderate number of tasks. If an application will contain a large number of tasks and if various task subsets will be relevant under different system operating modes, it may be necessary to dynamically manage the TCB linked list so that only relevant TCBs are linked into the list for each operational mode. Task priorities may also be adjusted under these conditions.

This completes our review of the CX2 example application program. One feature of real-time systems that this program did not demonstrate is support for interrupts. We will address this subject in the next chapter.

6

Hardware Interface Concepts

At this point we have established software techniques for supporting task scheduling and message passing in a real-time system. Another important aspect of these systems is the software that is required to interface to equipment. Although task scheduling and message passing in real-time systems are effectively supported by system level software that is part of an executive, equipment interfaces are more properly handled at the application program level. This contrasts with the approach taken by general-purpose computer systems that employ operating systems. In these machines, equipment interfaces are supported by drivers that are part of the system software. Often in real-time systems, timing constraints can only be met when application program operations are tightly coupled to equipment control. As a consequence, equipment interface software must be designed to meet the specific needs of the application and must be directly accessible. High performance applications cannot tolerate the overhead associated with a system call to an operating system driver and a driver that is not tailored to application requirements.

In this chapter we will briefly divert our attention from real-time system software to consider issues associated with equipment interfaces. Later, in Chapter 7, we will integrate these concepts into the structure of the executive that we have been developing and then continue to extend that executive's capabilities. Readers who are already familiar with equipment interfacing techniques may wish to scan this chapter briefly and continue on to Chapter 7.

6.1 THE EQUIPMENT INTERFACE: AN OVERVIEW

It is often the case that a substantial fraction of the total software activity on a project must be devoted to establishing equipment interfaces. This is a result of the fact that these interfaces are often complex and difficult to test. Moreover, it is not uncommon to discover that the information needed to establish an interface is simply not available. That is, documentation may be inaccurate, incomplete, or ambiguous. When this happens, one must usually write a separate test program to discover the actual operation of the hardware before a satisfactory system interface can be established.

Since the amount of time required to construct equipment interfaces is often unpredictable, it is good practice to establish them as early in the project effort as possible. Once this phase has been completed, the remaining activity may be more reliably scheduled. This approach also leaves time to recover, should a particular interface prove to be inadequate for the intended purpose or impossible to establish. The system design may then be changed before delivery deadlines become too pressing.

In the sections that follow, we will examine some basic concepts that are associated with most hardware interface designs. We will look at the interface from the software writer's point of view and will emphasize the operations that software must perform. Although the specific details of various device interfaces differ considerably, common methods are used by processors to access them. We will review these hardware techniques and then consider the software procedures that are required to support them.

Since the process of establishing interfaces to equipment is the part of a project where the software writer is most directly concerned with the hardware, any knowledge of hardware operations that the writer may possess will be useful. Without this background, the writer may need to work with a hardware designer to determine details of equipment operation. However provided, hardware expertise is very often needed during the construction and testing of an equipment interface.

6.2 THE PROCESSOR I/O INTERFACE

Communication with external devices is accomplished by means of registers that are part of the device or a device interface controller. The registers are mapped into a processor address space and may be accessed by program instructions. A typical interface contains status, control, and data registers. Bit fields in the status and control registers are assigned specific functions. Status registers report the current state of the device; control registers are used to change its state and thus control its operation. Data are transferred to and from the device through its data registers.

There are two basic methods used by processors to access device registers. They are often identified as port I/O and memory-mapped I/O. Processors that use port I/O map device registers into a separate I/O address space and communicate with them by means of special instructions that can access this space only. By contrast, processors that use memory-mapped I/O access device registers through the normal program memory address space by using the instructions provided to access memory. Typically, these registers are mapped into the high end of the processor's address space. In subsequent sections we will limit our attention to I/O operations for the 680X0 group of processors and therefore to memory-mapped I/O.

External equipment must also be able to signal the processor that an event has occurred. This is accomplished either by setting a bit (or bit field) in a status register or by means of an interrupt. If the status register method is used, the processor must poll (read periodically) the register to detect the event. For real-time systems this approach has at least two drawbacks. First, a polling loop takes time to execute. Thus, if several interfaces must be serviced, immediate and predictable response time cannot be guaranteed. Second, the polling loop wastes processor execution time that is normally needed to perform other operations.

In high performance systems the polling technique is seldom used. Instead, an external event is reported by means of an interrupt. A device typically accomplishes this by producing a high-to-low transition on an Interrupt Request line (IRQ*—the asterisk indicates active-low).

The interrupt mechanism is an important component of any high performance real-time system. Indeed, these systems are often referred to as "event-driven" and the primary mechanism used to signal events is the interrupt. As a consequence, it will be important for us to understand clearly the way in which a processor responds to interrupts. We will then be in a position to write efficient interrupt handling software.

In the next section we will review the signaling sequence that is performed by the 680X0 group of processors in response to an interrupt request. Although members of this group handle interrupts in essentially the same way, differences do exist. The reader should refer to the manual for a particular processor model for unique details and specific timing information. Our limited objective will be to present sufficient technical information to form a basis for the discussions of interrupt-related software topics to be presented in subsequent sections and chapters.

The entire sequence of hardware operations performed by a member of the 680X0 processor group in response to an interrupt request is summarized in Figure 6.1. The software operations that are needed to complete an interrupt response are also shown. This flow diagram will be helpful in focusing the discussion of the hardware sequence that will be presented in the next section. The software operations will be discussed in Section 6.4. This diagram should also be useful during program testing, when it is necessary to mentally reconstruct the sequence of events that occurs during an interrupt.

6.3 PROCESSOR INTERRUPT PROTOCOL

We will begin this section with a short functional overview of the hardware and software operations that occur as a result of an interrupt. We will then examine in detail the way in which this sequence of operations is actually carried out by the 680X0 group of processors.

In general, when a device requires service, it pulls an assigned interrupt request line low.

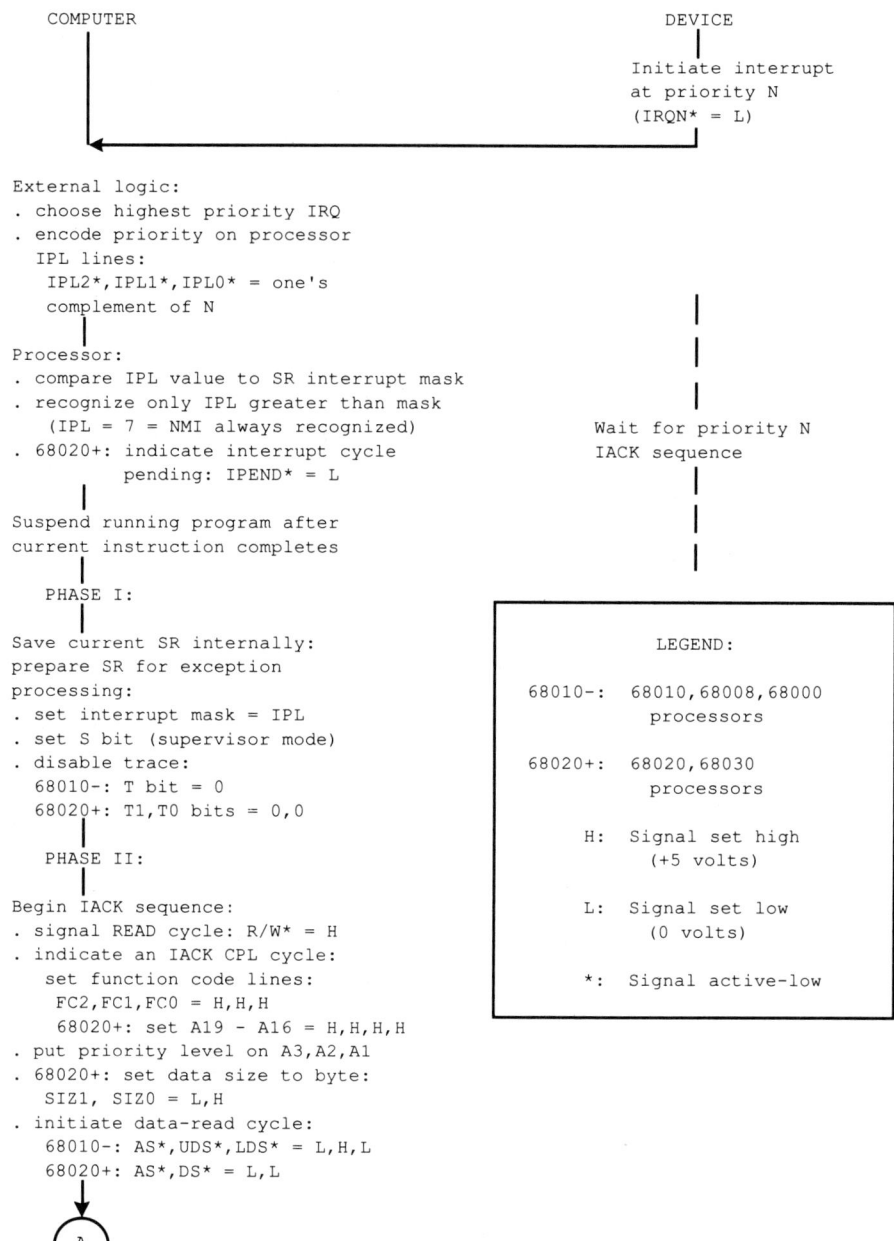

```
        COMPUTER                                    DEVICE
           |                                           |
           |                                  Initiate interrupt
           |                                  at priority N
           |                                  (IRQN* = L)
           └─────────────────────────◄─────────
External logic:
. choose highest priority IRQ
. encode priority on processor
  IPL lines:
    IPL2*,IPL1*,IPL0* = one's
    complement of N
           |                                           |
Processor:                                             |
. compare IPL value to SR interrupt mask               |
. recognize only IPL greater than mask                 |
    (IPL = 7 = NMI always recognized)          Wait for priority N
. 68020+: indicate interrupt cycle             IACK sequence
          pending: IPEND* = L                          |
           |                                           |
Suspend running program after                          |
current instruction completes                          |
           |
     PHASE I:
           |
Save current SR internally:
prepare SR for exception
processing:
. set interrupt mask = IPL
. set S bit (supervisor mode)
. disable trace:
  68010-: T bit = 0
  68020+: T1,T0 bits = 0,0
           |
     PHASE II:
           |
Begin IACK sequence:
. signal READ cycle: R/W* = H
. indicate an IACK CPL cycle:
  set function code lines:
    FC2,FC1,FC0 = H,H,H
    68020+: set A19 - A16 = H,H,H,H
. put priority level on A3,A2,A1
. 68020+: set data size to byte:
  SIZ1, SIZ0 = L,H
. initiate data-read cycle:
  68010-: AS*,UDS*,LDS* = L,H,L
  68020+: AS*,DS* = L,L
           |
           ▼
         ( A )
```

```
┌─────────────────────────────────────────┐
│                 LEGEND:                   │
│                                           │
│  68010-:  68010,68008,68000               │
│           processors                      │
│                                           │
│  68020+:  68020,68030                     │
│           processors                      │
│                                           │
│       H:  Signal set high                 │
│           (+5 volts)                      │
│                                           │
│       L:  Signal set low                  │
│           (0 volts)                       │
│                                           │
│       *:  Signal active-low               │
│                                           │
└─────────────────────────────────────────┘
```

Figure 6.1. 680X0 Processor Interrupt Response Sequence.

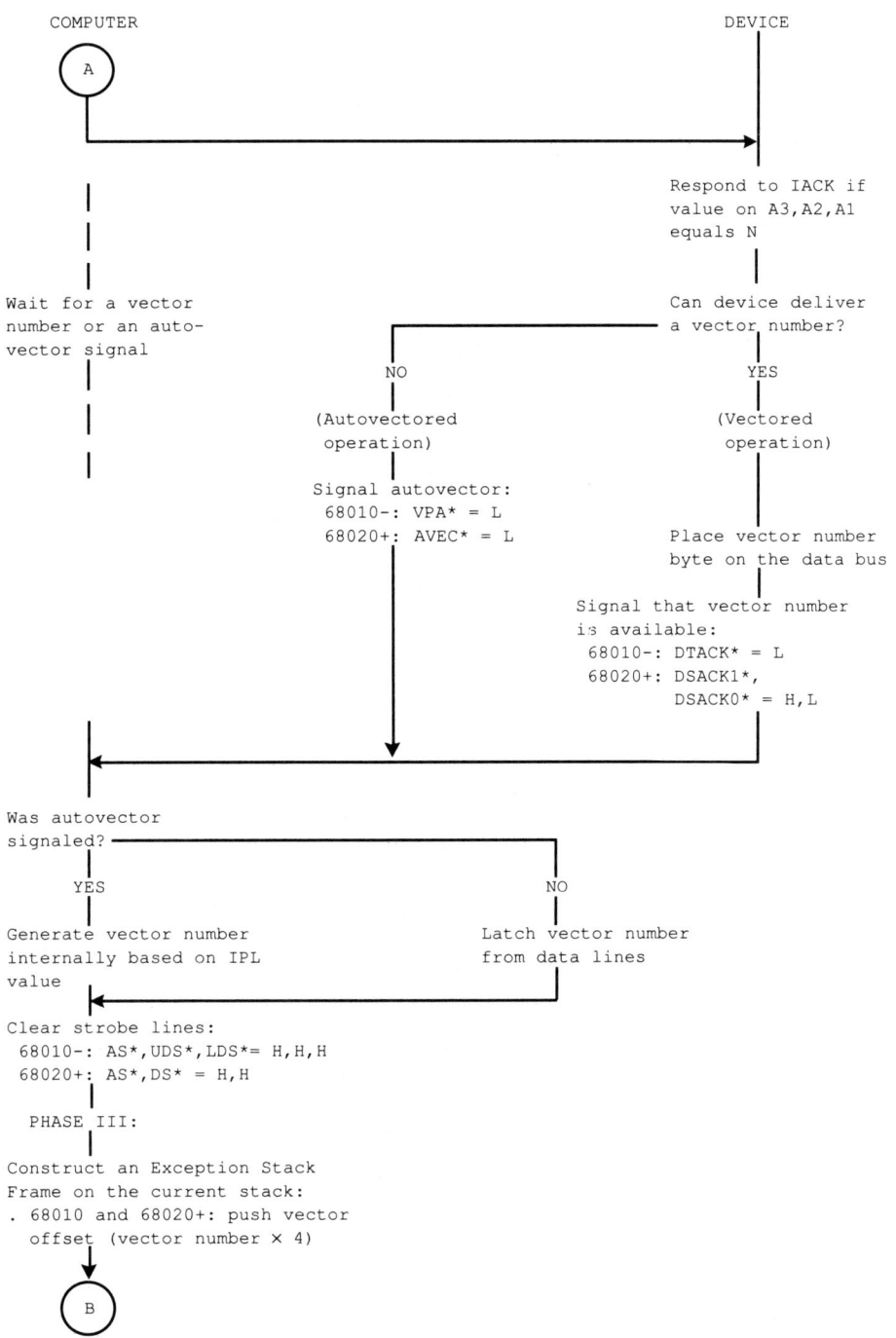

COMPUTER   DEVICE

A

Respond to IACK if
value on A3,A2,A1
equals N

Wait for a vector
number or an auto-   Can device deliver
vector signal   a vector number?

                        NO   YES

                   (Autovectored   (Vectored
                    operation)   operation)

                   Signal autovector:
                   68010-: VPA* = L
                   68020+: AVEC* = L   Place vector number
                                           byte on the data bus

                                           Signal that vector number
                                           is available:
                                            68010-: DTACK* = L
                                            68020+: DSACK1*,
                                                    DSACK0* = H,L

Was autovector
signaled?

      YES   NO

Generate vector number   Latch vector number
internally based on IPL   from data lines
value

Clear strobe lines:
 68010-: AS*,UDS*,LDS*= H,H,H
 68020+: AS*,DS* = H,H

   PHASE III:

Construct an Exception Stack
Frame on the current stack:
. 68010 and 68020+: push vector
  offset (vector number × 4)

B

(Continued on next page.)

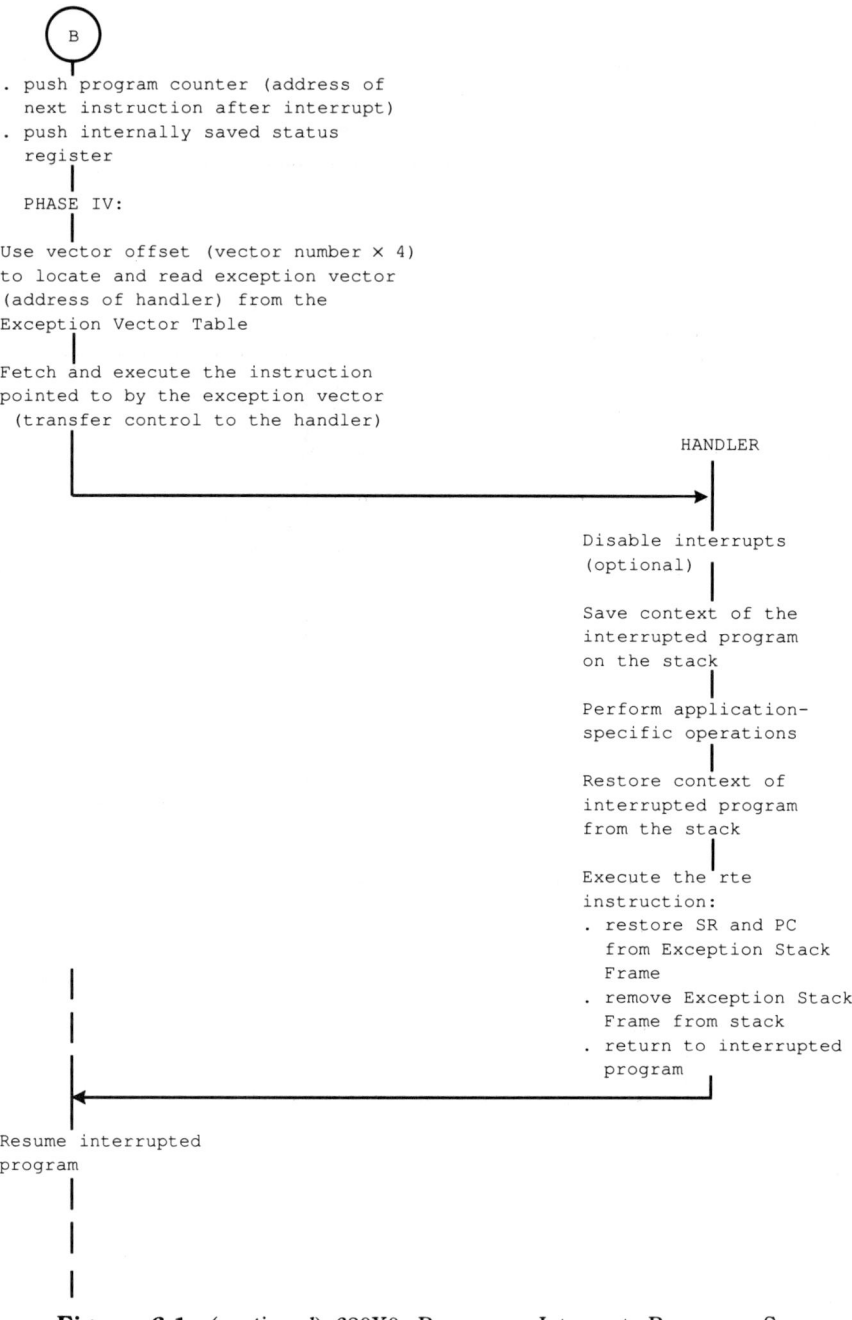

```
      ( B )
. push program counter (address of
  next instruction after interrupt)
. push internally saved status
  register

  PHASE IV:

Use vector offset (vector number × 4)
to locate and read exception vector
(address of handler) from the
Exception Vector Table

Fetch and execute the instruction
pointed to by the exception vector
 (transfer control to the handler)
```

```
                                          HANDLER

                                  Disable interrupts
                                  (optional)

                                  Save context of the
                                  interrupted program
                                  on the stack

                                  Perform application-
                                  specific operations

                                  Restore context of
                                  interrupted program
                                  from the stack

                                  Execute the rte
                                  instruction:
                                  . restore SR and PC
                                    from Exception Stack
                                    Frame
                                  . remove Exception Stack
                                    Frame from stack
                                  . return to interrupted
                                    program

Resume interrupted
program
```

Figure 6.1. (*continued*) 680X0 Processor Interrupt Response Sequence.

When the processor completes its current instruction, it checks its interrupt request lines and begins the interrupt response sequence. The processor immediately saves some of the interrupted program's context and then acknowledges the request by signaling the device. The device, in turn, supplies a pointer to the address of an appropriate interrupt service routine and the processor jumps to that address.

The interrupt routine first saves the remainder of the interrupted program's context and then proceeds to perform device-specific operations. When these operations have been completed, it restores the context of the interrupted program and returns processor control to the point of interruption. The interrupted program then continues as if no interrupt occurred.

Although this sequence would appear to be straightforward, many additional operations are hidden in the actual implementation of the interrupt response mechanism. It will be important to understand these details when it becomes necessary to find errors in an interrupt-driven, real-time program.

There may be several devices that need to request processor services by using the interrupt mechanism. Since devices operate asynchronously, their requests for service may occur simultaneously. The computer system must then decide which request to service first. That is, the system must order and service requests on the basis of priority.

In general, the 680X0 processor group supports interrupt requests at seven priority levels (the 68008 supports three). However, it is necessary for logic external to the chip to order interrupt requests from devices according to priority and to present one request at a time to the processor on its Interrupt Priority Level lines (IPL2∗, IPL1∗, and IPL0∗). The priority level must be binary encoded on these lines (one's complemented). When the processor completes its response to the current request, the external logic will then place the priority level of the next highest priority interrupt request on these lines. Thus, lower priority requests are held pending until the processor is able to accept them. These external operations are often performed by a single special-purpose chip.

When the processor receives an interrupt request on its IPL lines, it compares the requested level with the interrupt mask bit field in its status register. Except for the highest priority interrupt (level 7), if the priority level present on the IPL lines is equal to or less than the mask value, the interrupt request will be ignored by the processor. By contrast, a level 7 interrupt will be recognized even if the mask is set to seven. It is referred to as a Non-Maskable Interrupt (NMI). Thus, we see that the status register's interrupt mask field may be used to selectively disable interrupts at and below the level specified by the mask.

If an interrupt is not blocked by the mask, the processor then waits until any instruction currently being executed has completed. For 68020 and later models, the processor also asserts its Interrupt Pending line (IPEND∗) to signal external logic that it is about to respond to an interrupt. It then enters the first of four distinct phases in its interrupt response sequence.

To begin interrupt processing, the processor first saves a copy of the current status register in an internal register and then updates the interrupt mask in the active status register to reflect the priority of the interrupt to be processed. It also places the processor in supervisor mode (if it was not already there) by setting the status register's S bit and disables program trace mode (single stepping). Updating the interrupt mask blocks further interrupts at and below the level of the requesting interrupt. This completes the first phase of the response sequence.

In the second interrupt response phase the processor performs a so-called Interrupt Acknowledge (IACK) sequence. The purpose of this series of operations is to identify the program function that should be run to service the interrupt. As indicated earlier, this function is normally called an interrupt service routine or interrupt handler. The last instruction in the handler will cause the processor to return control to the point in the program where the interrupt occurred. Processing will then continue from that point—as if the interrupt had never occurred.

An IACK sequence consists of a series of hardware operations. The processor first sets its Read/Write line (R/W∗) high to indicate that a read cycle is about to begin. It then sets its Function Code lines (FC0, FC1, and FC2) high. These lines are used by the processor to indicate the type of CPU cycle about to be performed. In this case, the code indicates that the cycle will be an IACK. For 68020 and later models, the processor also sets address bus lines A16–A19 to signal the IACK cycle. In fact, it sets lines A0 and A4–A31, but only A16–A19 are significant.

Continuing the IACK sequence, the processor then places the interrupt priority level (as received from its IPL lines) on address lines A3, A2, and A1. Again, for 68020 and later models, it then signals that the cycle will consist of a byte-read operation with an appropriate code on its SIZ0 and SIZ1 lines. For earlier models this information is transferred by means of the data strobe lines (UDS∗ and LDS∗). The processor then asserts its address strobe and data strobe lines to initiate a data-read cycle. External logic must then interpret these signals and respond accordingly.

As indicated earlier, several devices may have requested interrupt servicing simultaneously—but at different priority levels. The processor indicates which request is being acknowledged by placing the interrupt's priority level on address lines A3, A2, and A1. The indicated device should then respond to the IACK.

There are two ways in which a device may respond to a processor IACK cycle. It may either supply a so-called vector number for the processor to read or it may signal the processor that it should generate its own vector number. In the latter case the number is called an autovector, since it is produced automatically by the processor. A unique value is generated for each request priority level. We will see shortly that the vector number is used to locate the address of the appropriate interrupt handler function.

If a vector number is to be provided externally, the device places the vector byte on the processor's data bus and signals the processor that it is available. For the autovector option, it simply indicates to the processor that it should generate its own vector number by asserting an appropriate control line (either VPA∗ or AVEC∗). In either case, after clearing the address and data strobe lines, the processor is left with an appropriate interrupt vector number. This completes the IACK cycle. The processor then enters the third phase of its response sequence.

Once the processor has determined the interrupt vector number, it must perform some operations that will allow it to resume execution of the interrupted program once the handler has completed. To accomplish this, it automatically constructs a so-called Exception Stack Frame on the current stack. This frame contains all of the information needed by the processor to return control to the point of interruption. Specifically, for all members of the 680X0 group, it at least contains the status register value that was saved internally earlier and the program counter for the next instruction to be executed when the handler completes. For 68010 and later processors it also contains the offset into the Exception Vector Table. This table is accessed as part of the next response phase.

Before examining the fourth and final processor response phase, it should be noted that, under normal operation, processor activity during the construction of an Exception Stack Frame is indivisible. That is, it cannot be interrupted by the occurrence of a higher priority external interrupt. In fact, a higher priority interrupt will not be recognized until after the first instruction in the interrupt handler has completed. This feature may be used to advantage if one desires to disable interrupts within the handler. As we will see in the next section, it may also be used to ensure that the context of the interrupted program is saved before another interrupt is serviced.

In the fourth phase of the processor's interrupt response sequence, the processor uses the vector number that resulted from the IACK cycle as an index into its Exception Vector Table, which is located in main memory. This table contains entries for the addresses of functions that should be executed in response to various processor exceptions. Among these are two sets of entries for interrupt handler functions. One set includes an entry for each interrupt priority level. A handler address is selected from this set if the processor has been directed to use the autovector method to access the table. The second set is reserved for user-defined entries. The processor uses a vector number supplied by an interrupting device to select an address from one of these entries. In either case, the address of an appropriate interrupt handler function must be present in the correct table location if the interrupt is to be properly serviced.

Once the processor has determined the address of the interrupt handler, it resumes program execution by fetching an instruction from that location. But the handler must perform certain additional operations to maintain program integrity. These will be examined in the next section.

6.4 INTERRUPT HANDLER PROTOCOL

Whether or not interrupts are disabled by the first instruction in an interrupt handler, the handler must take additional steps to preserve the context of the interrupted program. It is likely that the program was using processor registers to store address and data values. The contents of these registers must be saved so that they may be restored when control is returned to the program.

Strictly speaking, an interrupt handler need only save the contents of registers it intends to use. But if parts of the handler are written in C, it is not immediately evident which registers are used. Thus, it is good practice to save all processor registers—if timing considerations will allow. This will avoid a potential common programming error.

Consider a situation in which a handler changes a register that is not saved. The program will run until the changed register value causes the interrupted program to fault. Since interrupts occur asynchronously, the fault may occur at a different point in the program each time it runs. This is a very difficult error to find, since the symptoms are different each time it happens.

Even if a handler was originally written to save the registers that it uses, later program changes may cause additional registers to be used. This is especially true if parts of the handler are written in C. Saving all processor registers at the outset will avoid the problem. Moreover, we will see in Chapter 8 that if preemptive scheduling is used, saving and restoring all registers is mandatory.

The 680X0 group provides a single instruction for saving a specified set of registers (the **moveml** instruction) by pushing their contents onto the current stack. We may be assured that the context of the interrupted program will be saved if this is the first instruction executed by the handler, since, as we saw earlier, the first instruction will be completed before another higher priority interrupt is recognized by the processor. The **moveml** instruction may also be used to restore program context just before the handler returns control to the interrupted program. It does this by popping the previously saved register values off the stack and into the respective registers.

A handler must return control to the interrupted program by calling a special "return-from-exception" (**rte**) instruction. This instruction restores additional program context from the previously saved Exception Stack Frame and then removes the frame from the stack. In particular, it restores the interrupted program's status register value and its program counter. Control is then transferred to the instruction pointed to by the program counter—the next instruction following the interrupt.

Note that replacing the status register with the saved value restores the interrupt mask to the value present before the interrupt. Thus, if this value permits, pending interrupts at or below the priority level of the interrupt just completed may then be serviced.

It should also be noted that if interrupts are not disabled in a handler, it is possible for a lower priority handler to be interrupted by a higher priority interrupt. In fact, it is possible for a chain of successively higher priority interrupts (up to seven for the 680X0 group) to be recognized by the processor. In this case, the highest priority interrupt handler will run to completion and then return control to the next highest priority handler. In turn, this handler will complete and return to the handler with the next highest priority. This process will continue until all handlers have completed. Thus, interrupts are serviced properly in the order of their priority.

6.5 DEVICE INTERFACE SOFTWARE

From the discussion in the previous two sections, it is clear that application software must perform specific operations to support a device interface. Typically, certain actions must be taken during program initialization to put the device into a proper operating mode. If the device uses interrupts, it is also necessary to prepare the processor to accept them. Once real-time operation commences, software must be available to support device data transfers and interrupts.

One of the first steps normally performed in a real-time program is to make sure that all interrupts are disabled (except the NMI). This is accomplished by setting the status register's interrupt mask to seven. The program may then proceed to initialize itself and its device interfaces without interference from interrupts. Once these operations have been completed, it may then enable interrupts as part of its transition to real-time operation.

As indicated in Section 6.2, the operating state of a device interface is determined by the values present in its control registers. Device interfaces are often designed to operate in a variety of modes. The program must select an appropriate mode by writing values to device control registers. For example, a serial port's line discipline (i.e., baud rate, stop bits, parity, etc.) is selected through its control registers.

If a device uses interrupts and will supply a unique vector number in response to the processor's IACK cycle, the program must also write that vector number to a control register as part of device initialization. Typically, the priority level of the interrupt is selected by means of hardware straps or links on the processor or device interface board. In some cases a link is also available to select either vectored or autovectored operation.

In the previous section we saw that the processor responds to an interrupt by reading the address of an interrupt handler function from its Exception Vector Table. This value must be set during program initialization. The interrupt's vector number determines the location in the table where this address should be stored. Note that this operation and the enabling of interrupts are the only initialization operations needed by the processor, itself, to prepare for real-time interrupt activity.

The discussion to this point has been concerned with the basic mechanics of transferring information between a device and a processor. But it is often necessary for an interface to also be concerned with the actual content of the data that is transferred. For example, it may be necessary for the interface to be able to send a variety of commands to a device to cause it to respond with different types of information or to change its operating mode. Alternatively, the device may need to request specific services from the processor by means of a set of command messages. Thus, it may be necessary for a software interface to support a higher level communication protocol.

One may think of the functional organization of an interface as being analogous to the structure of a language. Both transfer information by means of a syntax (structure) and semantics (meaning, content). In the case of an interface, the lowest layer protocol (syntax) is concerned exclusively with the mechanics of information transfer—without reference to data content. But a higher level protocol is often needed to deal with message content (semantics). Indeed, a more complex interface may require several successively higher levels of communication protocol. Depending on the actual complexity of the interface, it may be worthwhile to explicitly structure the interface software to reflect these functional divisions.

In Chapter 7 we will examine the software operations required to support a specific device interface and the way they interact with the other application and system software components of an example real-time program. But, before leaving the subject of hardware interface concepts, it will be worthwhile to review the various ways in which interrupts are used to support device operations in a real-time system.

6.6 DEVICE USE OF INTERRUPTS

External devices may use the interrupt mechanism in a variety of ways. Generally speaking, it is employed to signal the occurrence of an event, but the event in question may have been explicitly requested by the software or may be the result of a hardware-initiated action. In fact, just the occurrence of an interrupt may be all that the processor needs to know to respond properly. On the other hand, the processor may require further communication with the device. In this section we will review a few of the ways in which devices use interrupts.

Probably the simplest application of the interrupt mechanism is in support of system timing. The external device in this case is usually a timer chip that may be programmed to produce interrupts at a specified periodic rate. In this case, all of the information needed by the processor is provided by the event itself. That is, the processor does not need to read additional data from the device to determine the nature of the event or to respond properly to its occurrence.

Note that, in situations where hardware produces interrupts at a regular rate, it is important for the program to be able to respond to an interrupt and complete its processing before the next interrupt is scheduled to occur. Otherwise, two interrupts will be merged into one and one will be lost. In the case of the timer, for example, this will result in the loss of a timer "tick." This problem may be avoided by assuring that interrupt priority is sufficiently high and that only essential processing is performed within the handler. Additional processing may be accomplished by a task that is awakened by the handler.

A device may also use an interrupt to signal the completion of an action requested by the application program. For example, the program might send a request to an analog-to-digital (A/D) converter device to collect a block of samples. When the device completes the operation, it could use an interrupt to inform the processor. The interrupt handler might then wake a task that would collect and process the data. In this case the program "expects" the interrupt, since the operation was initiated by the program. But it is also common for hardware to independently initiate a processor operation by means of an interrupt.

A system must often be constrained to operate within some performance "envelope." If a system parameter indicates that the equipment is approaching an operational limit, the hardware may signal an alarm condition via an interrupt. The program must then perform some action to relieve the condition. In this situation the interrupt is "unexpected" in the sense that it is not in response to a specific prior request made by the program.

It is clear that interrupts play an important role in coordinating the interaction between the various hardware and software components of a real-time system. In the next chapter we will review an example multitask real-time program that uses an interrupt to provide timing information to application tasks.

7

Example Application Program CX3

In Chapter 6 we explored various aspects of I/O programming, including the concept of the hardware interrupt. The purpose of this chapter is to investigate the software operations that are required to support interrupts in a real-time program. To do this, we will examine a specific example program that responds to interrupts. Since the program is an extension of the example program presented in Chapter 5, it also demonstrates the way in which interrupts are accommodated by the executive and the role that interrupts play in multitask application programs.

To avoid obscuring the issues, I have chosen the simplest possible source of interrupts for this program—a timer. Most computers provide one or more sources of timer interrupts. A timer is typically supplied as part of a multipurpose peripheral I/O chip. The primary purpose for the chip is to support some standard data transfer protocol. A timer is an added feature. Since no data must be read when a timer interrupt occurs, the interrupt handler required to service it is especially simple. It is hoped that the computer being used provides a source of timer interrupts. It should then be possible to reconstruct and run the program described in this chapter and compare its performance to the results discussed here. The only software differences should be in the areas of timer and interrupt vector initialization.

This chapter presents the software required to construct program CX3 by modifying a copy of program CX2, discussed in Chapter 5. The chapter begins with an overview of program operation and then proceeds to a detailed examination of software changes that are needed to convert the CX2 program. This includes the operations required to initialize a specific peripheral chip and to respond to timer interrupts from that chip. The chapter concludes with an evaluation of program performance, based on measurements made with a logic analyzer.

Program CX3 is a specific example of an interrupt-driven, multitask, real-time program using the executive described in Chapters 2–4. As such, it serves as a model for similar real-time programs that you may wish to construct for your own particular applications.

7.1 THE CX3 PROGRAM, A FUNCTIONAL DESCRIPTION

The structure of program CX3 is diagrammed in Figure 7.1. Comparing this figure to the diagram for program CX2 in Figure 5.1, it is evident that CX3 contains an additional task called **timer()**, queues **rtctim, contim,** and **timcon** and interrupt handler **duart()**. The figure also indicates that the **timer()** task has highest priority and that it communicates with the **consol()** task via queues **contim** and **timcon.** Since the names of the three new queues do not start with the letters "o" or "f," they are evidently not buffer pointer queues. Instead, the program uses message queues for these communication paths. This choice was made simply for the purpose of illustrating the use of message queues in an operational program.

Program CX3 is designed to receive and process timer interrupts from a Motorola 68681 DUART (Dual Asynchronous Receiver/Transmitter) chip. This is a popular multipurpose

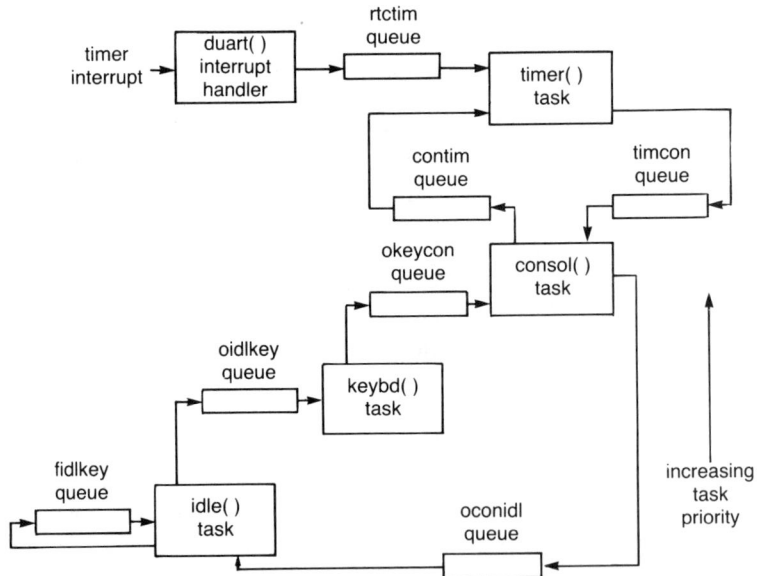

Figure 7.1. CX3 Program Structure.

chip that supports two RS-232 serial ports, a six-bit parallel input port, an eight-bit parallel output port, and a programmable counter/timer. Several of the chip's operations may cause interrupts, but only one interrupt line is supplied. As a result, the chip must be serviced by a single interrupt handler function that reads a chip status register to determine which operation caused the interrupt. In program CX3 this function is called **duart()**. Figure 7.1 indicates that it communicates with the **timer()** task via message queue **rtctim.**

In addition to performing all of the operations of program CX2, program CX3 adds a self-timing feature. The **consol()** task in CX3 sends a request to the **timer()** task for a timeout response after 1 second has elapsed. It uses queue **contim** to send the request and then wakes **timer()**. The **timer()** task, on receiving the request, uses messages received from interrupt handler **duart()** to measure the 1-sec delay. When the time interval has expired, it sends a message to **consol()** via queue **timcon** and wakes **consol()**. When **consol()** runs again, it receives the message, displays string "**tick . . .**" on the operator's terminal and repeats the sequence by sending another request for a one second timeout. This cycle is repeated as long as the main body of the program continues to perform the CX2 functions. That is, as long as the pointer to the message entered by the operator continues to be passed around the **idle()**, **keybd()**, **consol()** task loop.

Figure 7.2 shows the console display for a sample run. Note that the program performs both the pointer passing cycle and the timeout cycle simultaneously. Thus, all four tasks are being scheduled and run, based on their assigned priorities and the processing requirements of the application program.

Interrupt handler **duart()** sends messages to the **timer()** task via queue **rtctim.** As part of each transfer it wakes **timer()**. In turn, the **duart()** handler runs in response to interrupts from the 68681 chip. This chip is initialized to produce interrupts every 0.1 second. The content of the message sent to **timer()** by **consol()** is the number of 0.1-sec interrupt "ticks" in the requested timeout period. In this example program the number is ten. So the **timer()** task must receive ten messages from the **duart()** interrupt handler before returning a timeout message to **console()**. The content of the message sent from **duart()** to **timer()** is unimportant.

Note that tasks **timer()** and **consol()** are each awakened by two sources. The **timer()** task is awakened by **duart()** and **consol()**; **consol()** is awakened by **keybd()** and **timer()**. Since the source of a wakeup is not provided to a task, it is necessary for these tasks to determine this information independently. They do this by checking their input queues.

Since it is possible for a task to be awakened more than once before it is allowed to run, it should check all of its input queues and process all queued messages before suspending. In this situation one wakeup is sufficient to cause the task to satisfy all requests for service. But this will leave other unnecessary wakeups pending. When the task again runs, no messages (or pointers) will be in its input queues. The task must therefore be designed to check its input queues and suspend if they are empty. In Sections 7.6 and 7.7 we will see that tasks **timer()** and **consol()** are written to support this mode of operation.

To begin our study of the software changes required to produce program CX3 from a copy of program CX2, we will first review queue declarations and then proceed to examine initialization functions. We will then be prepared to inspect application tasks and the interrupt handler.

```
CX/68K  Executive, Version 1.0 (4/10/86)

(c)  1984  Walter S. Heath
     All rights reserved

This program demonstrates the task scheduling and
queue access capabilities of CX/68K.

This text is coming from the idle() task. The message you
enter below will be sent via queue 'idlkey' to the keybd()
task.  Keybd() will pass it on via queue 'keycon' to task
consol().  Consol() will send it back to the idle() task
via queue 'conidl'.

You will also be asked to enter the number of cycles this
loop will be repeated.

To exit the program type <CR> at any prompt.


Enter up to 8 characters:
ASDFGHJK

Enter number of repeat cycles (1 to 500000):
12345

I'm running . . .
tick . . .
tick . . .
tick . . .
tick . . .
tick . . .
tick . . .

ASDFGHJK

Enter up to 8 characters:
```
Figure 7.2. CX3 Application Program Console Display.

7.2 PROGRAM QUEUES

The CX3 program uses both buffer pointer queues and message queues. The queues for this program are declared in file **ques3.c,** shown in Figure 7.3. The function that is called by the executive to initialize them is also shown. This is actually the third time we have examined this figure. In Sections 4.1 and 4.3, we referred to it to see examples of queue declaration and initialization code. At that time we discussed these operations in detail. Moreover, the buffer pointer queues declared in this file are the same as those for example program CX2, described in Chapter 5. As a result, it will not be necessary to examine their operation again here. Instead, it will be sufficient to review this software in general terms.

File **ques3.c** includes files **qsymb.h** and **pqsymb.h.** These contain definitions of queue header data structures **que** and **pque,** respectively. Again, these files were discussed in Chapter 4 and are shown in Figures 4.1 and 4.6.

The **include** statements are followed by definitions of symbolic constants for the queue lengths. The buffer pointer queues contain room for ten pointers and the message queues are each four bytes long. These short queues are sufficient for this example program, since little buffering is needed to keep up with program execution.

Declarations for the three new message queues follow the pointer queue declarations. Each message queue declaration consists of a queue header and an array that will hold queued messages.

The **qinit()** function is called by executive function **cx()** to initialize application queue headers. For this example program it must initialize the four buffer pointer queues and the three message queues. The statements shown initialize each item in the header of each queue.

```
/*
 *      CX/68K Executive, Version 1.0      (4/10/86)
 *
 *      (c)  1984  Walter S. Heath, all rights reserved.
 *
 *      FILE QUES3.C
 *
 *      Application queues and queue initialization function.
 */

#include "pqsymb.h"
#include "qsymb.h"

/*
 *Declare the pointer queue lengths.
 */

#define FIKLNGTH            10              /*free lists              */

#define OIKLNGTH            10              /*occupied lists          */
#define OKCLNGTH            10
#define OCILNGTH            10
```

Figure 7.3. CX3 Program Queues. (*Continued on next page.*)

```
/*
 *Declare the message queue lengths.
 */
#define CTLNGTH            4
#define TCLNGTH            4
#define RTLNGTH            4

/*
 *Buffer pointer queue declarations.
 */
struct pque fidlkey                    ;/*idlkey queue free list header */
long fikbuf[FIKLNGTH]                  ;/*idlkey queue free list buffer */

struct pque oidlkey                    ;/*idlkey occupied list header    */
long oikbuf[OIKLNGTH]                  ;/*idlkey occupied list buffer    */

struct pque okeycon                    ;
long okcbuf[OKCLNGTH]                  ;

struct pque oconidl                    ;
long ocibuf[OCILNGTH]                  ;

/*
 *Message queue declarations.
 */
struct que contim                      ;/*consol()-timer() msg queue     */
char ctbuf[CTLNGTH]                    ;/*queue array                    */

struct que timcon                      ;/*timer()-consol() msg queue     */
char tcbuf[TCLNGTH]                    ;

struct que rtctim                      ;/*rtc()-timer() msg queue        */
char rtbuf[RTLNGTH]                    ;




/*
 *---qinit()
 *           This function initializes the application queues
 */
```

Figure 7.3. (*continued*) CX3 Program Queues.

```
qinit()
{
/*
 *Initialize the buffer pointer queues.
 */
fidlkey.full = 0                    ;/*queue-fill flags              */
oidlkey.full = 0                    ;
okeycon.full = 0                    ;
oconidl.full = 0                    ;

fidlkey.head = 0                    ;/*head pointers                 */
oidlkey.head = 0                    ;
okeycon.head = 0                    ;
oconidl.head = 0                    ;

fidlkey.tail = 0                    ;/*tail pointers                 */
oidlkey.tail = 0                    ;
okeycon.tail = 0                    ;
oconidl.tail = 0                    ;

fidlkey.lngth = FIKLNGTH            ;/*queue lengths                 */
oidlkey.lngth = OIKLNGTH            ;
okeycon.lngth = OKCLNGTH            ;
oconidl.lngth = OCILNGTH            ;

fidlkey.task = -1                   ;/*source task ID numbers        */
oidlkey.task = -1                   ;
okeycon.task = -1                   ;
oconidl.task = -1                   ;

fidlkey.pbuf = fikbuf               ;/*pointers to pointer queues    */
oidlkey.pbuf = oikbuf               ;
okeycon.pbuf = okcbuf               ;
oconidl.pbuf = ocibuf               ;


/*
 *Initialize the message queues.
 */
contim.lngth = CTLNGTH              ;/*queue lengths                 */
timcon.lngth = TCLNGTH              ;
rtctim.lngth = RTLNGTH              ;
```

(Continued on next page.)

```
contim.pbuf = ctbuf              ;/*buffer pointers              */
timcon.pbuf = tcbuf              ;
rtctim.pbuf = rtbuf              ;

contim.head = 0                  ;/*head pointers                */
timcon.head = 0                  ;
rtctim.head = 0                  ;

contim.tail = 0                  ;/*tail pointers                */
timcon.tail = 0                  ;
rtctim.tail = 0                  ;

contim.task = -1                 ;/*source task ID numbers       */
timcon.task = -1                 ;
rtctim.task = -1                 ;
}                                /*end of qinit() function       */
```

Figure 7.3 (*continued*) CX3 Program Queues.

7.3 PROGRAM INITIALIZATION FUNCTIONS

As with example program CX2, several functions must be called during program startup to initialize various task control and I/O device parameters. These are in addition to the queue initialization operations discussed in the previous section. Since most of these operations are similar to their counterparts in program CX2, we will review them only briefly and concentrate more attention on the new functions needed to initialize the timer.

7.3.1 The main() Function

The only difference between the **main**() function for the CX3 program, shown in Figure 7.4, and its counterpart for program CX2 is that it includes a different application symbol definition file, **apsymb3.h.** This file is shown in Figure 7.5. Note that the number of tasks is now four and that the task ID numbers have been adjusted so that the **timer**() task has highest priority. The remaining tasks have lower priority but maintain the priority order that they had in program CX2.

7.3.2 The TCB and Application Initialization Functions

The **api3.c** file, shown in Figure 7.6, contains TCB initialization function **initcb**() and application initialization function **apinit**(). The task stacks are also declared in this file. For

```
/*
 *      CX/68K  Executive,   Version 1.0   (4/10/86)
 *
 *      (c)  1984  Walter S. Heath, all rights reserved.
 *
 *      FILE CX3.C
 *                     Main function for runable demonstration program.
 *      REVISED:
 *            8/8/88
 */
#include "apsymb3.h"

extern short ntsks                      ;/*number of tasks defined        */
long cxst[256]                          ;/*cx()'s stack                   */

main()
{
/*
 *Initialize some application-dependent variables
 */
ntsks = NTSKS                           ;

/*
 *Call the CX/68K kernel
 */
cx()                                    ;

}                                       /*end of main()                   */

                                        /*end of CX3.C file               */
```

Figure 7.4. CX3 Main Program.

the CX2 program the corresponding file, **api2.c,** also contained vector initialization function **initvec(),** which was a null function since no vectors were required in that program. By contrast, the CX3 program does use an interrupt vector for the timer interrupt. An **initvec()** function is therefore required and is included in assembly language file **apio3.s.** This file will be examined in the next section.

File **api3.c** includes file **apsymb3.h.** In the last section we saw that a value of four is assigned to symbolic constant NTSKS in that file. So the **tcb[NTSKS]** declaration in file **api3.c** defines four task control blocks. An additional stack for the **timer()** task, **timst[],** is also declared. Function **initcb()** initializes all four TCBs.

The **apinit()** function calls function **ioinit().** In general, this function's purpose is to initialize I/O devices. We will see in Section 7.3.3.2 that, for the CX3 program, the function

```
/*
 *
 *      CX/68K  Executive, Version 1.0  (4/10/86)
 *
 *      (c)  1984  Walter S. Heath, all rights reserved.
 *
 *      FILE APSYMB3.H
 *
 *      This file contains application symbol definitions for
 *      demonstration program CX3.
 */

#define NTSKS                   4               /*number of defined tasks */

#define TIMEID                  0               /*task ID numbers         */
#define CONSID                  1
#define KEYBID                  2
#define IDLEID                  3


                                                /*end of APSYMB3.H file   */
```

Figure 7.5. CX3 Application Symbols.

initializes the timer chip. As in the case of program CX2, **apinit()** wakes the **idle()** task to get the application program started and then enables interrupts to the 68020 processor. Note that interrupts from the timer chip will not commence until they have been enabled at the timer chip. This will be accomplished in the **idle()** task.

7.3.3 The Application I/O Initialization Functions

Figure 7.7 shows file **apio3.s.** This file contains all of the assembly language application functions for program CX3. It is an expansion of file **apio2.s** for program CX2, which includes functions **_putch, _getline,** and **_getout.** These functions support terminal I/O. File **apio3.s** adds functions to initialize the timer and to service interrupts from it. Functions are also included to start and stop timer interrupts.

7.3.3.1 The Exception Vector Initialization Function

The **_initvec** function initializes exception vector locations. That is, for each specific exception vector that will be generated by the application, it writes the address of the appropriate exception handler function to the memory address pointed to by the vector. These addresses are located in low memory and are set aside by the processor specifically for this purpose. There are two types of exceptions that an application program can

```
/*
 *      CX/68K  Executive, Version 1.0   (4/10/86)
 *
 *      (c)  1984  Walter S. Heath, all rights reserved.
 *
 *      FILE API3.C
 *                  Application Initialization Functions and
 *                  Application Data Structures
 *      REVISED:
 *              8/8/88
 */
#include "cxsymb.h"
#include "apsymb3.h"

struct tcbdef tcb[NTSKS]                    ;/*task control blocks           */

long timst[256]                             ;/*timer()'s stack               */
long const[256]                             ;/*consol()'s stack              */
long keyst[256]                             ;/*keybd()'s stack               */
long idlst[256]                             ;/*idle()'s stack                */

short timer()                               ;/*declare tasks (for initcb())  */
short consol()                              ;
short keybd()                               ;
short idle()                                ;


/*
 *---initcb()
 *     This function initializes Task Control Blocks (TCBs).
 */

initcb()
{
tcb[0].tskadr = (short *)timer              ;/*task start addresses          */
tcb[1].tskadr = (short *)consol             ;
tcb[2].tskadr = (short *)keybd              ;
tcb[NTSKS - 1].tskadr = (short *)idle       ;

tcb[0].tsksp = (long)&timst[255]            ;/*task stack pointers           */
tcb[1].tsksp = (long)&const[255]            ;
tcb[2].tsksp = (long)&keyst[255]            ;
tcb[NTSKS - 1].tsksp = (long)&idlst[255]    ;

}                                  /*end of initcb()                          */
```

Figure 7.6. CX3 Initialization Functions. (*Continued on next page.*)

```
/*
 *---apinit()
 *     This function is called by the cx() function. It performs applica-
 *     tion-specific initialization operations.
 */

apinit()
{
ioinit()                        ;/*initialize I/O devices        */
wake(IDLEID)                    ;/*wake the idle() task          */
asm("  andw   #0xf8ff,sr    ")  ;/*enable interrupts             */

}                                /*end if apinit()               */

                                 /*end of API3.C file            */
```

Figure 7.6. (*continued*) CX3 Initialization Functions.

explicitly generate. One is the external hardware interrupt; the other is the internal software trap (the processor may generate several additional exceptions to signal errors).

The CX3 program is written to accept hardware interrupts from a 68681 DUART chip. The specific single board computer that CX3 is programmed to run on assigns the 68681's interrupt to processor interrupt level four and handles it as an autovector. We learned in Chapter 6 that, for this type of interrupt, the processor supplies the interrupt vector automatically. Specifically, it generates a unique vector for each interrupt level. For a level four interrupt it produces vector 70 hex. Hence, when a level four interrupt occurs, the processor calls the function specified by the address present in memory location 70 hex. Function **_initvec** must therefore place the address of the 68681 interrupt handler at that location. For the CX3 program, that is the address of function **_duarta**. We will examine this function shortly, but, first, we will complete our examination of timer initialization operations. The remaining operations are performed by function **_ioinit**.

7.3.3.2 The Timer Initialization Function

In Section 7.3.2 we noted that all I/O device initialization is performed by function **_ioinit**. For the CX3 program the only I/O device is the timer portion of the 68681 chip. So the **_ioinit** function must initialize this device. A processor accesses the 68681 by means of a set of sixteen eight-bit registers that are mapped into its address space. The specific addresses assigned to the chip's registers depend on the hardware design of the computer. The single board computer that was used to test program CX3 maps the registers starting at address ff0c0000 hex.

Function **_ioinit** configures the timer to produce interrupts at a rate of one every 0.1 second. This is accomplished by writing values to the Auxiliary Control Register (ACR), the Counter/Timer Upper Register (CTUR), and the Counter/Timer Lower Register (CTLR).

```
|****************************************************************************
| *
| *      CX/68K   Executive, Version 1.0    (4/10/86)
| *
| *      (c)  1984  Walter S. Heath, all rights reserved.
| *
| *      FILE APIO3.S
| *
| *      This file contains assembly language components of demonstration
| *      program CX3.  Functions are present to initialize I/O devices
| *      and exception vector locations.  It also contains the assembly
| *      language components of interrupt handlers, I/O devices and basic
| *      console I/O interfaces.
| *
| *      REVISED:
| *              8/8/88
|****************************************************************************
        .data
        .comm _duartst,1
| *
|*---initvec
| *      This function initializes locations pointed to by exception
| *      vectors.
| *
        .text
        .globl _initvec

_initvec:
        movl    #_duarta,0x70           |68681 interrupt; set auto vec. 4
        rts


| *
|*---ioinit
| *      This function initializes I/O devices.
| *
        .text
        .globl _ioinit

_ioinit:

| *
| *      Initialize the 68681 timer for 0.1 second interrupts. The count
| *      required is: NC = (.05 sec/half cycle)/TC, where TC is the
```

Figure 7.7. CX3 Application I/O Initialization Functions. (*Continued on next page.*)

```
|*      time for one count of the timer: TC = 1/(3.68684 mHz/16) =
|*      16/3.6864 mHz. So NC = .05(3.6864 X 10E+6)/16 = 11520.
|*
        movb    #0x70,0xff0c0004        |set ACR for TIMER; xtal; / by 16
        movb    #0x2D,0xff0c0006        |Set CTUR and CTLR for 0.1 second
        movb    #0x00,0xff0c0007        |interrupts (11520 counts).
        movb    #0x00,0xff0c0005        |disable TIMER interrupts in IMR
        rts


|*
|*---duarta
|*      This is the assembly language portion of the 68681 interrupt
|*      handler.  It calls C function duart().  duart() determines the
|*      source of the interrupt and then performs the appropriate
|*      operations before returning.
|*
|*      Notes: (1) Registers used must be saved by the FIRST instruction
|*                 executed.
|*             (2) For a preemptive interrupt handler it is necessary to
|*                 save/restore ALL registers.
|*
        .text
        .globl _duarta

_duarta:
        moveml #0xfffe,sp@-        |push all registers but SP

        movb    0xff0c0005,_duartst |get ISR
        movb    0xff0c000f,d0        |read STOP COUNTER to reset ISR

        jsr     _duart              |call C language duart()

        moveml sp@+,#0x7fff         |pop all registers but SP
        rte                         |return from exception (int.)
|*
|*---iostrt
|*      This function starts the I/O devices.
|*
        .text
        .globl _iostrt

_iostrt:
        movb    0xff0c000e,d0       |read START COUNTER to start timer
```

Figure 7.7. (*continued*) CX3 Application I/O Initialization Functions.

```
        movb    #0x08,0xff0c0005      |enable TIMER interrupts in IMR
        rts

|*
|*---iostop
|*      This function stops the I/O devices by disabling interrupts.
|*
        .text
        .globl _iostop

_iostop:
        movb    #0x00,0xff0c0005      |disable 68681 interrupts via IMR
        rts


        .data
        .comm  _outchr,4
        .comm  _inbuf,40

|*
|*---putch
|*      This function sends a character to the console CRT
|*
        .text
        .globl _putch

_putch:
        moveml #0x0004,sp@-           |save a5

        lea    _outchr,a5            |get address of _outchr
        movl   #4,d0                 |set putchar() routine #
        movl   a5@,sp@-             |load character to send
        trap   #15                   |enter monitor

        moveml sp@+,#0x2000          |restore a5
        rts

|*
|*---getlin
|*      This function gets a line of characters entered via the console
|*      keyboard
|*
        .text
        .globl _getlin
```

(Continued on next page.)

```
_getlin:
        moveml  #0x0004,sp@-        |save a5

        lea     _inbuf,a5           |get buffer-start address
        movl    #8,d0               |set getline() routine #
        movl    a5,sp@-                     |load buffer pointer
        trap    #15                 |enter monitor
                                    |character count returned in d0
        moveml  sp@+,#0x2000        |restore a5
        rts

|*
|*---getout
|*      This function provides re-entry to the monitor
|*
        .text
        .globl  _getout

_getout:
        movl    #0x07c,a5           |get level 7 (ABORT) vector addr
        jmp     a5@                 |jump to ABORT handler

|*
|*
|*                                  end of APIO3.S file
|*
```

Figure 7.7. (*continued*) CX3 Application I/O Initialization Functions.

The specific values that are written are explained in the function's header comment in the listing. Further details concerning specific bit-field assignments in the chip's registers are described in the 68681's documentation and will not be repeated here. Once the chip's control registers are set, the function disables chip interrupts by writing a zero to its Interrupt Mask Register (IMR). We mentioned in Section 7.3.2 that interrupts will be enabled at the appropriate time by the **idle()** task.

Note that if this program had been written for a computer that required vectored interrupts rather than autovectored interrupts, the **_ioinit** function would have also had to write a vector number to the chip's Interrupt Vector Register (IVR). The chip would then provide this vector number in response to an interrupt acknowledge (IACK) sequence from the processor. The processor would use this vector to locate the address of the appropriate interrupt handler and would then branch to that address.

Now that the timer has been initialized we may proceed to look at its interrupt handler. The handler is partitioned into two parts—one written in assembly language, the other in C. We will examine the assembly language portion in the next section. The C language part will be reviewed in Section 7.5.

7.4 THE ASSEMBLY LANGUAGE INTERRUPT HANDLING FUNCTIONS

The **_duarta** function, shown in Figure 7.7, contains several register operations that must be performed at the assembly language level and then calls C function **duart()** to perform application operations. These latter operations are more complex and are therefore more easily handled by C language statements.

The **_duarta** function begins by saving all of the processor's address and data registers (omitting the stack pointer address register, **a7**) on the currently active stack. In so doing, the handler preserves the context of the interrupted function. This context may then be restored after the handler completes its operations and before it returns control to the next instruction in that function. The interrupted function may then proceed as though no interruption occurred. Note that since a timer interrupt may happen at any time, the currently active stack could belong to the executive or to any of the defined tasks.

It should be kept in mind that when an interrupt occurs, the processor completes the current instruction and then saves the contents of the current program counter and status register. At that point the program counter points to the next instruction in the interrupted program. As we saw in Chapter 6, these register values are automatically pushed onto the current stack before control is transferred to the interrupt handler. Conversely, these values are automatically popped off of the stack and restored to their respective registers when the interrupt handler performs the **rte** (return-from-exception) instruction. The processor's status register is therefore properly saved and restored and control is automatically returned to the next instruction in the interrupted program.

Note that this interrupt handler saves and restores all of the processor's registers. As indicated in Chapter 6, it is actually necessary to save and restore only the registers that are used by the handler. But preserving all register values protects the program from a potentially difficult and common programming error. In Chapter 8 we will see that it is mandatory to do this in an interrupt handler that causes preemption of an interrupted task.

After saving processor registers, the **_duarta** function reads the 68681's Interrupt Status Register (ISR) and stores this value in global variable **_duartst**. This parameter will be tested by the C language **duart()** function to confirm that the 68681 interrupt was caused by its timer and not by some other on-chip service. The **_duarta** function then reads the chip's STOP-COUNTER register. This resets the ISR and prepares the chip to generate another timer interrupt. The function then proceeds to call C language function **duart()**. This function will be examined in the next section.

When **duart()** returns, **_duarta** must restore the saved context of the interrupted function and transfer control to the next instruction in that function. This is accomplished by restoring the contents of the processor's registers—including its program counter. The **moveml** (move-multiple) instruction restores the address and data registers (omitting the stack pointer, **a7**), and the **rte** (return-from-exception) instruction restores the status register and, finally, the program counter. The interrupted function then proceeds from the point of interruption.

7.4.1 Timer Interrupt
Start/Stop Functions

The CX3 program actually operates in two distinct modes. When it is waiting for input from the operator, it is operating in a "terminal-prompt" or non-real-time mode; once all necessary operator entries have been made, it switches to an interrupt-driven, real-time mode. Interrupts must be disabled during terminal-prompt mode and enabled during real-time mode. Functions _iostrt and _iostop, shown in Figure 7.7, perform these operations. In Section 7.7 we will see that they are called by the **idle()** task when program mode changes take place. Note that these functions are needed for this particular example program and may or may not be needed in an actual application program. The functions might also perform other mode-change operations in an application program.

The _iostrt function first reads the 68681's START-COUNTER register and then enables timer interrupts. Reading the register causes the timer to reload its countdown register with the value that was placed in registers CTUR and CTLR during chip initialization. The timer then proceeds to decrement this value. When it reaches zero, the chip generates a timer interrupt and repeats the sequence.

The _iostop function simply disables timer interrupts by clearing the bit assigned to the timer interrupt in the chip's Interrupt Mask Register (IMR).

7.5 THE C LANGUAGE
INTERRUPT HANDLER

We saw in Section 7.4 that the 68681 DUART interrupt handler _duarta calls C language function **duart()**. This function is included in file **timer3.c,** which is shown in Figure 7.8. In addition to **duart()**, this file contains the **timer()** task and associated data declarations. This task will be discussed in Section 7.6.

As mentioned in Section 7.4, **duart()** performs application-specific operations that are better handled by the higher level C language. As the listing indicates, the operations are quite simple. The function first checks the DUART's status register to make sure the interrupt was generated by the chip's timer. It then uses the **putq()** function to put a single-byte message in queue **rtctim** and then wakes the **timer()** task by calling executive function **wake()**. The **rtctim** queue establishes a communication link between **duart()** and the **timer()** task. When **timer()** runs, it checks the queue for messages.

Note that the content of message byte **intsig** is of no interest. The information that is being transferred is that an interrupt has occurred. That is conveyed by the fact that a message is present in the queue—not by its content. For this example program, the queue mechanism for communicating between an interrupt handler and a task could easily have been replaced with a simple global counter. The counter would be incremented by **duart()** and decremented by **timer()**. Each count would signify the occurrence of an interrupt. The queue was used to illustrate the more general case in which an interrupt handler has data to send to a task. Typically, an I/O device will cause an interrupt when it has data for the computer. For this more common situation the queue provides an efficient mechanism for transferring received data to a task.

```
/*
 *      CX/68K  Executive, Version 1.0  (4/10/86)
 *
 *      (c)   1984   Walter S. Heath, all rights reserved.
 *
 *      FILE TIMER3.C
 *
 *                      This file contains a general-purpose timer task
 *                      and the C portion of the interrupt handler. See
 *                      file APIO3.S for the assembly language part of
 *                      the interrupt handler and functions needed to
 *                      initialize the timer portion of the 68681.
 *      REVISED:
 *              8/8/88
 */
#include "apsymb3.h"
#include "qsymb.h"

extern struct que rtctim            ;
extern struct que timcon            ;
extern struct que contim            ;
extern char duartst                 ;

short tcount[NTSKS]                 ;/*timer count array                 */
static char sigmsg                  ;/*signal msg to timed-out task      */
static char tskmsg                  ;/*received countdown value          */

/*
 *---duart()
 *    This function performs the interrupt handler operations for the
 *    68681 DUART chip.  It is called by assembly language function
 *    _duarta (see file APIO3.S), which saves machine context before the
 *    call and restores it afterward.  Function duart() simply checks to
 *    see if the interrupt was from the chip's timer and then sends a
 *    "signal" byte via queue 'rtctim' to the timer() task and wakes it.
 */
char intsig                         ;/*interrupt signal msg              */
```

Figure 7.8. CX3 C Language Timer Interrupt Handler and Task. (*Continued on next page.*)

```
duart()

{
/*
 *Test 68681 status byte to determine if the interrupt was from the TIMER.
 *If is was, send a "signal" byte msg to the timer() task and wake it.
 */
if((duartst & 0x08) != 0){
      putq(&intsig,&rtctim,1)            ;
      wake(TIMEID)                       ;
}

}                                        /*end of duart()                */
```

```
/*
 *---timer()
 *
 *      This task provides interval timing for the other tasks.  A task
 *      initiates a timer by loading a countdown count into its timer
 *      output queue.  The countdown count is from 1 to 255.  One count
 *      = 100.0 msec (1/10th of a second, 25.50 seconds max.).  On an
 *      interrupt, timer() decrements each active timer's count and
 *      checks for a zero count.  On zero, the corresponding task is sent
 *      a message in its timer input queue and the task is awakened.
 *      Timer() then sets the task's countdown count to -1 (timer
 *      inactive).  Timer() then checks each task's timer-initiation
 *      queue and starts any new timers.  A timer may be stopped by
 *      sending it a -1 count.  It may be restarted with the same or
 *      another count at any time during the countdown.
 */

timer()
{
short i                                  ;/*timer-count array index       */
char tm                                  ;/*msg received from duart()     */

for(i = 0; i < NTSKS; i++)               /*disable all timer counters    */
      tcount[i] = -1                     ;

for( ; ; ){                              /*Start infinite loop . . .     */
sleep()                                  ;
```

Figure 7.8. *(continued)* CX3 C Language Timer Interrupt Handler and Task.

```
/*
 *Test each task timer input queue to see if a timeout should be started.
 *The while() loop clears the queue and gets the last entry.
 */

while(getq(&contim,&tskmsg) != -1)         /*If count is from consol(),   */
      tcount[CONSID] = tskmsg          ;
                                           /*Place tests for counts from  */
                                           /*other tasks here.            */
/*
 *Process each entry in the task timer count array, tcount[]; decrement
 *active counters and awaken tasks when their counts reach zero,
 *deactivate those timers. If more than one entry is present in queue
 *'rtctim', repeat.
 */
while(getq(&rtctim,&tm) != -1){            /*While duart() msgs present,   */
    for(i = 0; i < NTSKS; i++){            /*test all task counters.      */
        if(tcount[i] == -1)               /*If task's counter is inactive */
                continue                  ;/*go to next task's counter.   */
        else if (--tcount[i] == 0) {      /*If timeout reached,           */
                tcount[i] = -1            ;/*set task's timer to inactive. */



/*
 *Send a signal msg to timed-out task and wake the task.  The content of
 *'sigmsg' is immaterial.
 */
            switch(i){
            case CONSID:                   /*consol() task                */
                putq(&sigmsg,&timcon,1) ;/*put 'sigmsg'                    */
                wake(CONSID)             ;/*wake consol() after timeout    */
                break                    ;
                                           /*Place 'case' tests for other */
                                           /*tasks here.                  */

            }
        }
    }
}

                                           /* . . . end of infinite loop  */
}                                          /*end of timer() task          */
}

                                           /*end of TIMER3.C file         */
```

Figure 7.8. (*continued*) CX3 C Language Timer Interrupt Handler and Task.

A queue also provides buffering of received data. If several interrupts occur before the destination task is allowed to run, the data received by the interrupt handler will be buffered in the queue in the order in which they were received. When the task finally does run, it may then catch up with external events by processing all queued messages. This is especially useful when interrupts occur in bursts.

For this simple example program, it was not necessary to check to see if the **putq()** operation was successful (by testing its returned value). With a message length of one byte, four bytes in the queue's message buffer, and an interrupt rate of only one every 0.1 second, we could be assured that space would always be available. But in an actual application program it may be necessary to make the test. This is especially true if the processing load on the computer is uneven and/or interrupts occur in bursts. The problem of inadequate queue space may be alleviated by simply increasing the size of the message queue's buffer.

7.6 *THE TIMER() TASK*

In Section 7.1 we discussed the functional role of the **timer()** task. Briefly, it is designed to receive a timeout message from another task and to return a message to that task when the timout interval has elapsed. The requesting task is also awakened. The **timer()** task uses messages received from the **duart()** interrupt handler to measure time intervals. Although the task is designed to handle timeout requests from multiple tasks, in the CX3 program it accepts requests only from **consol()**. These requests are received via queue **contim** and responses are delivered via the **timcon** queue. Each timeout request message consists of a count of the number of tenth-second intervals in the requested timeout interval. For the CX3 program, this count is always ten.

Since the **timer()** task function, shown in Figure 7.8, is explained well and the operations performed are straightforward, it will not be necessary to discuss every operation in detail. Instead, I will comment generally on the functional operations that are performed and highlight points of interest.

The task begins by performing some initialization operations. Note that since these are located before the first call to **sleep()**, they are performed only once—during program initialization. Recall from Chapter 3 that the **tskinit()** function calls each application task and runs it to its first call to **sleep()**. These task initialization operations are performed at that time.

The first operation performed during task initialization is to set the entries in array **tcount[]** to minus one. Each entry in this array is assigned to a separate task. When a timeout request is received from a task, the count in the received message is placed in the entry in **tcount[]** assigned to that task. A minus one in an entry is used to indicate that no timeout request is pending for that task.

During normal operation the task is always entered from the **sleep()** function. At this point it checks its input queues from other tasks to see if any timeout requests have been posted. In the case of the CX3 program, the only source of timeout requests is the **consol()** task, so that **timer()** checks message queue **contim** from that task. If a timeout message is present, it is transferred to the entry in **tcount[]** assigned to the **consol()** task.

In the next section we will see that when **consol()** posts the timeout message, it also wakes the **timer()** task. Since **timer()** is the highest priority task in the program, it will run soon after **consol()** calls **sleep()**. As a consequence, the timeout countdown sequence will commence very soon after **consol()** makes the request.

The **timer()** task proceeds on to check the queue from the **duart()** interrupt handler function. If an entry is present, it checks each entry in the **tcount[]** array. First it checks to see if a timeout count is present and if one is, the count is decremented. It then checks for any remaining counts. If no more counts are present, it deactivates the counter (sets it to minus one) and then proceeds to send a timeout response message to the requesting task. Again, for the CX3 program the only requesting task is **consol(),** so it puts a message in queue **timcon** and wakes **consol()**. Note that, here again, the content of the message is unimportant—the presence of a message in the queue conveys the information.

Note that the **timer()** task uses a **while()** loop to check the **rtctim** queue. The loop continues until all entries in the queue have been removed. Thus, if several timer interrupts occur before the **timer()** task is allowed to run, all accumulated messages will be read and processed.

7.7 APPLICATION TASK MODIFICATIONS

At the beginning of this chapter, we noted that the CX3 program would be constructed from the copy of the CX2 program. To accomplish this, several changes were made to the **idle()** and **consol()** tasks. This section will complete our discussion of the CX3 program code by reviewing these changes. We will then be in a position to put the program together, run it, and measure its performance.

Figure 7.9 shows the **tasks3.c** file. This is a modified version of the CX2 program's **tasks2.c** file, which was examined in Section 5.5 and shown in Figure 5.9. Changes may be

```
/*
 *      CX/68K Executive, Version 1.0   (4/10/86)
 *
 *      (c) 1984  Walter S. Heath, all rights reserved.
 *
 *      FILE TASKS3.C
 *
 *              Tasks for Demonstration Program CX3.
 *
 *      REVISED:
 *              8/8/88
 */
#include "apsymb3.h"
#include "pqsymb.h"
#include "qsymb.h"
```

Figure 7.9. CX3 Application Tasks. (*Continued on next page.*)

```
extern struct pque fidlkey              ;/*buffer pointer queues         */
extern struct pque oidlkey              ;
extern struct pque okeycon              ;
extern struct pque oconidl              ;
extern struct que contim                ;/*message queues                */
extern struct que timcon                ;

char *getbpwt()                         ;/*declare returned values       */
char *getbp()                           ;

char dsp                                ;/*display control flag          */
long cycles                             ;/*execution cycles counter      */
char rcvd                               ;/*timer-msg-received flag        */
char timmsg                             ;/*timer msg byte                */

char *dsp0 = "\n\n\n\n" ;
char *dsp1 = "CX/68K  Executive, Version 1.0 (4/10/86)\n\n" ;
char *dsp2 = "(c)  1984  Walter S. Heath\n" ;
char *dsp3 = "     All rights reserved\n\n" ;
char *dsp4 = "This program demonstrates the task scheduling and\n" ;
char *dsp5 = "queue access capabilities of CX/68K.\n\n" ;
char *dsp6 = "This text is coming from the idle() task. The message you\n" ;
char *dsp7 = "enter below will be sent via queue 'idlkey' to the keybd()\n" ;
char *dsp8 = "task.  Keybd() will pass it on via queue 'keycon' to task\n" ;
char *dsp9 = "consol().  Consol() will send it back to the idle() task\n" ;
char *dsp10 = "via queue 'conidl'.\n\n" ;
char *dsp11 = "You will also be asked to enter the number of cycles this\n" ;
char *dsp12 = "loop will be repeated.\n\n" ;
char *dsp13 = "To exit the program type <CR> at any prompt.\n\n";

char *msg1 = "Enter up to 8 characters:\n" ;/*prompt message            */
char *msg2 = "\n"                ;/*line space message              */
char *msg3 = "Enter number of repeat cycles (1 to 500000):\n" ;
char *msg4 = "I'm running . . .\n"        ;

char *tim1 = "tick . . .\n"               ;

char idlbuf[10]                         ;/*array to store received msg   */

short inchrs                            ;/*number of char's input        */

char *idleptr                           ;/*idle() task msg pointer       */
char *keybptr                           ;/*keybd() task msg pointer      */
char *consptr                           ;/*consol() task msg pointer     */
```

Figure 7.9. (*continued*) CX3 Application Tasks.

```
/*
 * ---idle()
 *      This function is the lowest priority task.  For purposes of
 *      demonstrating the scheduler it contains a consol interface.
 *      The name is arbitrary.
 */

idle()
{
dsp = 0                              ;
cycles = -1                          ;

for( ; ; ){                          /*Start infinite loop . . .      */
sleep()                              ;

if(dsp == 0){                        /*Display full screen first      */
        dsp = 1                      ;/*time only.                     */
        conout(dsp0,4)               ;
        conout(dsp1,42)              ;
        conout(dsp2,27)              ;
        conout(dsp3,26)              ;
        conout(dsp4,50)              ;
        conout(dsp5,38)              ;
        conout(dsp6,58)              ;
        conout(dsp7,59)              ;
        conout(dsp8,58)              ;
        conout(dsp9,57)              ;
        conout(dsp10,21)             ;
        conout(dsp11,58)             ;
        conout(dsp12,24)             ;
        conout(dsp13,46)             ;
                                     /*Put pointer to data buffer     */
        putbpwt(idlbuf,&fidlkey,IDLEID)  ;/* idlbuf[] in free queue.   */
}
if(cycles > 0)                       /*If cycles are running,         */
     idleptr = getbpwt(&oconidl,IDLEID) ;/*just pull pointer in.      */

else{                                /*Else, prompt operator for input.*/

     iostop()                        ;/*stop I/O devices              */

     if(cycles == 0){                /*If previous run just finished, */
             idleptr = getbpwt(&oconidl,IDLEID);/*get buffer pointer.  */
             conout(msg2,1)          ;
             conout(idleptr + 1,*idleptr) ;/*display msg in buffer    */
             conout(msg2,1)          ;
                                     /*return pointer to free list    */
             putbpwt(idleptr,&fidlkey,IDLEID) ;
     }
```

(Continued on next page.)

```
                                            /*Get msg from operator to send.  */
        idleptr = getbpwt(&fidlkey,IDLEID) ;/*get pointer to free buffer      */
        do{
                conout(msg2,1)                  ;
                conout(msg1,26)                 ;/*prompt for message          */
                inchrs = conin(idleptr + 1,9) ;/*input entered char's          */
                *idleptr = inchrs               ;/*store # of chars in 1st byte */

        }while(inchrs > 8 )                     ;/*repeat for error input       */

        do{                                     /*Get cycles to run.           */
                conout(msg2,1)                  ;
                conout(msg3,45)                 ;/*prompt for cycles            */
                cycles = numin()                ;/*input cycles                 */

        }while(cycles < 1 || cycles > 500000) ;/*repeat for error input        */

        conout(msg2,1)                          ;
        conout(msg4,18)                         ;/*show "I'm running . . ."     */

        iostrt()                                ;/*start I/O devices            */
}
putbpwt(idleptr,&oidlkey,IDLEID)                ;/*output msg ptr to keybd()    */
cycles--                                        ;
wake(KEYBID)                                    ;/*wake the keybd() task        */

}                                               /* . . . end infinite loop.    */
}                                               /*end of idle() task           */

/*
 *---keybd()
 *     This function is the keyboard task (arbitrarily named).  It
 *     receives a message pointer from the idle() task and sends it to
 *     the consol() task.  It then wakes consol().
 */

keybd()
{
for( ; ; ){                                     /*Start infinite loop . . .    */
sleep()                                         ;

keybptr = getbpwt(&oidlkey,KEYBID)              ;/*get msg ptr from idle()      */
putbpwt(keybptr,&okeycon,KEYBID)                ;/*send it to consol() task     */
wake(CONSID)                                    ;/*wake the consol() task       */

}                                               /* . . . end infinite loop.    */
}                                               /*end of keybd() task          */
```

Figure 7.9. (*continued*) CX3 Application Tasks.

```
/*
 *---consol()
 *      This function is the console task (arbitrarily named).  It
 *      receives a message pointer from the keybd() task and sends it to
 *      the idle() task.  It then wakes idle().
 *
 *      It also sends a timeout message to the timer() task and wakes it.
 *      The timer() task returns a response after one second.  This task
 *      then prints out a "tick . . ." string to the console and restarts
 *      the timeout.
 */

consol()
{
rcvd = 1                                ;/*start timer-msg-received flag  */

for( ; ; ){                              /*Start infinite loop . . .      */
sleep()                                 ;

consptr = getbp(&okeycon)               ;/*check for a ptr from keybd()   */

if((int)consptr != -1){                  /*If wakeup from keybd() task,   */
        putbpwt(consptr,&oconidl,CONSID);/*send pointer to idle() task,   */
        wake(IDLEID)                    ;/*wake idle() to start over.     */
}
/*
 *Check the timer() task's return queue for a timeout response.  If one
 *is present, start another one second timeout.
 */
if(getq(&timcon,&timmsg) != -1){         /*If timer response received,    */
        rcvd = 1                        ;/*set timer-msg-received flag,   */
        conout(tim1,11)                 ;/*signal operator.               */
}

if(rcvd == 1){                           /*If start-first-timeout or      */
                                         /*timer re-start,                */

        rcvd = 0                        ;
        timmsg = 10                     ;/*select # of 1/10th seconds,    */

        putq(&timmsg,&contim,1)         ;/*send it to timer() task,       */
        wake(TIMEID)                    ;/*wake timer() task.             */

}

}                                        /* . . . end infinite loop.      */
}                                        /*end of consol() task           */

                                         /*end of TASKS3.C file           */
```

Figure 7.9. (*continued*) CX3 Application Tasks.

noted by comparing the two files. The reasons for making many of the changes are obvious. For example, the additions to the data declaration section at the beginning of the file are required to support the additional instructions that were added to the tasks. As a result, it will not be necessary to discuss each change individually. Instead, we will concentrate our efforts toward gaining an understanding of the functional operation of the functions.

Only two new statements have been added to the **idle()** task. These are calls to assembly language functions **iostop()** and **iostrt()**. In Section 7.4.1 we noted that the program switches between a non-real-time, terminal-prompt mode and a real-time, interrupt-driven mode. When the program is in the non-real-time mode, interrupts must be disabled. The **iostop()** function accomplishes this by disabling interrupts from the timer when this mode is entered. After the required operator prompts have been satisfied, function **iostrt()** is called as part of the transition to the real-time mode. This function enables timer interrupts.

It is evident from the listing that the **keybd()** task is unchanged, but several changes were made to the **consol()** task. These are needed to support its interaction with the **timer()** task.

Two tasks send messages to **consol()** and wake it. They are **timer()** and **keybd()**. Since **consol()** must check two input queues after each wakeup, it must use the primitive queue access functions. Instead of suspending a task if a queue is empty, these functions return minus one. The task may then continue on to perform other work. The **consol()** function first uses primitive function **getbp()** to check for a buffer pointer from **keybd()**. If one is present, it simply passes it along to the **idle()** task via queue **oconidl** and wakes that task. If a pointer is not found, it proceeds on to check the message queue from the **timer()** task, **timcon.**

If a timeout message is present in the **timcon** queue, **consol()** sets a flag and sends string "**tick . . .**" to the operator's consol. It then checks the flag. If it is set, it starts a new timeout sequence by placing a count message in queue **contim.** It then wakes the **timer()** task. Note that the flag is initially set when the **consol()** task is first initialized, during program startup. This gets the chain of timeout requests started.

Since the timer interrupt occurs at a 0.1-sec rate and the timeout message count is ten, the program will display the "**tick . . .**" message at a 1-sec rate.

7.8 PUTTING THE CX3 PROGRAM TOGETHER

The procedure for assembling, compiling, linking, and testing the CX3 program is essentially the same as that described for program CX2 in Section 5.6. In a Berkeley UNIX software development environment, assembly language files are assembled using:

as −o filename.o filename.s

and C language files are compiled using:

cc −c filename.c

The only significant difference is in the linker command, since different files must be linked:

**ld −x −T 1000 −o cx3 cx3.o tasks3.o ques3.o api3.o apio3.o\
timer3.o conio.o sys.o bptr.o quea.o cxn.o −1c**

Again, this statement links the program such that it starts at memory address 1000 hex. This can be changed to another address that is more convenient for a particular target computer.

Once the program has been successfully linked, it is ready to be loaded into the target real-time computer and tested. We will review the program's performance in the next section.

7.9 CX3 PROGRAM PERFORMANCE EVALUATION

It is interesting to observe the operation of the CX3 program, since interrupts occur asynchronously with respect to the ongoing **idle()**, **keybd()**, and **consol()** task operations and the task scheduling operations performed by **sched()**, **run()**, and **sleep()**. A variety of different task scheduling situations arise when the **timer()** task, which is awakened by the interrupt handler, must compete with the other tasks for access to the processor.

The way in which the executive handles requests for service will be observed by monitoring the program with a logic analyzer. The procedure is much the same as that described in Section 5.7 to "instrument" and observe the performance of the CX2 program. Statements are added that set and clear bits in a parallel port and the signals from the port are monitored with a logic analyzer. Since the CX3 program adds an interrupt handler and an additional task to the CX2 program, some additional instrumentation code is needed to monitor this program's performance.

In the next section we shall review the statements that must be inserted into the CX3 program to monitor its performance. Then, in Section 7.9.2, we will examine logic analyzer plots of program operation and will identify scheduling decisions that are made by the executive as the **timer()** task is awakened asynchronously at various points in the program.

7.9.1 Performance Test Setup

In Section 5.7.1 we reviewed several statements that were added to the CX2 program to set and clear bits in the port C parallel port of a Motorola 68230 Parallel Interface and Timer (PIT) chip to monitor the program's task scheduling activity. These statements must also be added to the CX3 program to monitor its performance. Some additional statements will also be needed to observe operation of the timer interrupt handler and the **timer()** task.

Figure 7.10 shows a section of file **apio3.s** that has been modified to include some of these statements. The **_ioinit** function contains code to configure port C of the 68230 chip as an output port and to initially set all of its bits high. These operations will be performed during program startup, when the executive calls this function.

```
|*
|*---ioinit
|*     This function initializes I/O devices.
|*
       .text
       .globl _ioinit

_ioinit:
|*
|*     Initialize the 68681 timer for 0.1 second interrupts. The count
|*     required is: NC = (.05 sec/half cycle)/TC, where TC is the
|*     time for one count of the timer: TC = 1/(3.68684 mHz/16) =
|*     16/3.6864 mHz. So NC = .05(3.6864 X 10E+6)/16 = 11520.
|*
       movb   #0x70,0xff0c0004     |set ACR for TIMER; xtal; / by 16
       movb   #0x2D,0xff0c0006     |Set CTUR and CTLR for 0.1 second
       movb   #0x00,0xff0c0007     |interrupts (11520 counts).
       movb   #0x00,0xff0c0005     |disable TIMER interrupts in IMR
|*
|*     Initialize the PIT port C for output.  Then set all bits.
|*
       movb   #0xff,0xff0e0004     |set port C for output
       movb   #0xff,0xff0e000c     |set port C to all 1's
       rts


|*
|*---duarta
|*     This is the assembly language portion of the 68681 interrupt
|*     handler.  It calls C function duart().  duart() determines the
|*     source of the interrupt and then performs the appropriate
|*     operations before returning.
|*
|*     Notes: (1) Registers used must be saved by the FIRST instruction
|*                executed.
|*            (2) For a preemptive interrupt handler it is necessary to
|*                save/restore ALL registers.
|*
       .text
       .globl _duarta

_duarta:
       moveml #0xfffe,sp@-          |push all registers but SP
       orb    #0x20,0xff0e000c      |set PIT port C, bit 5
```

Figure 7.10. An "Instrumented" Section of File apio3.s.

```
movb    0xff0c0005,_duartst  |get ISR
movb    0xff0c000f,d0         |read STOP COUNTER to reset ISR

jsr     _duart               |call C language duart()

andb    #0xdf,0xff0e000c      |clear PIT port C, bit 5
moveml  sp@+,#0x7fff          |pop all registers but SP
rte                          |return from exception (int.)
```

Figure 7.10. (*continued*) An "Instrumented" Section of File apio3.s.

Statements have also been added to the **_duarta** interrupt handler to set and clear bit 5 of port C. As a result, this bit will be high when the interrupt handler is executing and low otherwise. Note that the instruction that sets the bit is placed after the register-save instruction. The processor will always execute the first instruction in an interrupt handler before a higher priority interrupt is recognized. It is therefore very important for this first instruction to be the register-save instruction—so that the context of the interrupted function is preserved. Since the CX3 program has only one source of interrupts, this precaution is not strictly necessary for this program. But it will be important in the example programs that will be reviewed in Chapter 9.

Two statements must also be added to the **timer()** task. The first sets bit 6 of port C and should be placed just after the call to **sleep()**:

asm(" orb #0x40,0xff0e000c ") ;/*set PIT port C, bit 6 */

The second clears bit 6 and must be inserted just before the end of the task's infinite loop:

asm(" andb #0xbf,0xff0e000c ") ;/*clear PIT port C, bit 6 */

Again, these statements cause bit 6 of port C to be set when the **timer()** task is running and to be cleared otherwise.

At this point we are almost ready to begin monitoring the performance of the CX3 program. But before we begin, one further program adjustment is necessary. We will get much more stable logic analyzer displays if we disable the statement that outputs the "**tick . . .**" string to the operator's console. This statement is present in the **consol()** task, shown if Figure 7.9. It should be "commented out" as follows:

/* conout (tim1,11)   ;/*signal operator */

The program is now prepared for performance evaluation. A new binary image should be generated and logic analyzer probes should be attached to appropriate pins of port C. In the next section we shall examine the results of several test runs.

7.9.2 Performance Test Results

Figure 7.11a shows the results of a typical test run. Note that the plot traces have been arranged in ascending order of function priority. That is, **idle()** has lowest task scheduling priority, **timer()** has highest, and the **_duarta** interrupt handler (labeled DUART in the figure) may interrupt any task.

This particular plot shows a case in which the timer interrupt happened to occur when none of the monitored functions were executing. Since the interrupt happened just after **idle()** completed, the program was either entering **sleep()** or exiting **run()** in the process of returning control to **sched()**. The interrupt handler woke the **timer()** task and, since this task has highest scheduling priority, **sched()** chose to run it next. Clearly, this is entirely satisfactory performance, since the highest priority, awakened task ran immediately.

A different situation is shown in Figure 7.11b. Here again, the interrupt occurred outside of any monitored function. In fact, it happened just after **sched()** had run and the program was either entering **run()** or exiting **sleep()** in transition to the **keybd()** task. In this case **sched()** had already chosen **keybd()** to run before the interrupt handler woke **timer()**. So **keybd()** executes to completion and then **timer()** is allowed to run. This case shows suboptimal performance, since the highest priority, awakened task did not run next. This behavior is the result of the fact that the executive employs nonpreemptive task scheduling. We would prefer to have the **sched()** function "reconsider" its choice of the next task to run after an interrupt has occurred. In the next two chapters we will see how preemptive scheduling solves this problem.

Figure 7.11c shows yet another situation. Here, the interrupt took place while the **consol()** task was running. Again, the interrupt handler wakes the **timer()** task but control is returned to **consol()**. This is an example of typical nonpreemptive scheduling behavior. The **consol()** task is not preempted to allow the higher priority **timer()** task to run. Instead, it must wait until the interrupted task voluntarily relinquishes control of the processor by calling **sleep()** (or **pause()**). As with the case shown in the previous figure, this suboptimal behavior may be avoided by using preemptive scheduling.

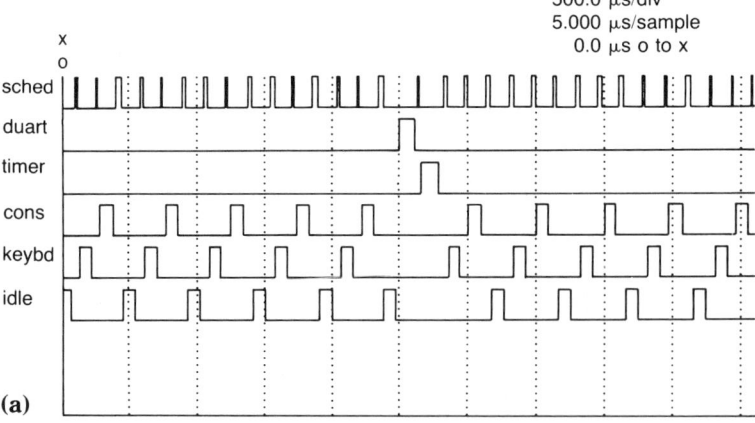

Figure 7.11a–d. CX3 Performance Test Results.

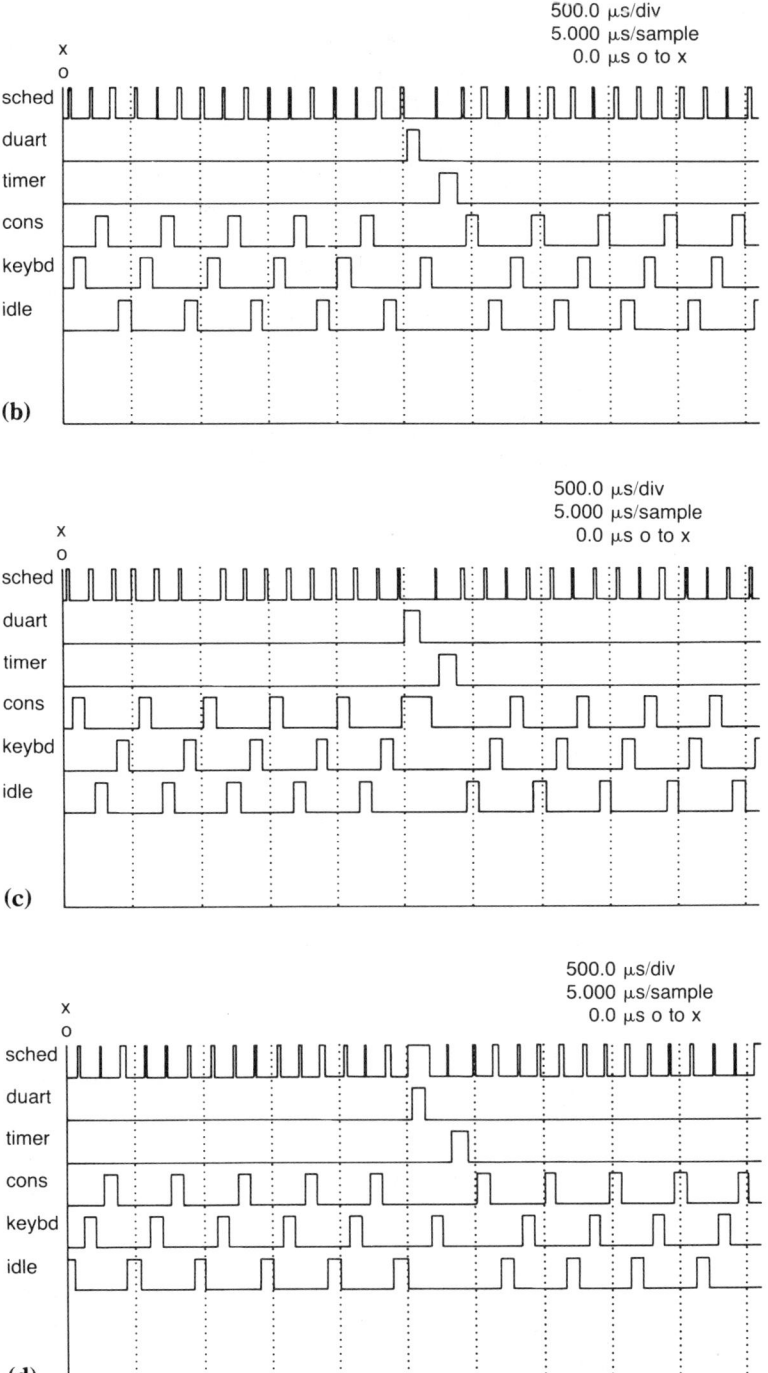

Figure 7.11a–d. (*continued*) CX3 Performance Test Results.

One more case of interest is shown in Figure 7.11d. This plot indicates that the interrupt occurred while **sched()** was running. Evidently **sched()** had proceeded past the point of choosing the next task to run, since **keybd()** runs next and the higher priority **timer()** task must wait. As in the case shown in Figure 7.11b, we would like to have **sched()** "reconsider" its choice after the interrupt.

It should be kept in mind that, although nonpreemptive scheduling is clearly suboptimal, its performance will be entirely adequate for applications of a certain class. In many situations it is not absolutely necessary for the highest priority, awakened task to run immediately. If task execution times are sufficiently short or if larger tasks cooperate by calling the **pause()** function at appropriate intervals to allow the scheduler to check for higher priority tasks, nonpreemptive scheduling may provide acceptable system performance.

When we examine preemptive scheduling in the next chapter, it will become clear that it increases the complexity of the executive. This naturally leads to somewhat slower task-switch times and a more complex debugging environment. A choice must therefore be made between the two scheduling techniques. The best solution in any particular application will depend on system performance requirements, project deadlines, and the ability of software writers to deal with the more complex preemptive environment. It is sometimes appropriate to use nonpreemptive scheduling during the initial stages of application program development and testing, and then to switch to preemptive scheduling at a later time to improve program performance.

8

Preemptive Task Scheduling

In Section 7.9.2, we reviewed the performance of an example application program that used nonpreemptive task scheduling and discovered that its performance was less than optimal for some applications. To reiterate, when an interrupt occurs in this environment and the interrupt handler wakes a task, that task is not allowed to run until the interrupted task voluntarily suspends. This is true even if the awakened task has higher priority.

In some applications this behavior is acceptable—in others it isn't. For example, if the interrupt is generated by some device to signal that it has completed an operation and is therefore going into a dormant state until another operation is initiated, it is probably not necessary for the awakened task to run immediately. The task might initiate another device operation when time permits. On the other hand, if the device is being driven by an external clock and is delivering a data sample on each interrupt and if that sample must be processed before the next sample is taken, then the task that is awakened by the interrupt handler to process the data must run immediately.

A specific example of this situation is a computer implementation of a phaselock loop. In a system of this type the amplitude of a received signal is sampled at a nominally periodic but adjustable rate. The objective is to track a zero-crossing of the signal. A phaselock loop algorithm accomplishes this by computing a sampling time for the next sample such that the amplitude of that sample will be closer to zero.

The calculation is based on the amplitude of the sample delivered by the hardware during the previous interrupt. Clearly, this calculation must be performed within some short and predictable time interval after a sample is received. The new sample time may then be delivered with sufficient lead time to allow the hardware to prepare to take the next sample. The task that is awakened by the interrupt handler to perform this calculation must therefore run immediately and must preempt any task that was running at the time of interruption. Once this high priority task has completed, the lower priority, interrupted task may continue.

In this chapter, the operations that must be performed to implement preemptive scheduling will be examined. We shall begin by reviewing design requirements and then examine a functional design, using block diagrams to show the sequence of events and flow of control. The issue of multiple levels of preemption will also be addressed. This is a situation in which an interrupt handler that is designed to preempt a running task is, itself, interrupted by a higher priority interrupt handler that must also preempt a running task. We shall demonstrate that multiple levels of preemption may be accommodated by a properly designed executive algorithm.

With the theory of operation firmly established we shall then look at the specific software changes that are needed to upgrade the executive described in Chapters 2 and 3 to support preemptive scheduling. Finally, the important subject of reentrancy, which imposes design constraints on the way both shared functions and shared data structures must be written in a preemptive environment will be discussed.

The concepts that are developed in this chapter will be applied to specific problems in Chapter 9. In that chapter we shall look at an example application program that incorporates preemptive scheduling and discuss the performance results for another program that demonstrates multiple level preemption.

8.1 DESIGN REQUIREMENTS

A preemptive scheduling operation is initiated by the occurrence of an interrupt. Clearly, if the interrupt occurs when no task is running, task preemption is not necessary. This situation arises when an interrupt occurs when the task scheduler is in the process of selecting the next task to run. Since the interrupt may occur at any point in this process, the scheduler may have already selected a task to run. But the preemptive interrupt handler may have awakened a different task of higher priority that must be run next. The handler must therefore be able to force the scheduler to "reconsider" its choice of the next task to run.

If the preemptive interrupt occurs when a task is running, the handler must suspend the task such that it may be reentered at the point of interruption the next time it is scheduled to run. Obviously, the entire context of the preempted task (the contents of the processor's registers, including its stack and stack frame points) must be saved so that it may be restored when the task is again run. The interrupt handler must also reschedule the suspended task (wake it) so that it will be resumed at some later time—when it again becomes the currently highest priority, awakened task. It must also wake the preempting task and must arrange for control to be transferred back to the scheduler so that this higher priority task may be selected to run next.

To summarize, a preemptive interrupt handler must:

- force the task scheduler to reselect the next task to run—if the interrupt occurs when the scheduler is running

- suspend a running task such that it may be reentered at the point of interruption when the task is next selected to run
- wake both the preempting and preempted tasks
- transfer control back to the task scheduler

In the next section we shall see that many of these operations may be performed by functions that we already have, and that the remaining operations may be implemented by making some relatively simple additions to our nonpreemptive executive.

8.2 FUNCTIONAL DESIGN

In the subsections that follow we shall examine the operation of a version of the non-preemptive executive that has been modified to support preemptive scheduling. Section 8.2.1 will review operation when a preemptive interrupt occurs while a task is not running—that is, when the scheduler is running. Preemption when a task is running will then be examined in Section 8.2.2. In Section 8.2.3 we shall inspect the way in which the processor's interrupt priority level is managed during preemption, and multiple level preemption will be addressed in Section 8.2.4.

8.2.1 Preemptive Interruption outside a Task

Figure 8.1 shows the sequence of events and the flow of control when a preemptive interrupt occurs while the task scheduler is running. The interrupt handler saves the interrupted function's context, performs some application-specific operations (such as I/O operations), and then wakes the task that must run next. It then tests flag **intask.** This is a flag that is set by **sleep()** (as the figure shows) just before a task is entered and is cleared when **sleep()** is reentered from a task. As a result, the flag is set when a task is running.

Since the interrupt occurred when a task was not running, **intask** is not set, and the interrupt handler proceeds to set flag **resched.** It then restores the calling function's context and returns control to the point of interruption in **sched().**

The scheduler then continues on and selects a task to run next—if it has not already done so. It then calls **run()** and **run()** transfers control to **sleep().** Function **sleep()** proceeds as usual but, before transferring control to the selected task, it checks to see if flag **resched** is set. If it is, it does not return to the selected task. Instead, after clearing **resched,** it loops back to **run()** and **run()** returns to **sched().** The scheduler then reselects the currently highest priority, awakened task and again calls **run().** That is, it "reconsiders" its choice of the next task to run, and, if the task that was awakened by the interrupt handler was missed during the previous selection, it will be properly selected this time. When **sleep()** is again entered, the **resched** flag will not be set and control will be transferred to the task awakened by the preemptive interrupt handler.

Note that if an interrupt occurs before **sched()** has made its first selection of a task to run, the task awakened by the handler will be selected immediately. But the algorithm will force

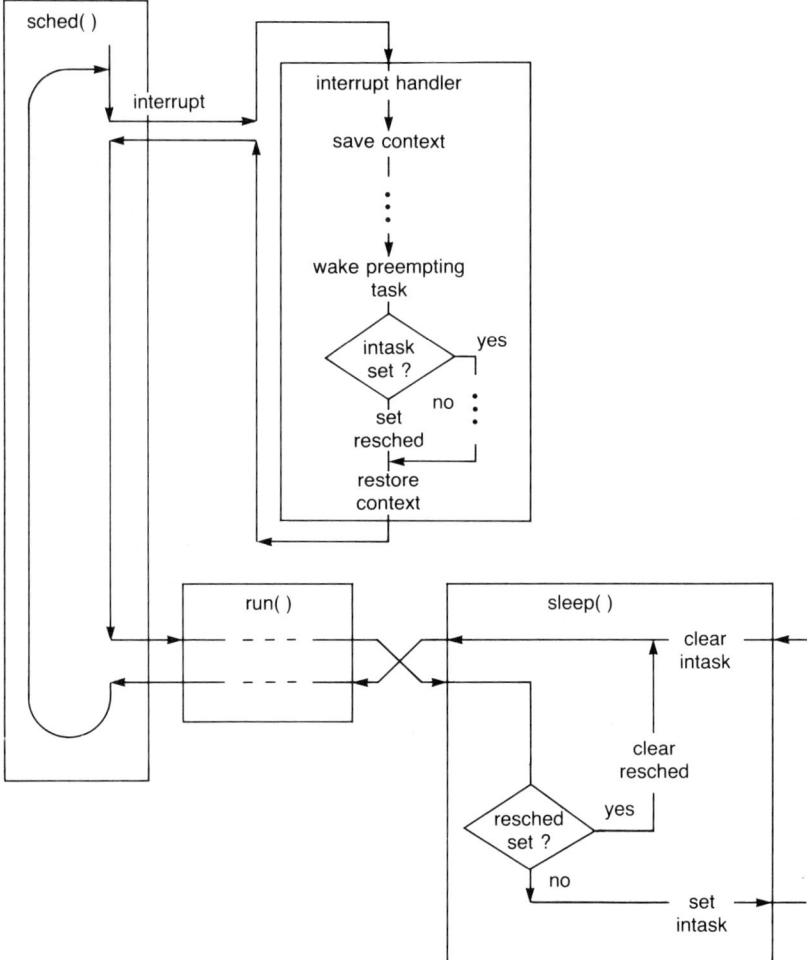

Figure 8.1. Preemptive Interrupt: Scheduler Running.

another redundant reselection. This is usually of little consequence, since scheduler execution time is fast. If desired, this redundancy could be removed by adding and testing another flag.

8.2.2 Preemptive Interruption within a Task

The situation is a bit more complex when a preemptive interrupt occurs within an application task. Figure 8.2 shows program flow for this case. The handler first saves the task's context on the currently active stack, which, in this case, is the task's stack, and then performs application-specific operations. It then wakes the task that will preempt the interrupted task and proceeds to test flag **intask.** Since a task was running when the interrupt occurred, **intask** will be set. As a consequence, the handler calls executive function **pause().**

In Section 3.2.2 we saw that function **pause()** effectively wakes the currently running task and then calls **sleep().** When **pause()** is called from an interrupt handler that has interrupted a task, the currently "running" task is the task that was interrupted. The task that is to be preempted is therefore reawakened.

The call to **sleep()** in **pause()** causes control to be transferred back to the task scheduler via **run().** The scheduler will then select the currently highest priority, awakened task, and will run it next. This will likely be the preempting task that was awakened by the interrupt handler.

At some point, the task to be run next will become the preempted task. The last call to **sleep()** that was made when that task's stack was active occurred when the **pause()** function called it in the preemptive interrupt handler, as shown in Figure 8.2. Consequently, when the scheduler again transfers control to the task, it will be entered via a return from this call. The interrupt handler will then restore the task's context and return control to the point of interruption in the task. The task may then proceed as though no preemption occurred.

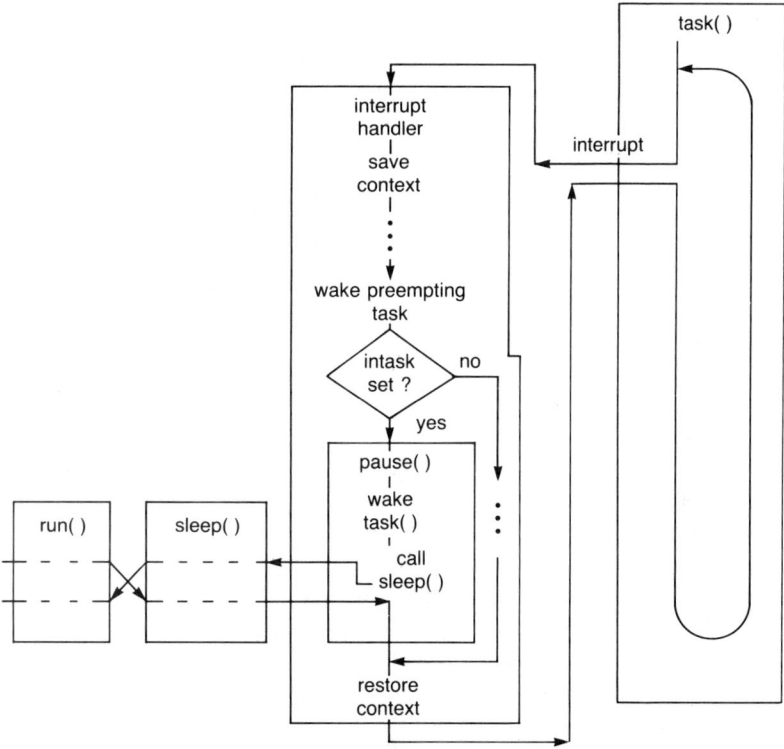

Figure 8.2. Preemptive Interrupt: Task Running.

8.2.3 Interrupt Priority
Management

One aspect of the design that has not yet been addressed concerns the way in which interrupt priority level is managed. When an interrupt occurs, the processor automatically raises its interrupt priority level to the level of that interrupt. For example, if the interrupt shown in Figure 8.2 has a level 4 priority, the processor will automatically disable any subsequent interrupts at levels 4 and lower. This level of interrupt masking will be maintained as long as the program does not explicitly change it or until the interrupt handler returns to the interrupted task. In the latter case, the level at the time interruption is restored.

In the design shown in Figures 8.1 and 8.2 the interrupt priority level is explicitly changed during the **run()**/**sleep()** transitions. All interrupts are disabled within these functions. But the level that was present when the functions were entered is restored when they are exited. For example, if the interrupt in Figure 8.2 has level 4 priority, interrupts at and below that level are disabled when **sleep()** is called from the interrupt handler. All interrupts are disabled in the **sleep()**/**run()** transition and level 4 priority is restored when **run()** returns to the scheduler. Thus, interrupts at and below level 4 will be disabled while the scheduler runs.

The interrupt level that existed when the scheduler was entered will be maintained (unless explicitly changed by another application task) until the preempted task is again selected to run and control is transferred back to it via the interrupt handler's return. At that point, the level that was present before the preemptive interrupt occurred will be restored.

What this means from the viewpoint of an application program is that, unless the priority level is explicitly changed by the preempting task, interrupts at and below the level of the preemptive interrupt will be disabled until the preempted task again runs. This is not unreasonable for most applications, since it keeps lower priority activity locked out until the preempted task again resumes. But if this behavior is unacceptable in a particular application, interrupts may be reenabled before the preempting interrupt handler transfers control to the scheduler. The procedure for accomplishing this will be described in Section 8.3.

8.2.4 Multiple Level Preemption

It is possible for an application program to require more than one level of preemptive scheduling. For example, a system may include more than one device that needs "immediate" attention. For such applications the executive must be capable of supporting multiple preemptive interrupts.

Figure 8.3 shows two types of multiple preemption when the task scheduler is running. In one case a preemptive interrupt handler of higher priority interrupts a handler of lower priority. In the second case the scheduler is interrupted again by a preemptive interrupt after **sleep()** has forced it to reselect a task. In each case the additional handler wakes a task and then sets flag **resched.**

The figure attempts to show that even if a second preemptive interrupt occurs, a task will not be run until the currently highest priority, awakened task has been selected. That is, as long as **resched** is again set by additional interrupt handlers, **sleep()** will continue to force a task reselection.

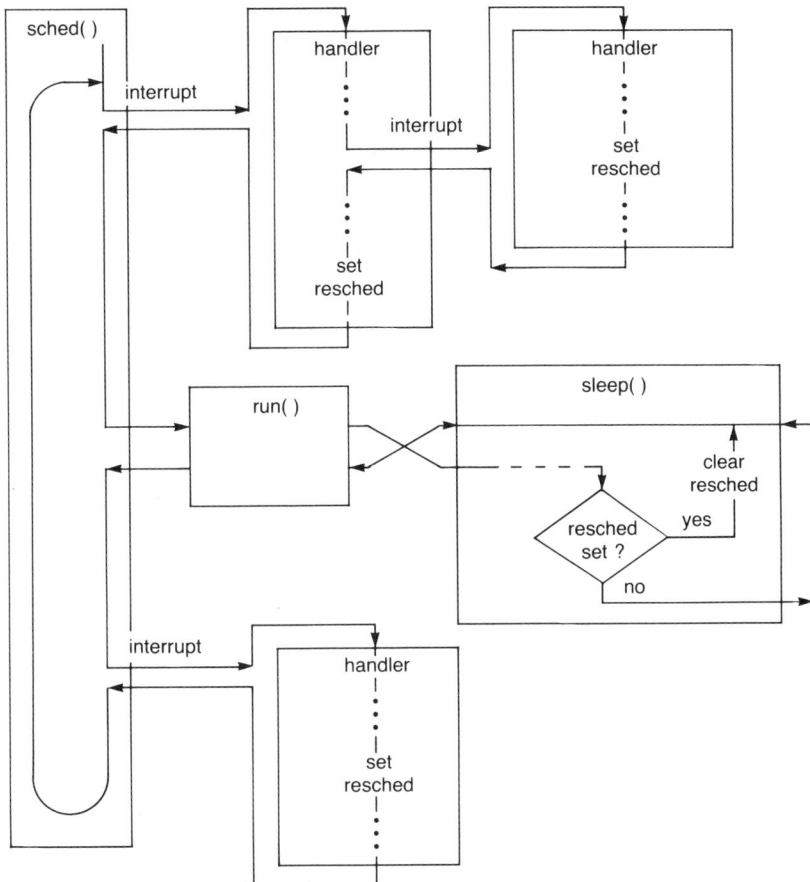

Figure 8.3. Multiple Preemption: Scheduler Running.

Note that it is possible for several reselection sequences to occur before a task is ultimately allowed to run. In fact, it is conceptually possible for an interrupt handler at each processor interrupt level to interrupt the handler for the next lower level. Obviously, it is highly unlikely for an actual application to require this many levels of preemptive scheduling, but such an application could be supported by this executive.

The case of multiple preemption when a task is running is shown in Figure 8.4. Here the first interrupt handler is interrupted by a higher level interrupt. In this case control will be transferred back to the scheduler from the higher priority handler. Since the task that was awakened by that handler will probably be highest priority, it will run next.

After the preempting task completes, if the lower priority handler was interrupted after it had awakened a task, that task will be run. On the other hand, if the interrupt occurred before this wakeup, the scheduler will wake the preempted task. The scheduler will then attempt to transfer control to that task via the **sleep()** return in the higher priority handler, and that handler will return to the initial interrupt handler.

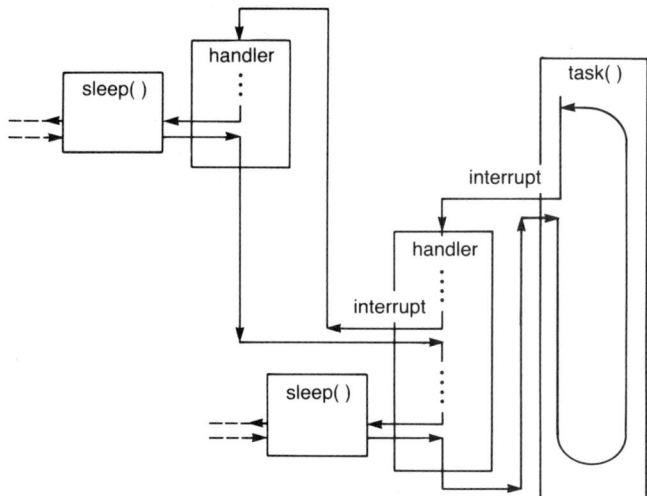

Figure 8.4. Multiple Preemption: Task Running.

After the initial handler has selected a task, control will be transferred to the scheduler and the preempting task that was awakened by this handler will be run. Once this task has completed, the preempted task will again be selected. It will run from the point of interruption after control is returned to it via the **sleep()** function return in the initial interrupt handler.

Note that in this sequence, the preempted task is selected to run twice. For this to work properly, the task must have been previously awakened twice. But two wakeups did occur since each handler actually called **pause()** and this function wakes the currently "running" task before calling **sleep()**. In this case, that task is the preempted task.

It should also be noted that, although Figure 8.4 shows two levels of preemption, it is clear that several levels could be accommodated by the same algorithm. Indeed, preemptive interrupts at each interrupt level supported by the processor could be handled.

An additional point that should be kept in mind is that the preempted task's stack is the currently active stack for all interrupt handler operations shown in the figure. This is true since **sleep()** restores that task's stack pointer each time it attempts to run the task. It is therefore important to be sure that this stack contains sufficient space to accommodate all of the context-switch and other stack operations performed by the handlers.

8.3 EXECUTIVE
CHANGES

In this section we will examine the software changes that are required to enhance the executive described in Chapters 2 and 3 with the features needed to support preemptive scheduling. We will see that surprisingly few changes are needed to add this new capability.

Figure 8.5 shows four sections of file **cx.c,** a preemptive version of the executive kernel. This file is a modification of file **cxn.c,** which was described in Chapter 3 and is shown in Figure 3.1. Figure 8.5 shows sections of **cxn.c** that were changed to support preemptive scheduling. All other sections of the file are the same as their counterparts in file **cxn.c.**

Figure 8.5a shows the file's data declaration section. The only changes here are the addition of two flags, **intask** and **resched.**

The **intask** flag is cleared after the TCB link list is initialized, as shown in Figure 8.5b. This indicates that a task is not running, and prepares the executive for the enabling of interrupts, which normally occurs in function **apinit().** The executive will then behave properly if a preemptive interrupt occurs before **sched()** has transferred control to the first task to run.

Figure 8.5c shows the modified **sleep()** function. First, the **intask** flag is again cleared. Since **sleep()** is called from a task, or from an interrupt handler that is preempting a task, this operation indicates that the program is leaving the task environment and is entering the scheduler.

The next addition to **sleep()** is the statement that clears flag **resched.** As indicated in the previous section, this flag is set by an interrupt handler if the preemptive interrupt occurs while the scheduler is running. As we shall see shortly, this causes **sleep()** to return control to **sched()** so that it may "reconsider" its choice of the next task to run.

After clearing **resched,** function **sleepa()** is called. This function transfers control to **run()** and **run()** returns to **sched().** After the scheduler has chosen the next task to run, **sleep()** is reentered via a return from function **sleepa().** At that point, flag **intask** is set, in preparation for the return to the task environment, and the previous status register value is restored. But before **sleep()** returns to the task, the **resched** flag is tested. If it is set, control is returned to the scheduler via a second call to **sleepa().**

As indicated in the figure, flags **intask** and **resched** are cleared and interrupts are disabled before **sleepa()** is called, as before. Function **sched()** then runs again and reselects the next task to run. It then returns control to **sleep()** via the return from the second **sleepa()** call. Again, **intask** is set and the previous status register value is restored. But before control is transferred to the selected task, flag **resched** is retested.

The use of a C language **while()** loop to test **resched** guarantees that control will continue to be transferred back to the scheduler as long as the **resched** flag is found to be set—that is, until no more preemptive interrupts occur while the program is in the scheduler. Thus, the **while()** loop assures that the scheduler has chosen the currently highest priority, awakened task when **sleep()** finally exits to a task.

It is worth reviewing the way in which interrupt priority is handled by **sleep().** It would appear that the processor's status register value is saved in variable **_cxsr** at the beginning of **sleep()** and then is restored from this variable later. However, the value stored by **sleep()** is actually restored by **run()** (see Figure 3.3b), and the value restored by **sleep()** was placed in **_cxsr** by **run().** Since a bit field in the status register determines processor interrupt priority, the priority level that exists when **sleep()** is entered is restored before **run()** exits to the scheduler. Similarly, the level when **run()** is entered from **sched()** is restored just before **sleep()** returns to the task environment.

It is also interesting to note that the changes to **sleep()** all involve additions to the nonpreemptive version. Thus, the modified executive will also support nonpreemptive task

```
/*
 * The  information  in  these  files  is  subject  to  change  without  notice.
 * Permission  to  make  backup  copies  for  personal  use  is  hereby  granted.
 * Programs  may  also  be  modified  to  suit  user  needs,  provided  that  the
 * copyright  notice  is  included  in  the  final  listings  and  reference  is  made
 * to  the  fact  that  modification  privileges  were  granted  by  the  author.
 *
 * The  distribution  or  use  of  all  or  part  of  the  source  code  in  a  commercial
 * product  or  service  offered  for  sale  is  not  authorized  and  constitutes
 * a  violation  of  the  program's  copyright  protection.  Binary  (machine
 * executable)  application  programs  that  are  produced  from  source  code  that
 * uses  all  or  part  of  CX/68K  may  be  sold  without  obtaining  a  license.
 *
 * These  programs  are  not  covered  by  a  warranty,  either  expressed  or  inplied.
 * The  author  will  not  assume  responsibility  for  any  damages  (including  con-
 * sequential)  caused  by  reliance  on  the  materials  presented,  including
 * but  not  limited  to  typographical  errors  or  arithmetic  errors.
 *
 *              CX/68K  Executive,  Version  1.0   (4/10/86)
 *
 *                   (c)  1984  Walter  S.  Heath
 *
 *                 A  Real-time  System  Executive
 *                           for
 *                   680X0  Computers
 *
 *     FILE CX.C    - Preemptive Version
 *
 *              Kernel Program and Scheduler.  Function cx() is
 *              called from the application main() function.
 *     REVISED:
 *           8/8/88
 */
#include "cxsymb.h"                /*CX/68K executive symbols     */
short ntsks                        ;/*number of tasks defined      */
short tidx                         ;/*task index                   */
short intask                       ;/*in-a-task (=1) flag          */
short resched                      ;/*rerun-sched() flag           */
extern struct tcbdef tcb[]         ;/*task control blocks (TCBs)   */
long cxsp                          ;/*cx()'s SP-save longword */
short cxsr                         ;/*cx()'s SR-save word          */
short *rtnadr                      ;/*sleep()'s return address     */
short *runadr                      ;/*run()'s re-entry address     */
short *tskaddr                     ;/*task's address               */
long *spaddr                       ;/*task's SP location in its TCB */
extern long cxst[]                 ;/*cx()'s stack                 */
long *cspadr                       ;/*cx()'s stack-start addr.     */
```

Figure 8.5a. Executive Kernel—Preemptive Version.

```
/*
 *Initialize task TCBs.
 */
initcb()                                ;

/*
 *Initialize each task.
 */
for(tidx = 0; tidx <= ntsks - 1; tidx++){
        tskaddr = tcb[tidx].tskadr      ;/*get task's start address        */
        spaddr = &tcb[tidx].tsksp       ;/*get task's SP location in its TCB  */
        tcb[tidx].tsksta = 1            ;/*initialize task wake flags      */
        tcb[tidx].tsksig = 0            ;
        tskinit()                       ;/*Call assembly language task     */
                                         /*initialization function.        */
}
rtnadr = runadr                         ;/*Change sleep()'s return addr    */
                                         /*so it returns to run().         */


/*
 *Initialize TCB link list.
 */
for(tidx = 0; tidx <= ntsks - 2; tidx++)
        tcb[tidx].tsklnk = tidx + 1     ;

tcb[tidx].tsklnk = 0                    ;/*close the loop                  */

intask = 0                              ;/*indicate not-in-a-task yet      */

/*
 *Initialize queue headers and semaphore structures.
 */
qinit()                                 ;

/*
 *Perform application-specific initialization operations.
 */
apinit()                                ;

sched()                                 ;/*call the scheduler              */
                                         /*( sched() never returns )       */
}                                        /*end of cx() function            */
```

Figure 8.5b. Executive Kernel—Preemptive Version. (*Continued on next page.*)

```
/*
 *---sleep()
 *     This function is called by a task to suspend its operation and
 *     transfer control back to the scheduler.  It is also called by
 *     function pause() (see below).
 *
 *     Note:  If only non-preemptive scheduling is to be used, code
 *            referencing `intask' and `resched' may be removed.
 */

sleep()
{
intask = 0                      ;/*leaving a task                           */

asm(" movw   sr,_cxsr       ")  ;/*save sr (save interrupt level)           */
asm(" orw    #0x0700,sr     ")  ;/*disable interrupts                       */

if(tcb[tidx].tsksig)            /*If current task should be                 */
                                /*rerun, leave last wake.                   */
      --tcb[tidx].tsksig        ;/*remove a task re-wake signal             */

else                            /*If current task should not be             */
      --tcb[tidx].tsksta        ;/*rerun, remove a task wake.                */

resched = 0                     ;/*clear rerun-sched() flag                 */

sleepa()                        ;/*call assembly lang. sleepa()             */

intask = 1                      ;/*entering a task                          */

asm(" movw  _cxsr,sr       ")   ;/*restore sr (interrupt level)             */

while(resched){                 /*while rerun-sched() requested,            */
      intask = 0                ;/*leaving a task                           */
      asm(" movw   sr,_cxsr  ")  ;/*save sr (save interrupt level)*/
      asm(" orw    #0x0700,sr ")      ;/*disable interrupts                 */
      resched = 0               ;
      sleepa()                  ;/*rerun sched()                            */
      intask = 1                ;/*entering a task                          */
      asm(" movw  _cxsr,sr   ") ;/*restore sr (interrupt level)             */
}
}                               /*end of sleep() function                   */
```

Figure 8.5c. (*continued*) Executive Kernel—Preemptive Version.

```
/*
*---preempt()
*      This function performs the operations that an interrupt handler
*      must perform to cause a running task to be preempted (suspended)
*      to allow the scheduler to run a higher priority task.  The
*      preempted task will resume running later (when its priority
*      becomes highest) at the point of interruption.  Several interrupt
*      handlers may call preempt().  A higher priority interrupt handler
*      will preempt a lower priority handler.  This function MUST ONLY
*      be called from an interrupt handler.
*
*      Flag 'intask' is set/cleared by sleep() to indicate that a task
*      was running when the preemptive interrupt occurred.  In this case
*      function pause() is called to reschedule (wake) the running task
*      and then suspend it (calls sleep()).  If a task was not running,
*      the scheduler (sched()) was.  In that case flag 'recsched' is set
*      by the handler. Function sleep() tests 'resched' just before
*      transfering control to the next task to run.  If it is set, it
*      sends control back to sched().  sched() then re-selects the highest
*      priority task to run.  This is done to handle the case in which
*      sched() has already chosen the next task to run before the
*      preemptive interrupt occurs.  The interrupt handler will probably
*      wake a higher priority task - which should be run next.
*
*      Note that when preemptive scheduling is used, "critical regions"
*      of code in the application program must be protected.  This is
*      the responsibility of the software writer.
*
*      Note also that for maximum performance, the operations performed
*      in preempt() may be coded in-line in the interrupt handler - to
*      save the call/return overhead of preempt().
*/

preempt()
{
if(intask)                      /*If a task was running,       */
        pause()                   ;/*preempt it.                */
else                            /*If sched() was running,      */
        resched = 1             ;/*rerun sched().               */


}                               /*end of preempt()             */

                                /*end of CX.C file             */
```

Figure 8.5d. (*continued*) Executive Kernel—Preemptive Version.

scheduling, as before. The operations that are performed in a particular interrupt handler will determine whether preemptive or nonpreemptive task scheduling takes place.

Figure 8.5d shows a new function that has been added to file **cx.c** to support preemptive scheduling. Function **preempt()** is designed to be called from an interrupt handler. It performs the operations that are required to cause preemption.

The function first tests the **intask** flag. If it is set, the interrupt occurred while a task was running, and function **pause()** is called. Otherwise, the scheduler was running and the function simply sets the **resched** flag.

As indicated in Section 8.2.3, if a preemptive interrupt occurs while a task is running, the processor's interrupt priority level will be maintained at the level of the handler that caused the preemption until the preempted task is again reentered. This behavior may not be acceptable in some applications. In that case, interrupts may be enabled by inserting the following statement before the call to **pause()** in **preempt()**:

asm("   andw #0xf0ff,sr   ") ;/*enable interrupts, */

Note that brackets must also be added to delimit the expanded scope of this conditional branch. With this addition, all interrupts will be enabled while the scheduler and higher priority tasks (including the preempting task) are run.

An alternative approach is to restore the priority level that was present before the interrupt occurred. This may be accomplished by setting the status register to the value that was pushed onto the stack by the processor in response to the interrupt:

asm("   movw sp@(76),sr ") ;/*restore interrupt level,*/

The displacement (76) in this instruction represents the offset that must be added to the current contents of the stack pointer to access the stored status register value. This offset may vary, depending on the compiler used.

The modifications to the executive kernel shown in Figure 8.5 and discussed in this section will assure that application tasks are scheduled preemptively. However, as the header comment for function **preempt()** indicates, the tasks that run in this environment must be written such that certain "critical regions" of code are compatible with preemptive scheduling. These special considerations will be examined in the next section.

8.4 REENTRANCY

In a preemptive scheduling environment it is possible for a task to be suspended at any point. Another task will then run before the preempted task is allowed to continue. Two basic problems may arise under these conditions. One concerns the use of shared functions by the preempted and preempting tasks; the other concerns access to shared data structures by the two tasks. We will examine these phenomena separately in the two subsections that follow.

8.4.1 Shared Function
Reentrancy

Consider a situation in which a task is executing a commonly used utility function when a preemptive interrupt occurs. It is possible for the preempting task to also call the same utility function. Thus, the function is reentered by the preempting task before the previous call to it in the preempted task is allowed to complete. Clearly, a potential problem exists, since data values that were set by the first function execution will be overwritten by the second. When the preempted task is again allowed to run, the utility function will continue with data values that are incorrect.

This scenario illustrates a problem that must be addressed for any function that will be called by a preempted task and also by a preempting task or an interrupt handler. For example, the compiler C and math library functions and the queue access functions discussed in Chapter 4 fall into this category, as do console I/O service functions that may be provided by a processor's PROM monitor. In general, any functions that are intended to be generally available for use by application program modules must be designed to cope with this reentrancy phenomenon.

It is clear that some method must be found to create a new set of local variables each time a utility function is called. Then, each instance of a function execution will have a separate set of local variables to work with. It happens that most C compilers provide a very efficient mechanism for accomplishing this.

C compilers typically declare space on the currently active stack for function variables that are declared to be of type automatic. This type designation is implicitly attached to variables that are declared within the scope of a function. When a function accesses an automatic variable, the compiler references it by means of an offset from a stack frame pointer. A new frame pointer is created each time the function is called. As a result, a new set of local variables is created each time the function is reentered. Thus, a function may be made reentrant by simply declaring all of its local variables to be of type automatic.

For the preemptive scheduling scenario described earlier, this method of achieving reentrancy will solve the indicated problem. When the task is preempted, the task's frame pointer is saved (by **sleepa()**). Likewise, when the task is allowed to continue, its frame pointer is restored. So, the frame of local variables that the preempted utility function was using will again be available when it resumes.

Recall that the queue access functions described in Chapter 4 are written to support reentrancy. All local variables are declared within the scope of their respective functions. As a result, they are treated as automatic variables by the compiler and space is allocated for them on the currently active stack each time a function is entered.

8.4.2 Shared Data Reentrancy

A similar reentrancy problem exists when preempted and preempting tasks access a common data structure. The problem occurs when a task is part way through the process of updating a shared data structure when it is preempted. The preempting task then accesses the structure and changes some entries. When the preempted task again runs, it will find a data structure that has been changed and therefore contains inconsistent entries.

This scenario describes a case of data reentrancy. That is, a data structure that was entered by one task is reentered by another—before the first task has finished. This is a problem that often occurs in database management systems that allow several users to access the same data records. A common solution is to use some form of record-locking mechanism (a semaphore, for instance) to limit access to only one user at a time.

Unfortunately, the record-locking approach is not usually valid for the real-time, preemptive environment, since a lockout placed on a data structure by the preempted task will keep the preempting task locked out forever. A different solution is called for in this situation.

An effective way to handle the problem is to simply disable interrupts during the "critical region" of code that accesses the data structure. Then, a preemptive interrupt will be held off until the data structure has been completely updated. This solution is entirely satisfactory in many applications. However, it may reintroduce the problem that preemptive scheduling was originally intended to solve—namely, the need to respond to interrupts either immediately or at least within a predictable maximum time interval. If interrupts are disabled by tasks for excessively long periods of time, interrupt response times may become unacceptably long.

On occasion, the items in a shared data structure are accessed such that a conflict never occurs. A case in point is the queue header data structure used to manage a queue. As we saw in Section 4.6, if one program component puts data into a queue and another takes data from it, the two components access different items in the data structure. The component that puts data manipulates the tail pointer; the receiving component uses the head pointer. As a result, no conflict occurs, and the queue access functions do not need to be treated as critical regions.

As in the case of the buffer pointer queue header, other special situations may present opportunities for unique solutions. In any case, the reentrancy phenomenon is a characteristic of the preemptive task scheduling environment that must be addressed. By contrast, if nonpreemptive scheduling is used, a task can maintain control of the processor (except for interrupt handling) until a shared function has completed or until a shared data structure has been completely updated. As a result, the reentrancy problem rarely arises.

9

Example Application Programs PCX3 and MPCX3

We began Chapter 8 by developing a list of requirements that an executive would need to satisfy for it to be able to support preemptive scheduling of application tasks. We then proceeded to construct a functional design for this executive by extending the design for the nonpreemptive executive described in Chapters 2 and 3. Finally, we determined the software additions that were needed to adapt this executive to also support preemptive scheduling. In this chapter we will examine application programs that demonstrate the concepts developed in Chapter 8.

Program PCX3 extends program CX3, which was described in Chapter 7, by adding preemptive scheduling of the **timer()** task. As such, it demonstrates single level preemptive scheduling. To demonstrate multiple level preemptive scheduling, program MPCX3 extends program PCX3 by adding a second, higher priority timer interrupt and a second timer task. The new timer interrupt handler causes preemptive scheduling of the additional timer task. Thus, the program contains two preemptively scheduled tasks.

The PCX3 program will be examined in Section 9.1; MPCX3 in Section 9.2. We will begin each section by reviewing program operation. A subsequent subsection will then present an analysis of program performance. Again, a logic analyzer will be used to reveal internal program activity.

9.1 THE PCX3 PROGRAM

We analyzed program CX3 in detail in Chapter 7. As shown in Figure 7.1, this program consists of the **idle()**, **keybd()**, **consol()** task loop, a timer interrupt handler, **duart()**, and the **timer**() task. The interrupt handler wakes the **timer**() task and the task is run nonpreemptively. That is, if another task is running when the interrupt occurs, that task is not suspended to let the higher priority **timer**() task run. Instead, the interrupted task is allowed to continue until it voluntarily suspends. Only then is the **timer**() task allowed to run. By contrast, the PCX3 program will force an interrupted task to suspend and will allow the **timer**() task to run immediately.

Few software changes are needed to produce PCX3 from the source files for CX3. In fact, only the **timer3.c** file needs to be changed. Figure 9.1 shows the first part of a new version of this file, called **ptimer3.c**. The only difference is the inclusion of the call to function **preempt**() in the **duart**() interrupt handler, as shown. All other sections of the file are the same as their counterparts in file **timer3.c**. As was discussed in Chapter 8, function **preempt**() causes an interrupted task to be suspended. On the other hand, if the interrupt occurs while the scheduler is running, it forces the scheduler to "reconsider" its choice of the next task to run.

If the program is being prepared in the Berkeley UNIX environment, the command to link is

**ld −x −T 1000 −o pcx3 cx3.o tasks3.o ques3.o api3.o apio3.o\
ptimer3.o conio.o sys.o bptr.o quea.o cx.o −1c**

Comparing this command to the corresponding command for program CX3, it is evident that, in addition to the new **ptimer3.c** file, this command links the preemptive executive kernel file **cx.o** instead of **cxn.o**. Otherwise, the programs are the same. Again, this program is linked to start at memory address 1000 hex; if desired, a different starting address may be used.

```
/*
 *
 *      CX/68K   Executive, Version 1.0   (4/10/86)
 *
 *      (c)   1984   Walter S. Heath, all rights reserved.
 *
 *      FILE PTIMER3.C - Preemptive version
 *
 *              This file contains a general-purpose timer task
 *              and the C portion of the interrupt handler. See
 *              file APIO3.S for the assembly language part of
 *              the interrupt handler and functions needed to
 *              initialize the timer portion of the 68681.
 *      REVISED:
 *              8/8/88
 */
```

Figure 9.1. PCX3 C Language Timer Interrupt Handler.

```
#include "apsymb3.h"
#include "qsymb.h"

extern struct que rtctim        ;
extern struct que timcon        ;
extern struct que contim        ;
extern char duartst             ;

short tcount[NTSKS]             ;/*timer count array                  */
static char sigmsg             ;/*signal msg to timed-out task       */
static char tskmsg             ;/*received countdown value           */

/*
 *---duart()
 *      This function performs the interrupt handler operations for the
 *      68681 DUART chip.  It is called by assembly language function
 *      _duarta (see file APIO3.S), which saves machine context before the
 *      call and restores it afterward.  Function duart() simply checks to
 *      see if the interrupt was from the chip's timer and then sends a
 *      "signal" byte via queue 'rtctim' to the timer() task and wakes it.
 */
char intsig                     ;/*interrupt signal msg               */

duart()
{
/*
 *Test 68681 status byte to determine if the interrupt was from the TIMER.
 *If is was, send a "signal" byte msg to the timer() task and wake it.
 */
if((duartst & 0x08) != 0){
      putq(&intsig,&rtctim,1)    ;
      wake(TIMEID)              ;
}

preempt()                       ;/*preempt a running task             */

}                               /*end of duart()                     */
```

Figure 9.1. (*continued*) PCX3 C Language Timer Interrupt Handler.

9.1.1 PCX3 Program
Performance Evaluation

The operation of program PCX3 may be monitored using the same techniques employed to monitor program CX3. In fact, the exact same statements must be added to set and clear bits in a parallel port. The operation of the resulting "instrumented" version may then be observed by connecting logic analyzer probes to the pins of the parallel port.

Figure 9.2a shows a typical logic analyzer plot of program performance. Note that the figure also includes a line showing the occurrence of the actual hardware interrupt (labeled "INT" in the figure). An additional probe was connected to the interrupt line from the 68681 DUART chip to generate this plot.

The figure indicates that, in this test run, the interrupt occurred when the **consol()** task was running. Shortly, thereafter, the line monitoring the **duart()** interrupt handler goes high. The line stays high until the **consol()** task is reentered via a return from the **duart()** handler. This occurs when the scheduler again selects the **consol()** task to run next. Likewise, the line monitoring the **consol()** task goes high when the task is initially entered and stays high, even though control is transferred out of the task. This line remains high until control is returned to the task and the task voluntarily terminates (calls **sleep()**). Thus, the rising and falling edges of the plots indicate when the indicated function is entered and exited, respectively; the fact that the line is high between these points does not necessarily indicate that the processor is actually executing code in that function.

When **duart()** called **preempt()**, control was transferred back to the scheduler (shown as point "a" in the figure). The scheduler then chose the highest priority, awakened task to run next. In this case that was the **timer()** task. This task ran and then returned control to the scheduler (indicated as point "b"). The **consol()** task was then reselected to run next. The last call to **sleep()** from the **consol()** task's environment (when its stack was active) occurred within **duart()**. Thus, control was returned to **duart()** via this **sleep()** return. The **duart()** handler then restored the **consol()** task's context and returned control to it at the point of interruption. Clearly, the **consol()** task was preempted to allow the **timer()** task to run.

A more complex event sequence is shown in Figure 9.2b. Here the **keybd()** task was preempted and **timer()** ran. The fact that **timer()** took longer to execute this time than it did for the case shown in Figure 9.2a indicates that the time interval measurement request made earlier by **consol()** completed during this execution. As a result, a timeout message was sent to **consol()** and **consol()** was awakened.

Since **consol()** has higher task scheduling priority than **keybd()**, it ran next. It received the timeout response from **timer()**, issued a new countdown request, and again woke **timer()**. Again, since **timer()** has highest priority, it ran next. This time it simply initiated the timeout countdown operation requested by **consol()** and suspended. Its execution time is therefore less.

After the second **timer()** execution, we see that **consol()** ran once more. This time its execution time was very short. This additional execution is accounted for by the fact that **keybd()** also woke **consol()** as part of the ongoing background process of passing the operator-entered message pointer from the **idle()** task to **consol()**. Evidently the interrupt occurred in **keybd()** after this wakeup had been posted. But why is **consol()**'s second execution time so short? The answer to this question lies in the design of the task.

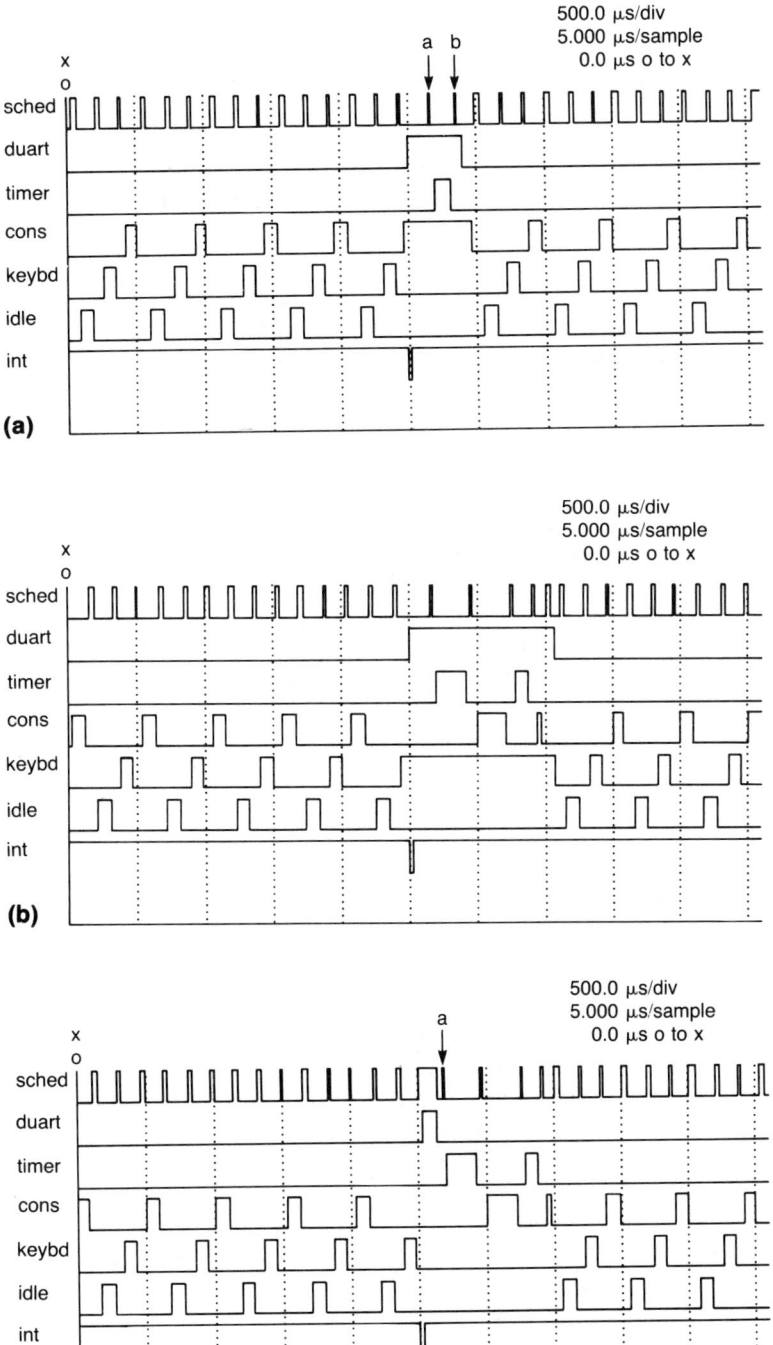

Figure 9.2a–c. PCX3 Performance Test Results.

The **consol()** task was written to check all of its input queues each time it runs and to perform any work that is indicated. Thus, it processed messages from both **timer()** and **keybd()** the first time it ran, leaving no work to be performed when it was awakened the second time. As a result, on the second wakeup it simply checked its input queues, found no messages, and suspended.

We may conclude from this behavior that under certain circumstances it is possible for a task to be awakened when no work is pending for it. Any task that is awakened by more than one source is subject to this phenomenon. Thus, it is important that these tasks be designed such that they will suspend if no work is available for them to do. Since **consol()** is awakened by **timer()** and **keybd()**, it must meet this requirement.

Returning to Figure 9.2b, after **consol()** completed the second time, the scheduler finally allowed **keybd()** to resume. Again, control was returned to it via the **duart()** interrupt handler. Note that, in this test run, both **timer()** and **consol()** ran twice—before the lower priority **keybd()** task was allowed to continue.

Figure 9.2c shows another interesting test run. Here the interrupt occurred while the scheduler was running. In this case, the **preempt()** function caused the scheduler to run again (indicated by point "a"). It correctly selected **timer()** to run next and the **timer()** and **consol()** tasks again interacted as before, in Figure 9.2b.

To summarize, the test runs shown in Figure 9.2 have verified that our modified scheduler algorithm is at least able to handle single level preemption. This is true whether the preemptive interrupt occurs within an application task or the scheduler itself. In addition, Figure 9.2b illustrated that if an application task may be awakened from more than one source, it must be written so that it will suspend if it finds that no messages are present for it to process in its input queues. What remains is to demonstrate that the executive is also able to support multiple level preemption.

9.2 THE MPCX3
PROGRAM

To demonstrate multiple level preemptive task scheduling, we will need at least two sources of interrupts. Since program MPCX3 is an extension of program PCX3, one interrupt source will be the timer interrupt from the 68681 DUART that was used in that program. Most single board computers contain several peripheral interface chips that are capable of generating timer interrupts. For program MPCX3 it was convenient to use the timer provided by the 68230 Parallel Interface and Timer (PIT) chip as the second interrupt source.

Figure 9.3 shows a block diagram of program MPCX3. By comparing this figure to the diagram for program PCX3 in Figure 7.1, it is clear that the MPCX3 program adds task **clock()** and an additional interrupt handler called **pit()** to that program. It also adds message queues **pitclk, conclk,** and **clkcon.**

It would appear from the figure that handler **pit()** and task **clock()** perform essentially the same operations as **duart()** and **timer()** did in program PCX3. This is true. In fact, **pit()** and **clock()** are "clones" of **duart()** and **timer(),** respectively, with only minor changes to

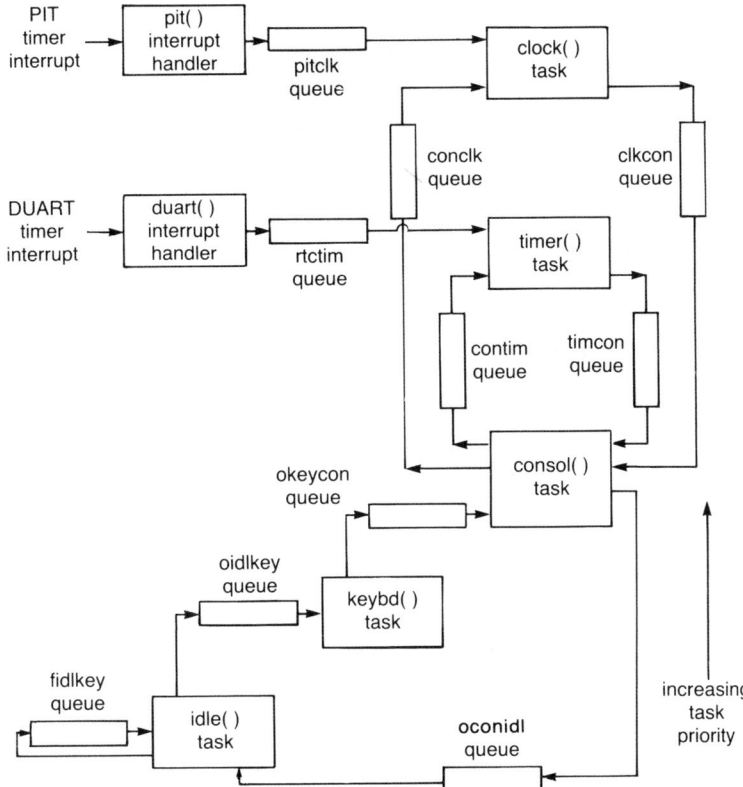

Figure 9.3. MPCX3 Program Structure.

access different queues. The only operational difference between these two sets of functions is that the PIT interrupt has higher priority than the DUART interrupt and **clock()** has higher task scheduling priority than **timer()**. In all other respects, the functions operate the same.

Interrupt handlers **pit()** and **duart()** preemptively schedule tasks **clock()** and **timer()**, respectively. Thus, by properly adjusting the rates of the two sources of interrupts such that they slowly "drift past" each other over time, it should be possible to cause multiple level preemptive events to occur during the various operational states of the remainder of the program. This will provide an effective test of the executive's ability to handle multiple level preemption.

Since most of the new functions for program MPCX3 are cloned from functions discussed earlier for programs PCX3 and CX3, we will not present and review them again here. The only programming details that will be addressed concern the generation and processing of timer interrupts from the PIT chip and changes to the **consol()** task.

As mentioned earlier, we would like to choose the PIT interrupt rate such that its interrupts drift slightly with respect to the interrupt stream from the DUART. The DUART interrupts were programmed to occur at a 0.1-sec rate. Thus, to accomplish our objective, we may choose a PIT interrupt rate that is a multiple of this value plus a "little more." The specific rate chosen should be such that it is possible to easily observe multiple preemptive events as they occur, using a logic analyzer. By trial and error an interrupt period of 0.501248 second was found to be acceptable.

Figure 9.4 shows the additions that are necessary in file **apio3.s** to support timer interrupts from the PIT. The **_ioinit** function contains code to initialize the chip's timer so that it will produce interrupts at a 0.501248-sec rate. It assumes that the chip's registers are mapped into the processor's memory space starting at address ff0e0000 hex. Note that the chip's parallel ports A and C are also set to output mode and are cleared. Both ports are used to monitor program activity.

The PIT timer initialization operations in **_ioinit** leave interrupts disabled. Interrupts are enabled and disabled in the application program by the **idle()** task when it calls functions **_iostrt** and **_iostop**, respectively. The figure shows the statements that must be added to these functions to enable and disable PIT interrupts.

As mentioned earlier, PIT timer interrupts have higher priority than the interrupts from the DUART. Peripheral interface chip interrupt priority is usually selectable by means of straps or links on the computer logic board. For program MPCX3 and PIT interrupt was strapped to cause a level 5 autovector interrupt; the DUART interrupt was strapped for level 4 operation.

Figure 9.4 shows the statements that are needed to initialize the exception vectors for level 4 and 5 autovector interrupts. It also shows the assembly language part of the PIT interrupt handler. Note that before the C language **pit()** interrupt handler function is called,

```
|*---ioinit
|*      This function initializes I/O devices.
|*
        .text
        .globl _ioinit

_ioinit:
|*
|*      Initialize the 68681 timer for 0.1 second interrupts. The count
|*      required is: NC = (.05 sec/half cycle)/TC, where TC is the
|*      time for one count of the timer: TC = 1/(3.68684 mHz/16) =
|*      16/3.6864 mHz. So NC = .05(3.6864 X 10E+6)/16 = 11520.
|*
        movb    #0x70,0xff0c0004      |set ACR for TIMER; xtal; / by 16
        movb    #0x2D,0xff0c0006      |Set CTUR and CTLR for 0.1 second
        movb    #0x00,0xff0c0007      |interrupts (11520 counts).
        movb    #0x00,0xff0c0005      |disable TIMER interrupts in IMR
```

Figure 9.4. MPCX3 Program Changes to File apio3.s.

```
|*
|*      Initialize the 68230 timer for 0.501248 second interrupts.  The 8 mHz
|*      clock is divided by the prescaler (8 mHz/32 = 250 kHz).  The
|*      counter preload register is set to 125312 (= 1e980 hex) to get
|*      250000/125312 = 1.995 Hz (or 0.501248 second) interrupts.  The clock
|*      is left disabled.
|*
        movl    #0x0001e980,0xff0e0012      |set Counter Preload Registers
        movb    #0xe0,0xff0e0010      |TCR: autovec, preload, prescaler
                                      |disable
|*
|*      Initialize PIT ports A and  C for output.
|*
        movb    #0xff,0xff0e0002      |set port A for output
        movb    #0x00,0xff0e0008      |set port A to zero

        movb    #0xff,0xff0e0004      |set port C for output
        movb    #0x00,0xff0e000c      |set port C to zero


        rts
|*
|*---iostrt
|*      This function starts the I/O devices.
|*
        .text
        .globl _iostrt

_iostrt:
        movb    0xff0c000e,d0         |read START COUNTER to start timer
        movb    #0x08,0xff0c0005      |enable 68681 interrupts via IMR

        orb     #0x01,0xff0e0010      |enable 68230 clock
        rts


|*
|*---iostop
|*      This function stops the I/O devices by disabling interrupts.
|*
        .text
        .globl _iostop

_iostop:
        movb    #0x00,0xff0c0005      |disable 68681 interrupts via IMR

        andb    #0xfe,0xff0e0010      |disable 68230 clock
        rts
```

(Continued on next page.)

```
|*
|*---initvec
|*      This function initializes locations pointed to by exception
|*      vectors.
|*
        .text
        .globl _initvec

_initvec:
        movl    #_duarta,0x70        |68681 interrupt; set auto vec. 4
        movl    #_pita,0x74          |68230 interrupt; set auto vec. 5
        rts

|*
|*---pita
|*      This is the assembly language portion of the 68230 (PIT) timer
|*      interrupt handler.  It calls C function pit().  pit() performs
|*      appropriate timer operations before returning.
|*
        .text
        .globl _pita

_pita:
        moveml #0xfffe,sp@-          |push all registers but SP
        orb    #0x01,0xff0e0008      |set PIT port A, bit 0

        movb   #0x01,0xff0e001a      |TSR: clear interrupt
        jsr    _pit                  |call C language pit()

        andb   #0xfe,0xff0e0008      |clear PIT port A, bit 0
        moveml sp@+,#0x7fff          |pop all registers but SP
        rte                          |return from exception (int.)
```

Figure 9.4. (*continued*) MPCX3 Program Changes to File apio3.s.

it is necessary to clear the interrupt by setting a bit in the chip's Timer Status Register (TSR). The code also includes statements to set bit zero of the chip's port A parallel port when the interrupt handler has control of the processor. This signal will be monitored when we look at program performance in Section 9.2.2.

For this test program, the **consol()** task must be able to send countdown requests and accept timeout responses from the **clock()** task as well as **timer()**. Figure 9.5 shows the additional statements that must be added to it to accomplish this. They essentially duplicate the code to communicate with **timer()**. Note that since PIT interrupts occur at a rate of about one every 0.5 second, the countdown message sent to **clock()** must contain a value of 2 to request a timeout interval of 1 second.

```
extern struct que conclk          ;/*message queues                        */
extern struct que clkcon          ;

char gotit                        ;/*clock-msg-received flag                */
char clkmsg                       ;/*clock msg byte                         */
char *tim2 = "    tock . . .\n"   ;/*console display string                 */
consol()
{
rcvd = 1                          ;/*start timer-msg-received flag          */
gotit = 1                         ;/*start clock-msg-received flag          */

for( ; ; ){                        /*Start infinite loop . . .              */
sleep()                           ;

consptr = getbp(&okeycon)         ;/*check for a ptr from keybd()           */

if((int)consptr != -1){            /*If wakeup from keybd() task,           */
     putbpwt(consptr,&oconidl,CONSID);/*send pointer to idle() task        */
     wake(IDLEID)                  ;/*wake idle() to start over             */
}
/*
 *Check the timer() task's return queue for a timeout response.  If one
 *received, start another one second timeout.
 */

if(getq(&timcon,&timmsg) != -1){  /*If timer response received,            */
     rcvd = 1                     ;/*set timer-msg-received flag,           */
     conout(tim1,11)              ;/*signal operator.                       */
}

if(rcvd == 1){                     /*If start-first-timeout or              */
                                   /*timer re-start,                        */

     rcvd = 0                     ;
     timmsg = 10                  ;/*select # of 1/10th seconds,            */

     putq(&timmsg,&contim,1)      ;/*send it to timer() task,               */
     wake(TIMEID)                 ;/*wake timer() task.                     */

}

/*
 *Check the clock() task's return queue for a timeout response.  If one
 *received, start another one second timeout.
 */
```

Figure 9.5. MPCX3 Program Changes to File tasks3.c. (*Continued on next page.*)

```
if(getq(&clkcon,&clkmsg) != -1){    /*If clock response received,         */
        gotit = 1                   ;/*set clock-msg-received flag,          */
        conout(tim2,15)             ;/*signal operator.                     */
}

if(gotit == 1){                         /*If start-first-timeout or         */
                                        /*clock re-start,                    */
        gotit = 0                   ;
        clkmsg = 2                  ;/*select # of 1/2 seconds,             */

        putq(&clkmsg,&conclk,1)     ;/*send it to clock() task,             */
        wake(CLCKID)                ;/*wake clock() task.                    */
}


}                                       /* . . . end infinite loop.        */
}                                       /*end of consol() task              */
```

Figure 9.5. (*continued*) MPCX3 Program Changes to File tasks3.c.

9.2.1 Program Operation

Figure 9.6 shows the operator's console display for a typical test run. Compared to program PCX3, this program generates the additional display line "**tock . . .**" during real-time operation. This line is output by the **consol()** task when the timeout request that it sends to the **clock()** task expires. Like the "**tick . . .**" messages, these messages are displayed at an approximate rate of one every second.

The figure indicates that occasionally a "**tock . . .**" message is missing. This is a result of the fact that the PIT timer is generating interrupts at a rate slightly slower than one every 0.5 second. The additional delay builds up relative to the timeout sequence for the "**tick . . .**" message until two displays of the latter message appear together. This behavior verifies that the timer interrupts from the two sources are, indeed, "drifting" with respect to each other, as desired.

9.2.2 Program Performance
Evaluation

Our objective in this section will be to see if the executive can properly perform multiple level preemption under typical operational conditions. We will accomplish this by examining logic analyzer plots of program MPCX3 test runs. Note that for these runs, the statements in **consol()** that send the "**tick . . .**" and "**tock . . .**" messages to the operator's console were "commented out." This eliminated program delays associated with these slow serial line output operations and, as a result, stabilized the logic analyzer display.

Figure 9.7a shows a plot of a test run in which a DUART interrupt occurred while the **keybd()** task was running. The **duart()** interrupt handler would normally wake the **timer()**

```
CX/68K  Executive, Version 1.0 (4/10/86)

(c)  1984  Walter S. Heath
     All rights reserved

This program demonstrates the task scheduling and
queue access capabilities of CX/68K.

This text is coming from the idle() task. The message you
enter below will be sent via queue 'idlkey' to the keybd()
task.  Keybd() will pass it on via queue 'keycon' to task
consol().  Consol() will send it back to the idle() task
via queue 'conidl'.

You will also be asked to enter the number of cycles this
loop will be repeated.

To exit the program type <CR> at any prompt.


Enter up to 8 characters:
ASDFGHJK

Enter number of repeat cycles (1 to 500000):
12345

I'm running . . .
tick . . .
     tock . . .
tick . . .
     tock . . .
tick . . .
     tock . . .
tick . . .
     tock . . .
tick . . .
     tock . . .
tick . . .
     tock . . .
tick . . .
tick . . .
     tock . . .

ASDFGHJK

Enter up to 8 characters:
```

Figure 9.6. MPCX3 Application Program Console Display.

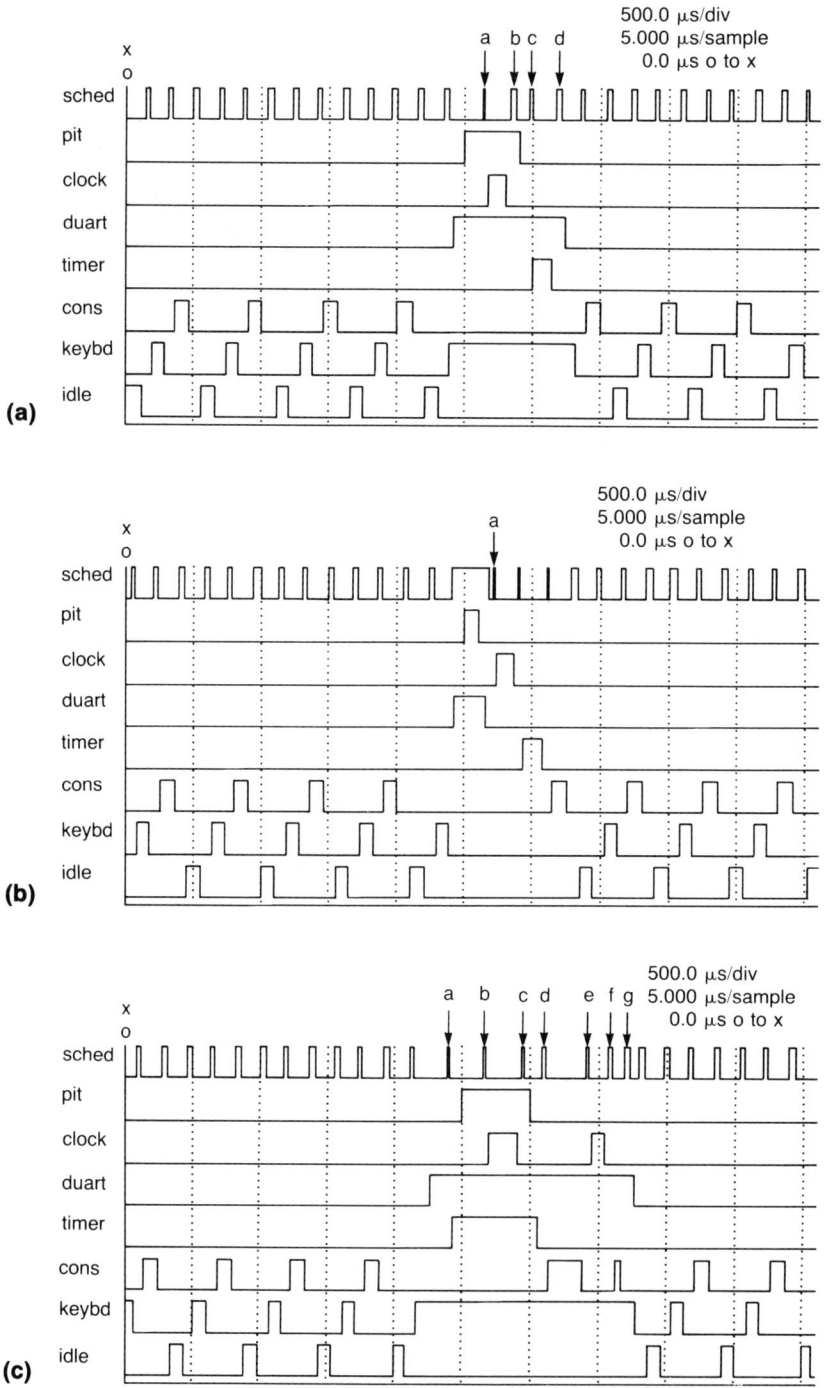

Figure 9.7a–d. MPCX3 Performance Test Results.

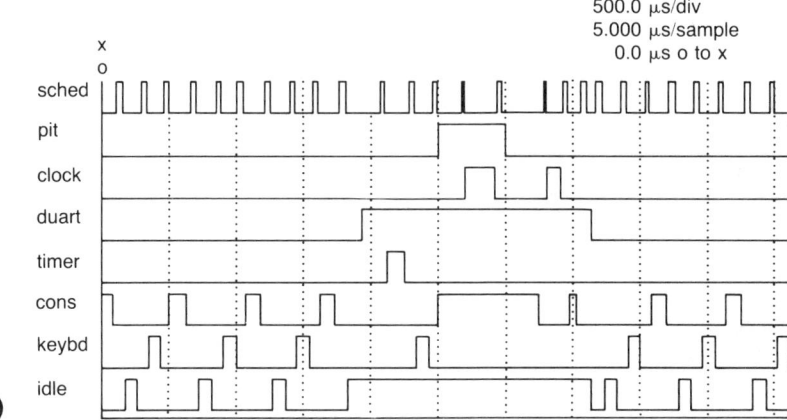

(d)

Figure 9.7a–d. (*continued*) MPCX3 Performance Test Results.

task and then preempt **keybd()** to allow it to run immediately. But, in this case, a PIT interrupt occurred shortly after the DUART interrupt.

Since the PIT interrupt has higher priority, the processor allowed it to interrupt the **duart()** handler. The **pit()** handler then woke the **clock()** task and, since this handler is also preemptive, control was returned to the scheduler (point "a" in the figure). The **clock()** task was then allowed to run next.

When **clock()** finished, the scheduler chose **keybd()** to run again (point "b"). However, the last **sleep()** call from the **keybd()** environment occurred in the **pit()** handler. So control is transferred back to **pit()** via that **sleep()** return. The **pit()** handler then completed and returned control to the **duart()** handler.

At this point the **duart()** handler was free to resume the preemptive scheduling of the **timer()** task. After waking **timer()**, it transferred control back to the scheduler (point "c") and **timer()** was selected to run next. Then, when **timer()** completed, control was once more returned to the scheduler (point "d").

Since **keybd()** was the only task remaining that was still awakened, the scheduler selected it to run next, but, again, the last call to **sleep()** from the **keybd()** environment was made from the **duart()** handler. So **duart()** was entered via a return from this **sleep()** call. At this point **duart()** restored the context of the **keybd()** task and returned control to the point of interruption in that task. The task then resumed its normal operation.

This rather complex test case has demonstrated that the executive is capable of supporting multiple level preemption when the interrupts occur while an application task is running. The basic scenario for this case was diagrammed in Figure 8.4. The other possible scenario was shown in Figure 8.3. In this case the preemptive interrupt chain begins while the scheduler is running. We need to examine a test run that demonstrates performance under these conditions.

Figure 9.7b shows a case in which the DUART interrupt occurred while **sched()** was running. Before the **duart()** handler was able to complete, a PIT interrupt occurred. Again, since the PIT interrupt has highest priority, it was allowed to interrupt the **duart()** handler.

The **pit**() handler then ran to completion and returned to **duart**(). Likewise, **duart**() completed and returned control to the point of interruption in **sched**().

The figure indicates that **sched**() made an attempt to run a task, but **sleep**() forced it to "reconsider" its choice (point "a" in the figure). It then chose to run the **clock**() task, which was the highest priority, currently awakened task.

After **clock**() finished, the scheduler chose **timer**() to run next. When this task completed, it ran **consol**(), which was awakened by **keybd**() before the preemptive interrupt chain began.

It is clear from this test case that the executive is also capable of supporting multiple level preemption when the interrupt chain begins while the scheduler is running. Thus, we have shown that the executive behaves properly for the two possible scenarios in which multiple level preemption may occur.

Before leaving this subject, it will be worthwhile for us to look at the plots for two more test runs. Since these runs are more complex, they will give us an appreciation for the level of scheduling activity that is likely to occur, even in programs that are relatively simple.

Figure 9.7c shows a plot of a test run in which the DUART interrupt once again occurred while **keybd**() was running. In this case the **duart**() handler had time to wake the **timer**() task and the scheduler was able to start it running (point "a" in the figure) before the PIT interrupt occurred.

The **pit**() handler proceeded to wake the **clock**() task and then preempted **timer**(). Since **clock**() was then the highest priority, awakened task, it was selected to run next (point "b").

When **clock**() completed, the scheduler chose **timer**() to resume (point "c"). However, the last call to **sleep**() from the **timer**() environment occurred in **pit**(). So control was returned to **pit**() via this **sleep**() return. The **pit**() handler then restored the context of the **timer**() task and returned control to the point of interruption in that task. The **timer**() task then completed.

At this point **consol**() was selected to run next (point "d"). Evidently, when the **clock**() task ran, it sent a timeout message to **consol**() and woke it, since the figure indicates that **clock**() ran again after **consol**() completed (point "e"). This would result if **consol**() sent it another countdown request and woke it.

When **clock**() finished running the second time, **consol**() ran again (point "f"). This additional wakeup of **consol**() came from **keybd**(), before it was initially interrupted. Judging from **consol**()'s short execution time, no messages were pending for it in its input queues, so that it suspended immediately.

The highest priority, awakened task at this point was **keybd**(), so that the scheduler chose it to run next (point "g"). Once again, the last call to **sleep**() in the **keybd**() environment occurred in the **duart**() handler. Control was therefore transferred back to **keybd**() via the **sleep**() return in **duart**() and **duart**()'s return to the point of interruption in **keybd**().

Note that in this test case, two tasks were preempted. The **keybd**() task was initially preempted by **duart**() to allow the higher priority **timer**() task to run. Then **timer**() was, itself, preempted by **pit**() to allow **clock**() to run.

The final test run that we will consider is shown in Figure 9.7d. In this case the **idle**() task was preempted by a DUART interrupt. Compared to the previous case, the PIT interrupt occurred somewhat later, relative to the DUART interrupt. As a result, both **timer()** and **keybd()** ran to completion before the **consol()** task was preempted by the **pit()** handler. From this point on the scheduling activity was very similar to that shown in Figure 9.7c.

To summarize, the test cases that were reviewed indicate that the executive is capable of preemptively scheduling high priority tasks under all possible operational scenarios. Indeed, it is fascinating to dynamically monitor this program's operation and watch it cope with the various scheduling situations as they arise. In every case, preempting tasks are allowed to run immediately—in order of their priority.

9.3 THE EXECUTIVE
IN SUMMARY

In Section 1.1, we observed that the operational environment for real time software appears at first glance to be "nothing less than chaotic," considering the varying demands of multiple I/O devices all operating asynchronously and competing for access to limited processor resources. We concluded that a formal program architecture was needed that could bring order to this potential chaos. In the intervening chapters we have systematically set about developing system software that could fulfill this need.

The executive design that has resulted from this effort is capable of providing an orderly and efficient environment for many real-time application programs. At the same time it has been reasonably successful in satisfying another important initial goal—namely, to provide system software that is relatively easy for users to understand and use.

In the end, every design is a compromise. This is particularly true for system software that is intended for general use in a wide variety of applications. Clearly, software that is designed with this goal in mind cannot possibly provide the most efficient environment for every possible application.

The executive that is presented in this book contains the basic core elements that are needed to support high performance real-time applications. Other features may be added to satisfy the requirements of specific applications. It is hoped that this executive's strengths outweigh its weaknesses and that it will be useful to designers of equipment that must satisfy the very demanding performance requirements so often associated with real-time systems.

10

Multiprocessor Systems

In Chapter 1, we observed that real-time systems must typically be able to service several I/O sensors in parallel. Since most computers contain only one central processing unit, some form of serial-to-parallel transformation is needed if these machines are to satisfy the simultaneous processing demands of real-time systems. In the intervening chapters we examined a real-time executive that meets this requirement by providing a means to quickly shift the processor's resources between several application tasks. Thus, if the processor is sufficiently fast, relative to the demands of the sensors, all I/O transfers and internal computing operations may be completed, and the system will appear to be operating in parallel.

But we know that a single processor system can only process a single thread of computations at any given time and that a certain amount of the processor's computing resources must be spent in supporting transfers between the several tasks of an application. There is therefore an upper limit to the level of system performance that a given processor is capable of supporting. If we are faced with an application that demands even greater performance, we must either choose a processor that can perform operations faster or resort to the use of several processors.

If a new application is essentially an extension of a previous design, we may be saved by the manufacturer of the processor if a version with a higher clock rate is available. Existing software may then run on the faster processor with few if any changes. But if the new design is not constrained by previous work, one should seriously consider the use of multiple processors.

At the outset, a multiprocessor architecture presents obvious technical advantages as well as additional design challenges. Clearly, an architecture that more nearly matches the parallel nature of real-time systems should lead to a design that uses processing resources more efficiently. With this approach, several threads of computation may be executed simultaneously and multiple sensors may be serviced at the same time. Thus, application tasks actually will operate in parallel and the system will be able to respond more quickly and predictably to external events. But with several operations occurring simultaneously, the problem of coordinating system activity presents a new design challenge. The system must have an efficient, fast, and reliable means for interprocessor communication and signaling.

One of the important recent advances of technology has been the introduction of nonproprietary system buses. A bus is an electronic communication "highway" over which multiple processors may converse with each other and with sensor interfaces. Physically, a bus consists of a printed circuit board containing parallel sets of tracks that are used to pass data and signals between processing elements. Processor and sensor interface cards plug into connectors on this so-called "backplane" and communicate by means of a strictly defined hardware signaling protocol. As long as all processing elements faithfully adhere to the protocol, successful communication and signaling may be accomplished without interference.

Buses have existed for almost as long as computers. The new innovation has been the willingness of manufacturers and others to introduce nonproprietary designs and to standardize bus protocols through international organizations. Once a standard has been established, manufacturers are then able to provide a wide range of processor and interface boards that operate harmoniously in a system. The result has been a rush of activity by several hundreds of companies to supply a vast array of processing elements.

Several bus architectures have been defined and standardized. They include the VMEbus, Multibus, Nubus, and STDbus, among others. Higher performance buses and extensions of existing bus designs are continually being introduced.

It is beyond the scope of this book to delve into the detailed theory-of-operation for any one bus design. The reader should refer to the appropriate printed bus specification for this material. Instead, since this book is primarily concerned with software topics, we will concentrate on the software writer's view of one particular bus design and then address the problem of providing efficient software for communicating between multiple processors via that bus. The VMEbus will be used for this exercise, since it is a high performance bus that has gained wide acceptance among real-time system designers. Since most bus architectures are similar at the functional level, the techniques developed for the VMEbus should be applicable to the other bus environments, as well.

10.1 VMEBUS SYSTEMS: AN OVERVIEW

One important advantage in using a standard, nonproprietary bus is that a designer may configure a computer system to meet the particular needs of an application. This contrasts sharply with the situation that existed in the recent past when it was necessary to adapt an application design to meet the capabilities of a standard computer system purchased as a package from a single manufacturer. The availability of a wide range of compatible processor and sensor interface boards from different manufacturers has increased the designers options immensely. To appreciate the significance of this, we can envision a system design that incorporates a variety of processing and interface elements.

Figure 10.1 shows a candidate multiprocessor system that includes several dedicated processing elements and sensor interfaces. Typically, a system will consist of one or more primary, high data rate and/or high priority sensors and a collection of lower priority interfaces to secondary support equipment. The figure shows a system in which a processor is dedicated to supporting a high priority interface and dispatching the data received from that interface to the other processors. These secondary processors might be assigned to computation or to high speed communication with other systems, as shown. A low priority processor might also be dedicated to auxiliary support functions such as an operator interface, program loading, and equipment environmental monitoring (e.g., temperature, pressure, vibration, etc.).

The figure also shows purchased interface cards that support standard communication protocols and custom cards that interface to custom-built equipment. These latter special-purpose interfaces may be constructed using wirewrap techniques.

The computer programs that run on the dedicated processors may consist of one or more tasks. A processor that is assigned to supporting a single interface and/or a single processing algorithm will often contain only one task. In that case, no task scheduler is required. On the other hand, the program for a processor that must support several interfaces (e.g., the auxiliary processor) will contain several tasks and will therefore require a scheduler. One requirement that is common to all processors is the need for efficient communication with its neighbors. We will address this subject in detail later in this chapter. But first, we need to become more familiar with the operation of the VMEbus.

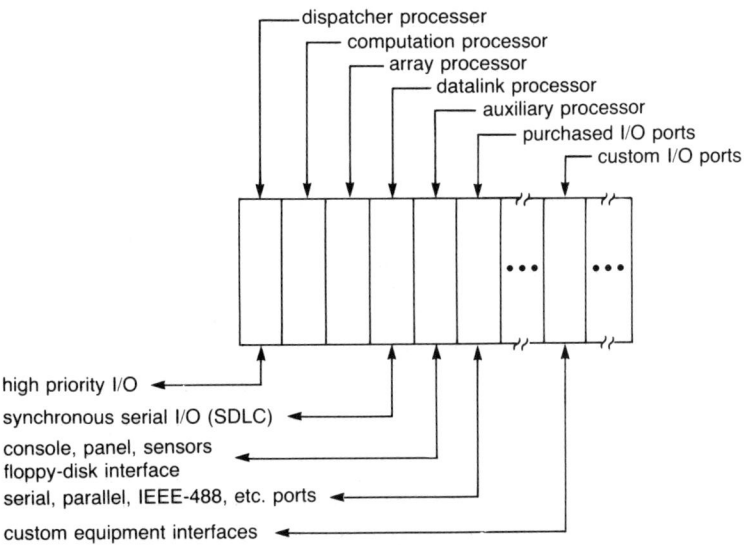

Figure 10.1. Candidate Multiprocessor VMEbus System.

10.2 A FUNCTIONAL
VIEW OF THE VMEBUS

Fortunately for the software writer, virtually all of the signaling protocols required to communicate over the VMEbus are handled by the hardware and are transparent to the computer program. This is not to say that the writer may ignore these protocols, however. As a practical matter, it is necessary to be very familiar with bus protocols to be able to effectively conduct system testing. But when software is being designed and written, one may usually take a higher level view and ignore many details of bus operation.

Figure 10.2 shows a simplified view of the VMEbus backplane. The bus supports 32-bit address and data transfers, seven levels of priority interrupts, four priority levels of bus arbitration, and several additional status and control lines that are required to support bus protocols. As indicated, the bus operates asynchronously. That is, instead of relying on a central clock to step bus interface logic through a data transfer protocol in a lock-step fashion, the bus relies on a sequence of "handshake" initiate/acknowledge signaling sequences to accomplish bus transfers. This approach has the advantage of allowing boards with differing operational speeds to communicate successfully.

The figure also indicates that the bus has a theoretical maximum transfer rate of 40 megabytes per second. This rate may be achieved in practice only when special block transfer bus operational modes are used with equipment that is designed to support these modes. Conventional transfers occur at rates substantially below this upper limit. Even so, these lower rates are sufficient for many high performance applications, and ongoing development efforts promise more convenient access to the faster rates in the near future.

The bus is designed to support memory-mapped transfers. That is, all transfers take place between addressed locations mapped into the address space of the bus. This includes transfers between processors and between a processor and sensor interfaces. With 32

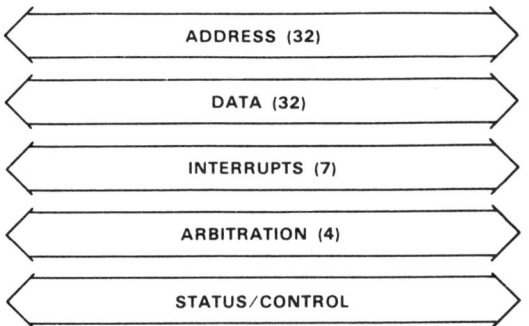

- **ASYNCHRONOUS**
- **THEORETICAL BANDWIDTH: 40 Mbytes/s**

Figure 10.2. VMEbus Backplane.

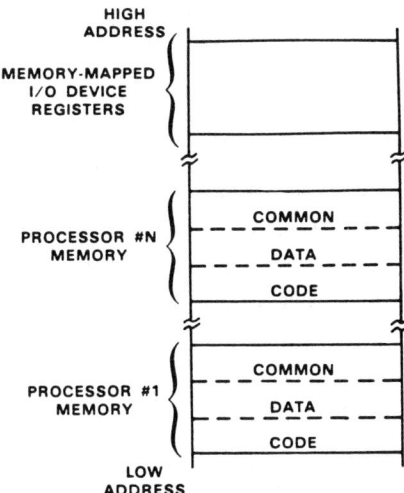

Figure 10.3. VMEbus Memory Map.

address lines, the bus provides direct access to about four gigabytes (4×10^9 bytes) of addressed locations.

Figure 10.3 shows a representative system address map. Included are the memories for two processors and the access registers for several sensor interfaces. The figure implicitly assumes that processor memory is dual ported. That is, it is accessible by the processor through one port and from the bus through another. This arrangement is especially efficient in multiprocessor systems, since it allows one processor to access the memory of another by simply generating addresses in that processor's mapped memory range.

Typically, the actual physical addresses occupied by processor memory and sensor interface registers may be selected by switches or links on each board. Thus, it is possible to map system components into fixed, nonoverlapping regions of the bus address space.

From a software writer's standpoint, the VMEbus may be viewed as indicated in Figure 10.3 for most purposes. That is, it may be thought of as a collection of memory regions and sensor interface registers that are mapped into the address space of a bus. This model is adequate with respect to data transfers across the bus. Of course, one must also be concerned with other aspects of bus operation, such as interrupt priority assignments and arbitration levels, when putting a complete system together.

The figure indicates that processor memories are partitioned into code, data, and common regions. The code and data regions represent the normal partitions of a processor program that are generated by a compiler and linker. On the other hand, the common region is a space that is explicitly allocated by the program to support interprocessor communication. In the next several sections we will be concerned with examining a method for establishing this region and with formal procedures for transferring data between processors through data structures in it.

10.3 ESTABLISHING A COMMON MEMORY REGION

Communication between processors in a VMEbus system may be accomplished by means of variables and data structures that are located in common memory regions. A common region may be placed in a processor's dual ported memory or on a separate memory card. The choice of location is usually governed by bus usage considerations. Since the bus is a common communication highway for all processors, it is a point of potential data transfer congestion. As a result, a primary objective in VMEbus system design should be to optimize bus throughput. In computer terminology throughput is often referred to as bandwidth—a term borrowed from radio communication technology.

Bus bandwidth may be preserved by choosing the locations of communication variables and data structures such that accesses across the bus are minimized. For example, it would be unwise to place a variable that must be polled by a processor in memory that is accessed across the bus. The polling activity would waste bus cycles. Instead, the variable should be placed in the processor's local memory—perhaps in a common region, if it must be updated occasionally by another processor. These software design considerations are dependent upon the application and become evident as a design unfolds.

Figure 10.4 shows an example of the use of common memory. The figure illustrates communication between processors SRC and DST by means of variables and buffer pointer queues declared in common memory region **sdcom.** The region includes signal flags **ready** and **go,** error and status variables **srcerr** and **srcstat,** and a set of buffer pointer queues **osrcdst** and **fsrcdst** that establish a buffered communication link between the processors. We will use this specific model in the sections that follow to illustrate software techniques that may be used to support interprocessor communication.

Note that a common region similar to **sdcom** may be established in the dual-ported memory of each processor in a system. The software designer then has considerable flexibility in deciding where specific variables and data structures should be located.

A system's efficiency may be enhanced by paying close attention to the location of pointer queues and their data buffers. For example, in the case shown in Figure 10.4, it would be appropriate in some applications to place queue **osrcdst** in the SRC processor's common memory and the **fsrcdst** queue in the DST processor's common. The actual message buffers may also be located in either processor's memory. These decisions must be based on the way in which the application program uses the queues. Again, the overriding consideration is the need to preserve bus bandwidth.

10.3.1 The Common Memory Data Structure

To establish a common data region one must first declare the structure of the data in that region. Figure 10.5 shows include file **sdcom.h.** This file contains a declaration for the

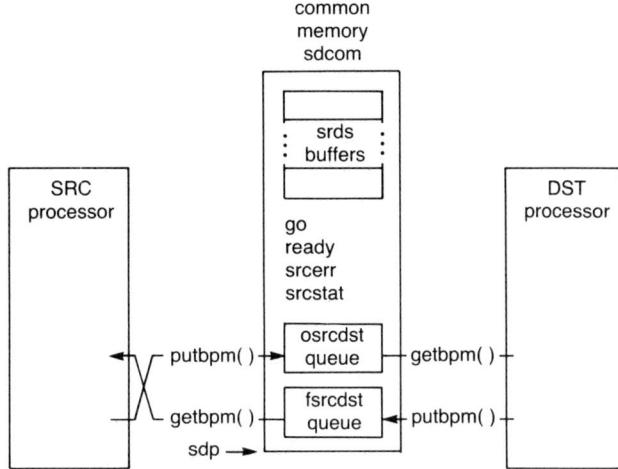

Figure 10.4. An Example Common Memory Region.

structure of the **sdcom** common that is shown in Figure 10.4. It includes two queues and the variables and flags discussed in the previous section. Note that queue headers are declared to be structures of type **pquem**. This is a different header than structure **pque** defined in Chapter 4 for buffer pointer queues that are used within a single processor program. We will examine this new header in Section 10.4.1.

Include file **sdcom.h** also defines symbolic constant **SDSTART.** As the figure indicates, this constant will be used to establish the physical memory address of the start of common **sdcom.** In this example we have chosen that address to be 480000 hex.

At this point we have declared the structure of common **sdcom** and have defined its starting address. What remains is to explicitly define a data structure of type **sdcom** that starts at address **SDSTART.** We should then be able to access data items in that region.

10.3.2 Defining a Common Region

Common **sdcom** is defined by declaring a pointer to a structure of type **sdcom** and then initializing that pointer to the desired starting address. Figure 10.6 shows the code required to accomplish this. The figure shows file **sdques.c** which includes function **qinit().** Recall that this is the function that is called by the executive to initialize all application queues. In this example the queues are located in common **sdcom.**

The file begins by defining variable **sdp** to be a pointer to a structure of type **sdcom.** The first executable statement in **qinit()** initializes **sdp** to the physical memory address defined

```
/*
 *      CX/68K Executive, Version 1.0 (4/10/86)
 *
 *      (c) 1984  Walter S. Heath, all rights reserved.
 *
 *      FILE SDCOM.H Example Interprocessor Common Data
 *                   Structure Declaration.
 */

#define      SDSTART      0x480000      /*common physical start address */

/*
 *Declare lengths of pointer queues.
 */
#define FSDLNGTH     10                 /*SRC-DST free queue length     */
#define OSDLNGTH     10                 /*SRC-DST occupied queue length */

/*
 *Declare the common data area's structure.
 */
struct sdcom{
      struct pquem fsrcdst             ;/*srcdst queue free list header */
      long fsdbuf[FSDLNGTH]            ;/*srcdst queue free list buffer */

      struct pquem osrcdst             ;/*srcdst occupied list header   */
      long osdbuf[OSDLNGTH]            ;/*srcdst occupied list buffer   */

      long srcstat                     ;/*SRC processor status          */
      short srcerr                     ;/*SRC processor errors          */
      short ready                      ;/*SRC-ready flag                */
      short go                         ;/*SRC-go flag                   */

      struct{                           /*SRC-DST message buffers       */
            short mbuf[1024]           ;/*a buffer                      */
      }srds[FSDLNGTH]                  ;

}                                      ;
                                        /*end of SDCOM.H file           */
```

Figure 10.5. Example Common Data Structure Declaration.

```
/*
 *      CX/68K Executive, Version 1.0 (4/10/86)
 *
 *      (c)  1984  Walter S. Heath, all rights reserved.
 *
 *      FILE SDQUES.C
 *
 *      Example interprocessor communication queues and
 *      queue initialization function.
 */
#include "pqsymbm.h"
#include "sdcom.h"

/*
 *Declare a pointer to common structure sdcom.
 */
struct sdcom *sdp                       ;/*pointer to sdcom structure    */

/*
 *---qinit()
 *
 *      This function initializes the application queues.
 */

qinit()
{
short i                                 ;/*working index                 */

/*
 *Initialize the pointer to common sdcom.
 */
sdp = (struct sdcom *)SDSTART           ;

/*
 *Initialize the queue headers.
 */
sdp->fsrcdst.sema = 0                   ;/*semaphores                    */
sdp->osrcdst.sema = 0                   ;

sdp->fsrcdst.full = 0                   ;/*queue-full flags              */
sdp->osrcdst.full = 0                   ;

sdp->fsrcdst.head = 0                   ;/*head pointers                 */
sdp->osrcdst.head = 0                   ;
```

Figure 10.6. Multiprocessor Buffer Pointer Queue Initialization.
(*Continued on next page.*)

```
sdp->fsrcdst.tail = 0                    ;/*tail pointers                  */
sdp->osrcdst.tail = 0                    ;

sdp->fsrcdst.lngth = FSDLNGTH            ;/*queue lengths                   */
sdp->osrcdst.lngth = OSDLNGTH            ;

sdp->fsrcdst.count = 0                   ;/*number-of-ptrs-present count    */
sdp->osrcdst.count = 0                   ;

sdp->fsrcdst.pbuf = sdp->fsdbuf          ;/*pointers to pointer queues      */
sdp->osrcdst.pbuf = sdp->osdbuf          ;

/*
 *Load the free list buffer pointer queue with pointers to buffers.
 */
for(i = 0; i < FSDLNGTH; i++)
      putbpm(sdp->srds[i].mbuf,&(sdp->fsrcdst)) ;
}
                                              /* end of SDQUES.C file       */
```

Figure 10.6. (*continued*) Multiprocessor Buffer Pointer Queue Initialization.

by symbolic constant **SDSTART** (in this example, 480000 hex). In so doing, it establishes a pointer to a data structure of type **sdcom** that starts at address **SDSTART.** The program may then use this pointer to access any variable or data structure declared within **sdcom.**

If the programs running in two processors establish identical pointers to the same common, they may communicate by means of data items defined in that region. For example, the SRC processor in Figure 10.4 might set the status variable in **sdcom** with statement

$$sdp->srcstat = statsend ;$$

and DST might read it using

$$statrcv = sdp->srcstat ;$$

Figure 10.6 shows additional examples of accesses to variables in common **sdcom.** Function **qinit()** initializes the headers for queues **fsrcdst** and **osrcdst** and then loads the free queue with pointers to message buffers. In the latter operation it calls primitive queue access function **putbpm().** This function and several others that are designed to support message passing between processors will be examined in the next section.

10.4 MULTIPROCESSOR BUFFER POINTER QUEUE ACCESS FUNCTIONS

Functions to access buffer pointer queues defined in a common data region are present in file **bptrm.c,** shown in Figure 10.7. The first two functions in this file, **putbpm()** and **getbpm(),** are the primitive functions that actually transfer buffer pointers to and from a queue. They are similar to the **putbp()** and **getbp()** functions described in Chapter 4 that support transfers within a processor. But, unlike these functions, the new functions use a semaphore flag in a queue's header to gain exclusive access to a queue while a transfer is being made. The functions therefore avoid the queue header reentrancy problem discussed in Section 4.6, but, in so doing, they introduce a potential system deadlock problem—if the functions are used for transfers within a single processor. This phenomenon will be explored later in Section 10.6. Fortunately, if the functions are used to transfer data between separate processors via a common data region, both the header reentrancy problem and the possibility of system deadlock are avoided.

```
/*
 *      CX/68K   Executive,    Version  1.0    (4/10/86)
 *
 *      (c)   1984   Walter S. Heath, all rights reserved.
 *
 *      FILE BPTRM.C Buffer Pointer Manipulation Functions,
 *               Multiprocessor Pointer Passing Support.
 *               All functions are reentrant.
 */
#include "pqsymbm.h"

/*
 *---putbpm(pointer,dest) "Put a buffer pointer - multiprocessor version"
 *
 *      This function puts pointer 'pointer' at the tail of the queue
 *      pointed to by 'dest'.  If the queue's semaphore flag is set
 *      (access blocked), it returns -2.  If access is not blocked but
 *      the queue is full, it returns -1.  Otherwise it returns zero.
 */
```

Figure 10.7. Multiprocessor Buffer Pointer Queue Access Functions. (*Continued on next page.*)

```
putbpm(pointer,dest)
char *pointer                    ;
struct pquem *dest               ;
{
short trytail                    ;/*trial tail                          */

/*
 *If queue is full, return -1.
 */
if(dest->full == 1)
       return(-1)                ;

/*
 *Call getset() to check the status of the queue's semaphore.
 */
if(getset(dest) != 0)                /*If the semaphore is set,         */
       return(-2)                ;/*return -2 (queue is blocked).        */

/*
 *Access to the queue is granted.  See if the queue will be full after the
 *new pointer is stored; set 'full' flag if true.
 */
trytail = dest->tail + 1         ;/*compute a trial tail pointer         */

if(trytail == dest->lngth)           /*If pointer should be wrapped,     */
       trytail = 0               ;/*wrap it.                             */

if(trytail == dest->head)            /*If queue will be full,            */
       dest->full = 1            ;/*indicate queue is full.             */

/*
 *Store 'pointer' in the queue and update the tail pointer; return zero.
 */
dest->pbuf[dest->tail] = (int)pointer   ;

dest->count++                    ;/*increment pointer count             */
dest->tail = trytail             ;
dest->sema = 0                   ;/*reset the semaphore flag            */
                                 /* (unblock the queue)                 */
return(0)                        ;
}                                    /*end of function putbpm()          */
```

Figure 10.7. (*continued*) Multiprocessor Buffer Pointer Queue Access Functions.

```
/*
 *---getbpm(source)    "Get a buffer pointer - multiprocessor version"
 *
 *      This function gets a buffer pointer form the queue pointed to by
 *      'source'.  If the queue's semaphore flag is set (access blocked) it
 *      returns -2.  If access is not blocked but no pointers are present,
 *      it returns -1.  Otherwise the function returns the pointer.
 */

char *getbpm(source)
struct pquem *source               ;
{
char *pointer                      ;/*buffer pointer value returned        */

/*
 *If queue is empty, return -1.
 */
if(source->count == 0)
        return((char *)-1)         ;

/*
 *Call getset() to check the status of the queue's semaphore.
 */
if(getset(source) != 0)            /*If semaphore is set,                  */
        return((char *)-2)         ;/*return -2 (queue is blocked).        */

/*
 *Remove a pointer from the queue.
 */
pointer = (char *)source->pbuf[source->head++] ;

source->count--                    ;/*decrement pointer count              */
source->full = 0                   ;/*indicate queue is not full           */

if(source->head == source->lngth)  /*If pointer should be wrapped,         */
        source->head = 0           ;/*wrap it.                             */

source->sema = 0                   ;/*reset the semaphore flag             */
                                    /* (unblock the queue)                 */
/*
 *Return the pointer.
 */
return(pointer)                    ;
}                                   /*end of getbpm() function             */
```

(Continued on next page.)

```
/*
 *---putbpr(pointer,dest,retsem,retfull) "Put a buffer pointer or retry"
 *
 *      This function calls putbpm() to put pointer 'pointer' in the queue
 *      pointed to by 'dest'.  If the queue's access is blocked, it retries
 *      the call 'retsem' times.  If the queue is full, it retries the call
 *      'retfull' times. The function returns the value (finally) returned
 *      by putbpm().
 */

putbpr(pointer,dest,retsem,retfull)
short *pointer                      ;
struct pquem *dest                  ;
short retsem                        ;
short retfull                       ;
{
long retval                         ;/*putbpm() value returned                */

/*
 *Call putbpm() while the returned value is negative and more repeat
 *requests remain.
 */
do{
      retval = putbpm(pointer,dest)     ;
      if(retval == -2)              /*If queue's semaphore is set,       */
            --retsem                ;/*decrement its retry counter.       */

      else if(retval == -1)         /*If the 'dest' buffer is full,      */
            —retfull                ;/*decrement its retry counter.       */

}while((retval == -2 && retsem >= 0) || (retval == -1 && retfull >= 0)) ;

return(retval)                      ;
}                                         /*end of putbpr() function            */

/*
 *---getbpr(source,retsem,retempt)    "Get a buffer pointer or retry"
 *
 *      This function calls getbpm() to get a pointer from the queue
 *      pointed to by 'source'.  If the queue's access is blocked it
 *      retries the call 'retsem' times.  If the queue is empty, it
 *      retries the call 'retempt' times.  The function returns the
 *      value (finally) returned by getbpm().
 */
```

Figure 10.7. (*continued*) Multiprocessor Buffer Pointer Queue Access Functions.

```
getbpr(source,retsem,retempt)
struct pquem *source                    ;
short retsem                            ;
short retempt                           ;
{
long retval                             ;/*getbpm() value returned              */

/*
 *Call getbpm() while the returned value is negative and more repeat
 *requests remain.
 */
do{
        retval = (long)getbpm(source)     ;
        if(retval == -2)                /*If queue's semaphore is set,         */
                --retsem                ;/*decrement its retry counter.        */

        else if(retval == -1)           /*If 'source' buffer is empty,         */
                --retempt               ;/*decrement its retry counter.        */

}while((retval == -2 && retsem >= 0) || (retval == -1 && retempt >= 0)) ;

return(retval)                          ;
}                                       /*end of getbpr() function             */

                                        /*end of BPTRM.C file                  */
```

Figure 10.7. (*continued*) Multiprocessor Buffer Pointer Queue Access Functions.

Since primitive functions **putbpm()** and **getbpm()** and the previously described **putbp()** and **getbp()** functions use the same techniques to move buffer pointers to and from a queue, it will not be necessary to describe those operations again here. Instead, we will concentrate on the operations that are unique to the new functions. We will start by examining the structure of the header for the queues that are accessed and then look at the way in which a semaphore flag is used to grant exclusive access to a queue. We will then return to Figure 10.7 and review the unique operations performed by the new queue access functions.

10.4.1 The Multiprocessor Buffer Pointer Queue Header

Figure 10.8 shows include file **pqsymbm.h.** This file contains a declaration for the multiprocessor buffer pointer queue header, **pquem.** Comparing this header to the **pque** header declared in Figure 4.6 for pointer queues used within a single processor, it is evident that, although most entries are the same, some variables needed to maintain queues between

```
/*
 *      CX/68K   Executive,   Version 1.0   (4/10/86)
 *
 *      (c)   1984   Walter S. Heath, all rights reserved.
 *
 *      FILE PQSYMBM.H
 *
 *          Pointer queue data structure declaration
 *          for multiprocessor buffer pointer queue
 *          functions in file BPTRM.C.
 */

struct pquem{                         /*buffer pointer queue header   */
     char sema                   ;/*access semaphore               */
     char full                   ;/*queue-full flag                */
     short head                  ;/*head pointer (index)           */
     short tail                  ;/*tail pointer (index)           */
     short lngth                 ;/*queue length (# of entries)    */
     short count                 ;/*count of pointers in queue     */
     long *pbuf                  ;/*pointer to array of ptrs       */
}                                 ;

                                      /*end of PQSYMBM.H file         */
```

Figure 10.8. Multiprocessor Buffer Pointer Queue Header Declaration.

processors are different. This header includes new items **sema** and **count** and omits variable **task.** Briefly, the **sema** flag is the semaphore that is used to limit access to the queue to one processor at a time. Variable **count** simply maintains a count of the number of entries in the queue. It is used to quickly determine whether a queue contains any entries and during program testing. Finally, the **task** variable is omitted since a task in one processor may not be directly awakened by a task in another.

10.4.2 Queue Semaphore
Interrogation Function

As indicated in Figure 10.7, the primitive queue access functions call function **getset()** to test the semphore flag in the header of a queue. This assembly language function is shown in Figure 10.9. We will review this function's operation and then establish its role in limiting access to a queue.

The **getset()** function first sets the program's frame pointer and then saves address register **a0** on the stack. It then copies the function's calling argument into **a0**. Since this argument is a pointer to a queue header and the first data item in that header is a byte containing the queue's semaphore flag, register **a0** then points to the semaphore.

```
|*****************************************************************************
|*
|*      CX/68K Executive, Version 1.0      (4/10/86)
|*
|*      (c)  1984  Walter S. Heath, all rights reserved.
|*
|*      FILE SEMA.S
|*
|*      Assembly language component of multiprocessor buffer pointer
|*      queue access functions.
|*
|*****************************************************************************

|*
|*---getset(queptr)
|*      This function gets the setting of the semaphore flag for the
|*      buffer pointer queue pointed to by 'queptr'.  It sets the flag
|*      in the same operation.  The function returns the initial flag
|*      setting.  This function is used to support multiprocessor
|*      communications.  It is called by functions putbp() and getbp()
|*      in file BPTRM.C.
|*
        .text
        .globl _getset

_getset:
        link    a6,#0               |set the frame pointer, a6
        movl    a0,sp@-             |push a0

        movl    a6@(8),a0           |copy 'queptr' to a0
        tas     a0@                 |test-and-set the MSB of '*queptr'
        beq     NOTSET              |Branch if semaphore is not set.
|*                                   Semaphore was set, so
        movl    #1,d0               |set the returned value.
        bra     EXIT

NOTSET:
|*                                   Semaphore was not set, so
        movl    #0,d0               |clear the returned value.

EXIT:
        movl    sp@+,a0             |pop a0
        unlk    a6                  |restore the old frame pointer

        rts
|*
|*                                   end of SEMA.S file
|*
```

Figure 10.9. Queue Semaphore Interrogation Function.

The processor's test-and-set (**tas**) instruction is used to interrogate the semaphore. This is a special-purpose instruction that performs an indivisible read-modify-write operation on a memory location. That is, it first reads the location and sets the processor's N (negative) and Z (zero) status bits according to the value received. It then writes a one into the high order bit of the same memory location. These two operations are performed without relinquishing control of the memory. Thus, it is not possible for another processor to access the same memory location between these two operations. We will examine the functional significance of this sequence of operations shortly. But first, we will complete our review of the **getset**() function.

After the test-and-set instruction, the function tests the processor's Z status flag. Based on this value, it returns a one if the semaphore was found to be set or a zero if it was not. To summarize, the function tests the queue's semaphore flag, sets the flag, and then returns a value that indicates the condition of the flag before it was set. Let us now consider how this curious sequence of operations is able to guarantee exclusive access to a queue.

As shown in Figure 10.7, the primitive functions that call **getset**() test the value that it returns and only continue with a queue access operation if this value is zero. When they have completed their operation, they clear the flag. Thus, a queue operation will be performed only if the queue's semaphore is found to be cleared. Since **getset**() leaves the semaphore set, no other program component may access the queue while this operation is in progress.

Note that it is necessary to use an indivisible instruction to interrogate the semaphore. If separate instructions were used to test the flag and then set it, a situation could arise in which two processors test the flag, find it cleared, and set it. Each processor would then proceed to perform a queue access operation under the assumption that it had exclusive access to the queue. As a consequence, the semaphore's role in providing exclusive access would have been defeated.

It is worth noting that the VMEbus specification supports indivisible instructions. Consequently, a processor that performs a test-and-set operation on a memory location that is accessed across the bus will maintain exclusive access to the bus through both instruction operations. We may therefore be assured that the semaphore technique will guarantee exclusive access to a queue in a VMEbus system containing processors on separate boards.

It is also worth noting that the **getset**() function may be used to control access to data structures other than queues. For example, you may wish to define a different kind of structure for passing data between processors. If several items must be changed each time it is updated and all changes must be made before the destination processor is allowed to read it, a semaphore may be used to limit access to the structure. The **getset**() function will perform the necessary semaphore operations if the first item in the structure is declared to be the semaphore.

10.4.3 The putbpm() and getbpm() Primitive Functions

The two primitive queue access functions shown in Figure 10.7 differ from the **putbp**() and **getbp**() functions described in Chapter 4 in only two ways. As we saw in the previous section, each tests a queue's semaphore flag by calling function **getset**(). It then clears that flag when its queue access operation has been completed. This effectively blocks access to the queue by another processor while the queue operation is being performed. The second difference concerns the manipulation of the **count** variable that has been added to the queue's header. This is used to keep track of the number of entries currently present in the queue.

The **count** entry was added for two reasons. First, it provides a way for the **getbpm()** function to quickly determine if the queue is empty without having to sacrifice the overhead associated with reserving the queue. If **count** is zero, the function returns a minus one immediately. By contrast, the **getbp()** function must perform a compound test of the queue's **head, tail,** and **full** variables to make the same decision. The use of the counter is therefore much more efficient for applications in which a queue is likely to be empty for a large percentage of the attempts to get a pointer. We will see in the next section that this situation occurs frequently for queues that are used to pass data between processors. The cost of providing this service is, of course, the execution time for the additional code required to maintain the counter.

The second reason for including the counter is to aid program testing. It is very convenient to be able to determine the number of entries in a queue immediately by looking at the **count** variable in a queue's header. Without this parameter, the number of entries must be computed by hand using the header's **head, tail,** and **lngth** values.

As indicated in the figure, both primitive functions return minus two if queue access is blocked (via the semaphore) and minus one if the operation fails for lack of an entry or storage space. In Section 10.4.5 we will see that these values are used by higher level functions **putbpr()** and **getbpr()** to provide enhanced services.

10.4.4 Using the Interprocessor Buffer Pointer Queues

Now that we have established specific software techniques for defining and accessing buffer pointer queues in a common region, we need to give some consideration to the way in which these queues may be used in an actual application.

In a typical single processor program, a task places a pointer in a queue and then wakes the task that will receive it. But in a multiprocessor system it is not as easy for a task in one processor to wake a task in another. The most convenient technique for implementing this operation is to use the processor-to-processor interrupt or so-called "mailbox" interrupt facility provided by the VMEbus. Using this mechanism a processor may cause an interrupt in a second processor by writing to a specific location that is designated as a mailbox by that processor. The associated interrupt handler may then wake a receiving task. It may even cause the preemption of a running task, if necessary.

The disadvantage of using an interrupt is that the receiving processor must suffer the overhead associated with processing the interrupt each time a message pointer is received. Often the receiving processor is busy processing the previously received message or with some other task and is not able to respond immediately to the new data. In such cases it is more appropriate for the sending processor to simply queue the message pointer without interruption. The receiving processor will then check the queue when it is ready. It is possible to envision several situations in which this approach makes sense.

In Section 10.1 we considered the candidate multiprocessor system shown in Figure 10.1. In this system, one processor is dedicated to dispatching data received from a high priority port to other processors that are assigned to process that data. In a system such as this, a program that runs in a receiving processor might consist of a single task that receives data, processes them, and passes them on to another processor or output port. Once a message has been processed, the receiving processor would typically check its input queue for another message pointer. If none is available, it has no useful work to do until another pointer arrives. Clearly, in this case, it makes sense for the task to spend its time polling the input queue for the arrival of the next message pointer. A tight polling loop will provide faster response than the mailbox interrupt mechanism described earlier.

Situations also arise in which it is appropriate for a program to poll an output queue. In the case of a processor that is dedicated to performing a single computation, it is often necessary for the results from the current computation to be passed on before new data may be accepted. If the processor's output queue is full, it may poll the queue until space becomes available.

Queue polling may also be an appropriate choice for a processor program that is not dedicated to performing a single task. For example, the program for the auxiliary processor in Figure 10.1 might consist of several tasks. When the processor is not busy with requests for service from its assigned I/O ports, it might run a lowest priority background task that polls for message pointers from other processors.

In general, if a processor must be notified immediately of a change in the status of one of its interprocessor queues, the mailbox interrupt mechanism may be used to provide the signal. On the other hand, if it is more important for the processor to continue its operations until it reaches an appropriate point before checking its queues, then the program should use polling. In the latter case it is convenient to define some utility functions that automate the polling procedure.

10.4.5 Extended Functions
putbpr() and getbpr()

The **bptrm.c** file shown in Figure 10.7 also contains extended functions **putbpr()** and **getbpr()**. In general, these functions perform a queue access operation by calling one of the primitive functions **putbpm()** or **getbpm()** and, if the operation fails, they try again. The number of retries is specified by the arguments passed to the functions.

There are two ways in which a queue access operation may fail. First, the primitive function might find that a queue is blocked. That is, its semaphore flag is set. This indicates that the queue is currently being accessed by another processor. In this case the primitive function returns a minus two. A queue access will also fail if the requested operation cannot be accomplished. In the case of **putbpm()**, this occurs if the queue is full; for **getbpm()**, it happens when the queue is empty. In either case, the primitive function returns minus one.

As indicated in the figure, the polling functions test the value returned by the primitive function call. If this value is negative, they decrement the appropriate retry counter and test to see if the queue should be polled again. On the other hand, if the primitive function was successful, they return immediately. In either case, the functions return the value returned by the last primitive function call.

In the actual application the queue access functions may be used to poll a specified number of times or until the requested operation is successful. For example, in the example case shown in Figure 10.4, the SRC processor might attempt to put pointer **srcptr** in queue **osrcdst** using statement:

$$\textbf{if((retval = putbpr(srcptr,\&(sdp->osrcdst),10,5)) < 0)}$$

In this case, **putbpr()** will poll up to ten times if the queue is blocked and as many as five times if the queue is full before returning. The statement checks for success or failure of the operation and the SRC program must then respond accordingly. Meanwhile, the DST processor might be polling the same queue using the primitive **getbpm()** function

$$\textbf{while((long)(dstptr = getbpm(\&(sdp->osrcdst))) < 0) ;}$$

This loop will continue until a valid pointer is received.

Note that, since DST is continuously polling the queue, it is likely that SRC will find the queue blocked occasionally (when DST is actually removing an entry). Consequently, it is important for the **putbpr()** statement in SRC to request several retries of the semaphore test.

This example case also illustrates another important point concerning the placement of queues in processor memories. The implied assumption in this example is that DST finishes its work and then pools queue **osrcdst** for a pointer to another message to process. It is also assumed that SRC occasionally has a pointer to deliver to DST. Thus, the queue is often empty and DST spends time polling it. In this situation it would be inappropriate for the **osrcdst** queue to be located in the common region of the SRC processor, since DST would then have to poll across the bus. This would waste bus bandwidth unnecessarily. Instead, the queue should be located in the DST processor's common. The example illustrates a general rule: a queue should be located in the memory of the processor that will access it most often.

10.5 COMPENSATING FOR MEMORY ACCESS OFFSET

The dual ported memory on some VMEbus processor boards is accessed differently depending on which port is used. If it is accessed by the on-board processor, the memory starts at address zero. On the other hand, if it is accessed from the bus, its starting address is selected by switches or links on the board. For example, if a variable is located at address 80000 hex when accessed by the on-board processor and the board's memory has been mapped into the VMEbus address space starting at 400000 hex, then the same variable must be accessed by an off-board processor at address 480000 hex. This situation will obviously have an impact on our procedures for establishing common regions. Let us again use the example case illustrated in Figure 10.4 to determine the adjustments that are needed.

The SRC processor may establish common region **sdcom** in its dual ported memory starting at address 80000 hex by setting its **sdp** pointer to this value. But if thie memory is mapped into the VMEbus starting at 400000 hex, the DST processor must initialize its **sdp** pointer to 480000 hex to access the same common. That is, it must add the VMEbus base offset of the SRC processor's memory to the location of the common within that memory. With this minor adjustment the techniques described earlier for passing variables and flags between processors may still be used. But the changes needed to support buffer pointer queues in the common region are somewhat more complex.

If the **osrcdst** queue is located in the SRC processor's common and SRC wishes to send a message pointer to DST via this queue, it must adjust the pointer to compensate for the different address ranges seen by the two processors. That is, it must add the VMEbus base offset of its memory to the pointer. The queue header also contains a pointer that must be adjusted depending on the memory port used to access the queue. This is the **pbuf** pointer. It points to the queue's array of pointers. Since these adjustments are necessary for every queue access, it is most convenient to incorporate them into the primitive functions that perform the actual access operations.

If we adopt the convention that the pointer values actually present in a queue should be correct for off-board references, the primitive functions **putbpr()** and **getbpr()** discussed earlier may still be used to access the queue from the VMEbus side. We will then need different primitive functions for accesses by the on-board processor.

Figure 10.10 shows a file that contains primitive functions **lputbpm()** and **lgetbpm()**.

```
/*
 *      CX/68K  Executive,  Version 1.0  (4/10/86)
 *
 *      (c)  1984  Walter S. Heath, all rights reserved.
 *
 *      FILE LBPTRM.C Local Buffer Pointer Manipulation Functions,
 *                 Multiprocessor Pointer Passing Support.
 *                 All functions are reentrant.
 */
#include "pqsymbm.h"

/*
 *---lputbpm(pointer,dest,membase)
 *           "Local put a buffer pointer - multiprocessor version"
 *      This function puts pointer 'pointer' at the tail of the queue
 *      pointed to by 'dest'.  If the queue's semaphore flag is set
 *      (access blocked), it returns -2.  If access is not blocked but
 *      the queue is full, it returns -1.  Otherwise it returns zero.
 */
```

Figure 10.10. Local Processor Buffer Pointer Queue Access Functions.

```
lputbpm(pointer,dest,membase)
char *pointer                          ;
struct pquem *dest                     ;
long *membase                          ;
{
short trytail                          ;/*trial tail                          */
long *lpbuf                            ;/*local pointer to pointers     */

/*
 *If queue is full, return -1.
 */
if(dest->full == 1)
        return(-1)                     ;
/*
 *Call getset() to check the status of the queue's semaphore.
 */
if(getset(dest) != 0)
        return(-2)                     ;/*If blocked, return -2        */

/*
 *Access to the queue is granted; see if the queue will be full after the
 *new pointer is stored; set 'full' flag if true.
 */
trytail = dest->tail + 1               ;/*compute a trial tail pointer        */

if(trytail == dest->lngth)             /*If pointer should be wrapped,        */
        trytail = 0                    ;/*wrap it.                            */

if(trytail == dest->head)              /*If queue will be full,               */
        dest->full = 1                 ;/*indicate queue is full.              */

/*
 *Store 'pointer' in the queue and update the tail pointer; return zero.
 */
                                       /*get local ptr to ptrs              */
(long)lpbuf = (long)dest->pbuf - (long)membase ;
                                       /*put global ptr                     */
lpbuf[dest->tail] = (int)pointer + (long)membase ;

dest->count++                          ;/*increment pointer count */
dest->tail = trytail                   ;
dest->sema = 0                         ;/*reset the semaphore flag           */
                                        /* (unblock the queue)              */
return(0)                              ;
}                                       /*end of function lputbpm()          */
```

(Continued on next page.)

```
/*
 * ---lgetbpm(source,membase)
 *            "Local get a buffer pointer - multiprocessor version"
 *      This function gets a buffer pointer form the queue pointed to by
 *      'source'.  If the queue's semaphore flag is set (access blocked) it
 *      returns -2.  If access is not blocked but no pointers are present,
 *      it returns -1.  Otherwise the function returns the pointer.
 */

char *lgetbpm(source,membase)
struct pquem *source           ;
long *membase                  ;
{
char *pointer                           ;/*buffer pointer value returned      */
long *lpbuf                             ;/*local pointer to pointers          */

/*
 *If queue is empty, return -1.
 */
if(source->count == 0)
        return((char *)-1)      ;

/*
 *Call getset() to check the status of the queue's semaphore.
 */
if(getset(source) != 0)
        return((char *)-2)              ;/*return -2 if queue blocked        */

/*
 *Remove a pointer from the queue; advance the head pointer; wrap it if
 *necessary.
 */
                                /*get local ptr to ptrs                      */
(long)lpbuf = (long)source->pbuf - (long)membase ;
                                /*get local ptr                              */
pointer = (char *)(lpbuf[source->head++] - (long)membase) ;

source->count--                         ;/*decrement pointer count           */
source->full = 0                        ;/*indicate queue not full           */
if(source->head == source->lngth) /*If pointer should be wrapped,           */
        source->head = 0                ;/*wrap it.                          */
source->sema = 0                        ;/*reset the semaphore flag          */
                                         /* (unblock the queue)              */
/*
 *Return the pointer.
 */
return(pointer)                 ;
}                                       /*end of lgetbpm() function          */
```

Figure 10.10. (*continued*) Local Processor Buffer Pointer Queue Access Functions.

These functions may be used by the local processor to access queues defined in its common region. Since these functions are very similar to **putbpm()** and **getbpm()** described earlier, it will only be necessary to review their differences here.

Note that both functions declare an additional calling argument, **membase.** This is the VMEbus starting address of the memory containing the common region. For the example case cited earlier, its value would be 400000 hex.

The **membase** parameter is used in the queue access calculations at two points. First, it is used to compute a local pointer to the array of stored message pointers, **lpbuf.** Here the memory base address must be subtracted from the array pointer **pbuf** stored in the queue's header. The second application of **membase** concerns the adjustment of the message pointer itself. In the case of **lputbpm(),** the memory base address must be added to the pointer before it is stored; in the **lgetbpm()** function it must be subtracted from the pointer that is removed from the queue.

To support the polling technique for accessing queues, it is also convenient to define a set of local polling functions, **lputbpr()** and **lgetbpr().** Clearly, these functions will be very similar to the **putbpr()** and **getbpr()** functions defined earlier. They differ only in that they include the additional argument **membase** and call primitive functions **lputbpm()** and **lgetbpm(),** rather than **putbpm()** and **getbpm(),** respectively.

It is worthwhile to review the way in which these new queue access functions are used in an actual application. We will once more use the example case shown in Figures 10.4–10.5 as a starting point for this discussion and will concern ourselves with the changes that are needed to compensate for memory access offset.

The first changes concern the way in which the queues are initialized by function **qinit().** Figure 10.11 shows the required adjustments. In general, they involve modifying pointers by an amount specified by symbolic constant **SDBASE** and the substitution of function

```
/*
 *      CX/68K Executive, Version 1.0 (4/10/86)
 *
 *      (c)  1984  Walter S. Heath, all rights reserved.
 *
 *      FILE LSDQUES.C - Memory access offset version.
 *
 *      Example interprocessor communication queues and
 *      queue initialization function.
 */
#include "pqsymbm.h"
#include "lsdcom.h"


/*
 *Declare a pointer to common structure sdcom.
 */
struct sdcom *sdp                        ;/*pointer to sdcom structure    */
```

Figure 10.11. Queue Initialization When Memory Access Offset Must Be Accommodated. (*Continued on next page.*)

```c
/*
 *---qinit()
 *
 *      This function initializes the application queues.
 */
qinit()

{
short i                                 ;/*working index                 */

/*
 *Initialize the pointer to common sdcom.
 */
sdp = (struct sdcom *)(SDSTART - SDBASE) ;

/*
 *Initialize the queue headers.
 */
sdp->fsrcdst.sema = 0                   ;/*semaphores                    */
sdp->osrcdst.sema = 0                   ;
sdp->fsrcdst.full = 0                   ;/*queue-full flags              */
sdp->osrcdst.full = 0                   ;
sdp->fsrcdst.head = 0                   ;/*head pointers                 */
sdp->osrcdst.head = 0                   ;
sdp->fsrcdst.tail = 0                   ;/*tail pointers                 */
sdp->osrcdst.tail = 0                   ;

sdp->fsrcdst.lngth = FSDLNGTH           ;/*queue lengths                 */
sdp->osrcdst.lngth = OSDLNGTH           ;

sdp->fsrcdst.count = 0                  ;/*number-of-ptrs-present count  */
sdp->osrcdst.count = 0                  ;

sdp->fsrcdst.pbuf =
  (long *)((long)(sdp->fsdbuf) + SDBASE) ;/*pointers to pointer queues   */

sdp->osrcdst.pbuf =
  (long *)((long)(sdp->osdbuf) + SDBASE) ;

/*
 *Load the free list buffer pointer queue with pointers to buffers.
 */
for(i = 0; i < FSDLNGTH; i++)
      lputbpm(sdp->srds[i].mbuf,&(sdp->fsrcdst),SDBASE) ;
}
                                        /* end of LSDQUES.C file         */
```

Figure 10.11. (*continued*) Queue Initialization When Memory Access Offset Must Be Accommodated.

lputbpm() in the free queue initialization operation. The **SDBASE** constant is defined as follows:

#**define SDBASE 0 × 400000** /∗**memory base offset** ∗/

This statement is added to file **sdcom.h** to form include file **lsdcom.h.**
 The SRC processor might get a pointer from queue **fsrcdst** using statement

srcptr = lgetbpr(&sdp − >fsrcdst),5,5,SDBASE) ;

It would probably then fill the buffer with data and send the pointer to DST using statement

lputbpr(srcptr,&(sdp − >osrcdst),5,5,SDBASE) ;

As noted earlier, DST may use functions **putbpr()** and **getbpr()** to access the queues.

10.6 SEMAPHORE PROTECTION OF QUEUES AND SYSTEM DEADLOCK

In Section 4.6 we discussed the reentrancy phenomenon as it relates to the queue header data structure. To review, a data structure will be reentered when a program component that is manipulating items in the structure is abruptly suspended (by interruption and possibly preemption) and another program component makes changes in the same structure. When the suspended function is again allowed to run, it will find a data structure that contains modified and possibly inconsistent data items. If the data structure is a queue header, these changes cannot be tolerated, since queue entries may be lost or overwritten.

We discussed three methods for avoiding queue header reentrancy. One technique mentioned briefly involved the use of a semaphore. Since we have now established this method for protecting queues when they are used to communicate between processors, we are in a position to evaluate its use for communication within a single processor.

It should be clear that primitive queue access functions **putbpm()** and **getbpm()** could also be used to support communication between tasks in a single processor system. But certain precautions must be observed in the design of the application program to avoid the possibility of system deadlock. We will examine the problem by considering an example.

Consider a case in which a low priority task is accessing a queue by calling either **putbpm()** or **getbpm().** It finds the queue's semaphore flag cleared and sets it. At some point in its queue access operations, an interrupt occurs and the handler preempts the running task to allow a higher priority task to run. If this task then tries to access the same queue, it will fail, since the queue's semaphore is set. If the preempting task cannot continue until its queue access operation is successful, a deadlock situation will exist: The preempting task cannot proceed until the queue becomes unblocked, and this will not occur since the low priority task that blocked it has been suspended. Clearly, this and similar situations must be avoided by proper design of the application program. For example, a task that encounters a blocked queue could suspend (call **sleep()**) to allow the lower priority task to free the queue. As an alternative, the lower priority task could disable interrupts while it assesses the queue.

Note that if the queue is accessed using the **putbp()** and **getbp()** functions described in Chapter 4, the deadlock problem will not occur and queue header integrity will be maintained—as long as only one task puts pointers into the queue and only one other task takes pointers from it. Semaphore protection of a queue header is useful when several tasks must access the same queue—and then, only when the application program may be written such that system deadlock cannot occur.

10.7 MULTIPROCESSOR SYSTEM INITIATION

In Chapters 11 and 12 we will discuss methods for loading and physically starting programs in a multiple processor system. In this section we will address the question of coordinating the initial operations in these programs such that the sequence is the same each time it occurs.

As we will see in Chapter 11, processor programs may be started either manually or automatically, but, in either case, the precise timing of these events cannot be guaranteed. As a result, it is appropriate to allow each processor program to independently run through its initialization procedure to a point where further operation will require coordination with other processors. At that point, each processor should pause and wait for the other processors to reach a similar point. Once all processor programs have completed their initialization operations, they may be signaled to continue in an appropriate order.

In Section 10.3 we introduced the concept of the common data region and used the example common shown in Figure 10.4 for illustration. Among other items, this common contains two flags called **ready** and **go.** These flags may be used to coordinate program initiation.

Typically, the processor that provides the operator's console interface to the system also controls the initiation sequence. When each of the other processors completes its initialization operations, it sets the **ready** flag located in its common and then polls its **go** flag. But when the control processor completes its initialization, it polls the **ready** flags of the other processors. When it determines that all have been set, it sets the **go** flags in these processors in a sequence that is appropriate for the application. The processors then begin operation in an orderly and repeatable sequence.

Note that for this procedure to work properly the control processor must clear the **ready** and **go** flags in the commons of the other processors before they are started. As a consequence, the program in the control processor must be started first.

11

Program Development, Loading, and Initiation

In the preceding chapters, we focused our attention on software design techniques that have been found to be useful in the construction of real-time systems. Our efforts were directed toward satisfying the very demanding requirements of these systems when they are actually in operation, but little was said concerning methods for writing the programs, loading them into the target equipment and starting them running. These are important issues, since they have a major impact on the efficiency of the software development process and the flexibility of the ultimate target system. We will address these subjects in this chapter.

As in Chapter 10, we shall be primarily interested in target systems that are based on the VMEbus technology. Both single and multiple processor systems will be addressed. We shall discuss various alternatives for accomplishing three steps in the software development process: writing, loading, and starting programs. Our emphasis will be on nonproprietary techniques that you may implement by writing support software for standard host and target computer products. Where possible, example software will be presented and reviewed. We shall emphasize techniques that the reader may use immediately to begin writing and testing real-time programs.

11.1 WRITING REAL-TIME PROGRAMS

In Chapter 5 we noted that the software presented in this book was prepared on a Sun-3 workstation. What made this host especially convenient was the fact that it uses the same processor as many target VME processor boards—namely the 68020. This meant that the

C compiler and assembler that is included with Sun's Berkeley UNIX-based operating system could be used immediately to write programs for target systems. The operating system's considerable support for the other aspects of software development was also available. But real-time software may also be developed just as effectively using other hosts and operating systems.

Cross compilers and assemblers are readily available for producing 680X0 code on hosts that use a different central processor. These tools may even generate code that is more efficient than the language processors provided by UNIX. The computing capacity of an alternative host may also be more appropriate for the size of the project you plan to undertake. In some cases a smaller host, such as a PC, may be adequate; for larger projects a minicomputer or mainframe may be needed. In any case, one should make sure that the software tools being considered can generate programs that will run on the target embedded system.

Programs that are written to run on a host are linked to operate in the operating system's virtual address space. The program linker produces code that is appropriate for this environment. But in an embedded system the program runs in physical address space and must be linked to start at a prespecified, fixed address. So it is important to determine whether the linker being considered has an option that will allow specification of the program's starting physical address. For some linkers (e.g., the Berkeley UNIX linker) it is possible to independently specify the starting addresses of both code and data segments. Separate segments are essential for ROM-based systems.

One should also determine the C compiler's method for maintaining function context. Most C compilers establish a frame on the stack for calling arguments and locally defined variables. This behavior is assumed by the task scheduler described in Chapter 3. It is also required to support reentrancy, as described in Chapter 4. The compiler's C and math libraries should also support reentrancy.

Some compilers may be more strict when variables with differing data types are equated. One may need to use the type casting feature of the C language to explicitly transform variables to the same data type in these situations.

We have seen that it is very convenient to be able to insert assembly language statements into C language programs. The executive's **sleep()** function uses this feature to save and restore the processor's status register, and it was also used to set and clear bits in a parallel port during system performance monitoring. Not all C compilers make provision for inline assembly language statements. One should make sure that the candidate compiler does.

Finally, it is also important that the software development toolkit includes a utility for producing a memory map of a linked program. In UNIX this is the **nm** utility. The map is needed during program testing to locate functions and global variables.

There may be characteristics of a set of software tools that render them unusable for embedded systems development. For example, if the optimizer for a compiler optimizes code across function calls, it may be difficult or impossible to save and restore the context of tasks. Keep in mind that most software tools are not designed for the production of real-time, embedded systems. So it is necessary to exercise considerable caution in adopting a particular set for this purpose. It would be prudent to try the tools on a test program before making a final commitment. The example application programs described in the earlier chapters of this book would be appropriate for this purpose.

11.2 LOADING REAL-TIME PROGRAMS

One aspect of the software development process that needs to be more seriously addressed by industry is the procedure for transferring programs from a host to a target system. Since this is the interface between equipments built by different manufacturers, it is an area where cooperation and agreement is needed. It is clearly an area where standards need to be established.

One de facto standard is available and is supported by most manufacturers of target processor boards. This is the so-called S-record method for transferring programs via a serial line. Developed originally by Motorola, this method essentially divides each byte of a program image file into two four-bit "nibbles" and encodes them as ASCII characters. The encoded data may then be transferred over a serial line as ASCII text. In the target processor the nibbles are recombined into bytes and loaded into program memory.

The S-record method will be examined in considerable detail in the next several sections. We will present and review software utilities that are needed in a host to convert program image files to S-records and download them to a target system. This will provide you with an initial method for transferring files so that you may begin testing programs in your target system without delay. But as the sizes of your programs increase, you may discover that transfer delays associated with this method become unacceptable.

The time required to transfer a file using the S-record method depends primarily on the baud rate of the serial line and the size of the file. But the fact that each image file byte is converted into two ASCII bytes essentially halves the effective baud rate. In addition, we will see shortly that each record in an S-record file contains additional control bytes that further reduce the effective transfer rate. The net result is that it can take several minutes to transfer a file for a program of moderate size. For example, it takes about 1 minute to transfer a 16K byte file over a 9600 baud line. This delay can have a substantial impact on the total time required to debug a program. A faster method is clearly needed.

We will look at an alternative method for transferring program image files in Chapter 12. This technique employs a floppy disk to transport files between host and target. A byproduct benefit of this approach is that it is not necessary for the two computers to be physically connected by a cable. Of course, this is also true if programs are burned into PROMs, but the floppy disk method is more convenient when programs must be changed regularly and during initial program testing.

Each program loading technique has its advantages and limitations. Whether one of the methods described in this book will be useful will depend on the type of system being built and the environment within which it will be required to operate.

11.2.1 The S-Record Method

Motorola has defined a set of standard data records, called S-records, for representing the content of a binary program image file as ASCII text. These records may be transferred over a serial line using standard techniques. In the target system, each record is interpreted by a utility provided by the processor's PROM monitor. The utility loads the contents of a

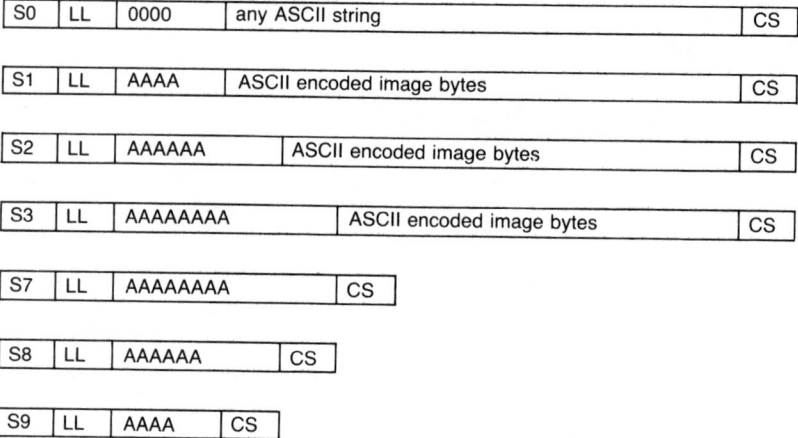

Figure 11.1. S-Record Formats.

record into specified locations in the processor's memory. Through a series of such transfers an entire program may be downloaded from a host to a target system.

Figure 11.1 shows the formats of the seven defined S-records. The symbols shown in the records represent ASCII bytes. Each record is terminated with carriage return (CR) and line feed (LF) characters (not shown). An example file of S-records is shown in Figure 11.2.

As indicated, each record begins with a two-byte record type designator. Different records perform different functions. An **S0** record must be sent at the beginning of a transfer. It identifies the file being transferred and notifies the target processor that program image records will follow.

Records **S1–S3** transfer actual binary image data. They differ only in the size of the field alloted for representing the starting address of the data (the **A . . . A** field). Sixteen-, 24-, and 32-bit addresses may be represented.

After all binary image data have been transferred, a termination record must be sent. Records **S7–S9** are provided for this purpose. Strictly speaking, a termination record with

```
S0 06 0000 484452 1B

S2 14 100000 4E56000033FC0001001040F242790010 FA
S2 14 100010 40EA4279001040EC33FC000100103C48 E6

S2 14 103C20 0000000000000000000000000000000000 7F
S2 14 103C30 0000000000000000000000000000000000 6F
S2 08 103C40 00103C40 DF

S9 03 0000 FC
```
Figure 11.2. Example S-Record File.

an address field that matches the size of the corresponding field in the preceding binary image records should be sent; but, in practice, most target processors will accept any terminator record, and the **S9** record is usually sent since it is the shortest.

The record type designator characters are followed by two characters (**LL** in Figure 11.1) that specify the number of bytes represented by the remainder of the record. Note that each byte is represented by the two ASCII characters that encode the four-bit nibbles of the byte. So the number of ASCII characters in the remainder of the record is actually twice the value indicated in the **LL** field.

As mentioned earlier, the next field in binary image records contains an ASCII representation of the starting address for the program bytes that follow. Records with three different sizes for this field are provided to accommodate target processors with corresponding address bus sizes. Most modern processors have at least a 24-bit address bus, so that the **S1** record is of little current value. On the other hand, program sizes seldom exceed 24 bits. If they do, a different transfer method should be found, since the S-record method will probably be too slow. As a result, the **S2** record format, which supports 24-bit addresses, is most commonly used to transfer program image data.

The address field in the termination records is occasionally used to indicate the program's starting address. In theory, a program could then be downloaded and started automatically by the PROM monitor; but, in practice, this feature is usually not supported, and programs are started by other means (see Section 11.3).

In **S0** records the address field always contains four ASCII zeros and serves no functional purpose. The next field in this record may contain any ASCII string. It could be displayed on the target system's console to identify the file being downloaded, but, again, this feature is seldom supported by PROM monitors.

The address field in the program image records is followed by an ASCII representation of the program bytes to be transferred by the record. Again, each byte is divided into two four-bit nibbles that are encoded as ASCII characters.

Every S-record is terminated with two bytes representing the checksum of all bytes encoded in the record following the record type designator field. The checksum is formed by simply summing the bytes represented in these fields, truncating the sum to a single byte, and one's complementing the result. This value is then converted to ASCII and stored in the two-byte **CS** field at the end of the record. When a record is downloaded, the target system compares its computed checksum to the **CS** field and returns an appropriate response to the host. The host may or may not wait for this response. Typically, the chance of an error occurring is so low that it is not worth the additional delay associated with waiting for each reply.

As indicated earlier, the monitors in most target processors contain a utility that will accept S-records and load the represented data into the specified memory locations; but we will need to provide our own utilities on the host to construct S-records from program image files and send them via a serial line to the target system. In the next three sections we will examine a set of utility programs that are appropriate for a Sun-3 host running the SunOS 3.2 version of UNIX. They should also work with little or no modification on other hosts that run an operating system based on Berkeley UNIX. It should also be possible to adapt them to run on other hosts.

11.2.2 Generating S-Records

Figure 11.3 shows a listing for utility program **srecs.** As the file header indicates, this utility may be used to create a file of S-records from a program image file generated by the UNIX linker. Since the listing is thoroughly commented, we will not review the program's operation in detail. Instead, we will simply highlight a few points of interest and indicate some modifications that may be needed to accommodate different target systems.

```
/*
 *      FILE SRECS.C
 *
 *      This program reads the load module file named in the first
 *      argument of its command line and generates the S-record output
 *      file named in its second argument.  The output file is suitable
 *      for downloading to a single board computer.  The input file load
 *      module MUST have the format of a Unix "a.out" file, as produced
 *      by the Unix "ld" linker.  An example linker command is:
 *
 *              ld -X -T 100000 -o userfile.a userfile.o -lc -lm
 *
 *      An example srecs calling syntax is:
 *
 *              srecs userfile.a userfile.sr
 */
#define PMODE 0644              /*RW for owner, R for others       */
#define BUFSIZ      16          /*input buffer size (bytes)        */

int f1,f2                       ;/*file descriptors                */

union{
    struct{                     /*a.out file header structure      */
        short   mach            ;/*machine type                    */
        short   fmagic          ;/*Unix "magic number"             */
        long    tsize           ;/*text size (bytes, even)         */
        long    dsize           ;/*data size (  "      "  )         */
        long    bsize           ;/*bss size                        */
        long    ssize           ;
        long    entry           ;/*program-start address           */
        long    rtsize          ;
        long    rdsize          ;
    }head                       ;
    unsigned char inbuf[32]     ;/*sturcture overlay buffer        */
}u                              ;
```

Figure 11.3. A Utility to Generate S-Records.

```
int nr                                ;/*read byte count                    */
long filsiz                           ;/*object file size (bytes)            */
char strec[] = "S00600004844521B";/*start record (S0)                       */
char serec[] = "S9030000FC"          ;/*end record (S9)                      */
char recend[] = {'\r','\n',0}         ;/*end of a record (CR,LF,NUL)         */
long ldaddr                           ;/*load address                        */
char outbuf[100]                      ;/*S-record output buffer              */
long outidx                           ;/*outbuf[] index                      */
long count                            ;/* # of bytes read from input         */
long i                                ;/*working index                       */
int chksum                            ;/*checksum calculation variable       */
unsigned int inchr                    ;/*input character                     */
unsigned int digit                    ;/*output digit                        */


main(argc,argv)
int argc                                ;
char *argv[]                            ;
{
/*
 *Check the number of input arguments.
 */
if(argc != 3){
      printf("One input file and one output file needed\n") ;
      return                            ;
}
/*
 *Open the input file; create output file.
 */
if((f1 = open(argv[1],0)) == -1){
      printf("Can't open %s\n",argv[1]) ;
      return                            ;
}
if((f2 = creat(argv[2],PMODE)) == -1){
      printf("Can't create %s\n",argv[2]) ;
      return                            ;
}

/*
 *Output the S0 header record.
 */
```

(Continued on next page.)

```
if(write(f2,strec,16) != 16){
     printf("Can't write S0 header record to %s\n",argv[2]) ;
     return                              ;
}
/*
 *Output the record-end string.
 */
if(write(f2,recend,3) != 3){
     printf("Can't output record-end string(1)\n") ;
     return                              ;
}
/*
 *Read the file header; check it and get the file size (text & data only)
 *and program entry point.
 */
if((nr = read(f1,u.inbuf,32)) <= 0){
     printf("Can't read %s header\n",argv[1]) ;
     return                              ;
}
else{
    if((u.head.fmagic != 0407) && (u.head.fmagic != 0413)){
        printf("Illegal input file header; fmagic = %o\n",u.head.fmagic) ;
          return                         ;
    }
    filsiz = u.head.tsize + u.head.dsize ;/*get file size              */
    ldaddr = u.head.entry                ;/*get program entry point    */
}

/*
 *Read bytes from input; form S2 records and output them.
 */
do{
     if(filsiz > BUFSIZ){                      /*chose record size          */
          count = BUFSIZ           ;
          filsiz -= BUFSIZ         ;
     }
     else{
          count = filsiz           ;
          filsiz = 0               ;
     }
     if((nr = read(f1,u.inbuf,count)) <= 0){
          printf("Can't read %s\n",argv[1]) ;
          return                   ;
     }
```

Figure 11.3. (*continued*) A Utility to Generate S-Records.

```
/*
 *Build the S2 header, the count and the load address; start checksum
 *calculation.
 */
        outidx = 0                       ;/*start the index                */
        outbuf[outidx++] = 'S'           ;/*store 'S2'                     */
        outbuf[outidx++] = '2'           ;
        chksum = count + 4               ;/*start checksum calculation     */
                                          /*(+4 is for length & addr. bytes)*/
        intasc(count + 4,2)              ;/*convert length; store it       */
        chksum += ((ldaddr >> 16) & 0xFF);/*Add 3 byte load address        */
        chksum += ((ldaddr >> 8) & 0xFF) ;/*to checksum.                   */
        chksum += (ldaddr & 0xFF)        ;
        intasc(ldaddr,6)                 ;/*convert & store load address   */
        ldaddr += count                  ;/*advance load address           */
/*
 *Now read each byte from inbuf[]; add it to the checksum; convert &
 *store it.
 */
        for(i = 0; i < count; i++){
                inchr = u.inbuf[i]       ;
                chksum += inchr          ;
                intasc(inchr,2)          ;
        }
/*
 *One's complement the checksum; AND off all but the lower byte; store it.
 */
        chksum = ~chksum & 0xFF          ;
        intasc(chksum,2)                 ;
/*
 *Now output the contents of outbuf[].
 */
        if(write(f2,outbuf,outidx) != outidx){
                printf("Can't write an S2 record\n") ;
                return                   ;
        }
/*
 *Output the record-end string.
 */
        if(write(f2,recend,3) != 3){
                printf("Can't output record-end string(2)\n") ;
                return                   ;
        }
}while(filsiz > 0)                       ;/*repeat while bytes remain      */
```

(Continued on next page.)

```
/*
 *Output the file-termination S9 record.
 */
if(write(f2,serec,10) != 10){
      printf("Can't write final S9 record\n") ;
      return                    ;
}
/*
 *Output the record-end string to terminate the S9 record.
 */
if(write(f2,recend,3) != 3){
      printf("Can't write record-end string(3)\n") ;
      return                    ;
}
}                                     /*end of main() function           */

/*
 *-intasc(intgr,nchrs)
 *     This function converts the binary number in 'intgr' to 'nchrs'
 *     of ASCII hex digits and places them in array outbuf[].  If more
 *     than 'nchrs' hex digits exist in 'intgr' or if 'nchrs' is out of
 *     range (1 to 6), it informs the operator and exits the program.
 */

intasc(intgr,nchrs)
unsigned int intgr                ;
int nchrs                         ;
{
switch(nchrs){
   case 6:
      digit = intgr/0x100000     ;/*get sixth digit                  */
      intgr %= 0x100000          ;/*save remainder                   */
      if(digit > 0xF){
            printf("intasc() input integer too large\n") ;
            exit(0)              ;
      }
      if(digit > 9)              /*convert it to ASCII               */
            digit += ('A' - 10) ;
      else
            digit += '0'         ;
      outbuf[outidx++] = digit   ;/*store it                         */
                                  /*Note: processing falls thru!!     */
```

Figure 11.3. (*continued*) A Utility to Generate S-Records.

```
case 5:
    digit = intgr/0x10000          ;/*get fifth digit              */
    intgr %= 0x10000               ;
    if(digit > 9)                   /*convert it to ASCII          */
            digit += ('A' - 10)    ;
    else
            digit += '0'           ;
    outbuf[outidx++] = digit       ;

case 4:
    digit = intgr/0x1000           ;/*get fourth digit             */
    intgr %= 0x1000                ;
    if(digit > 9)                   /*convert it to ASCII          */
            digit += ('A' - 10)    ;
    else
            digit += '0'           ;
    outbuf[outidx++] = digit       ;


case 3:
    digit = intgr/0x100            ;/*get third digit              */
    intgr %= 0x100                 ;
    if(digit > 9)                   /*convert it to ASCII          */
            digit += ('A' - 10)    ;
    else
            digit += '0'           ;
    outbuf[outidx++] = digit       ;

case 2:                             /*etc.                         */
    digit = intgr/0x10             ;
    intgr %= 0x10                  ;
    if(digit > 9)
            digit += ('A' - 10)    ;
    else
            digit += '0'           ;
    outbuf[outidx++] = digit       ;
```

(Continued on next page.)

```
case 1:
   if(intgr > 9)
        digit = intgr + ('A' - 10) ;
   else
        digit = intgr + '0'         ;
   outbuf[outidx++] = digit         ;
   break                            ;

default:
   printf("intasc() illegal nchrs: nchrs = %d\n",nchrs) ;
   exit(0)                          ;
}                                    /*end of switch              */
}                                    /*end of intasc() function   */
```

Figure 11.3 (*continued*) A Utility to Generate S-Records.

The UNIX linker produces a program file that has a so-called "a.out" file structure. The file begins with a specific header. A duplicate header structure is defined in the **srecs.c** program and is overlayed by buffer **inbuf[]**. The program uses **inbuf[]** to load an image file's header into the structure and then accesses fields in it using structure entries. It should be noted that the header structure shown in Figure 11.3 is appropriate for a.out files generated by the SunOS 3.2 version of UNIX. Other flavors and versions of UNIX may employ a different header structure. For these systems the header structure shown should be modified to accommodate the differences.

Once the header is loaded, the program checks the file type to be sure it is a program image file and then reads text and data sizes and the program-start address (the address of the program's **main()** function). It then proceeds to read 16 byte blocks of program image data from the file and construct **S2** records from them. This process continues as long as image data remains in the file. Each record is output to the file specified by the program's second calling argument. Finally, an **S9** file-termination record is output and the utility terminates.

For some target processors S-records are received through the same serial port used by the console. In this case, it is convenient to send the command that selects the download mode before sending the first S-record. This may be implemented by simply including a text line containing the command (e.g., **L01**) as the first line in the S-record file.

The manuals for some target processors indicate that a fixed number of ASCII zeros should be sent between S-records. This gives the processor time to interpret and process each record before another one arrives. These strings may be included in the S-record file, as required, or inserted during the actual download operation; but since sending these zeros delays the transfer, it is worthwhile to experiment with the actual number of characters needed. Often they may be eliminated altogether.

11.2.3 Downloading S-Records

Once S-records have been produced by utility **srecs,** a way must be found to transfer them to the target system. Figure 11.4 shows a listing for a program that will perform this operation. Again, this second utility is well commented, so we will only discuss a few details.

```
/*
 *      FILE DWNLD.C
 *
 *      This program downloads the S-records file specified by its first
 *      argument to a single board computer that is connected to the
 *      serial port specified by its second argument.
 *
 *            An example calling syntax is:
 *
 *            dwnld userfile.sr /dev/ttyb
 *
 *      Note that the tty port MUST NOT be configured into the Unix
 *      system (i. e., the /etc/ttys file entry for ttyb must start
 *      with a zero.  Then re-boot Unix).
 */
#include <sys/ioctl.h>
struct sgttyb data                   ;/*output port characteristics   */

#define BUFSZ 2048                    /*transfer buffer size           */

int f1,f2                            ;/*I/O file descriptors           */
char buf[BUFSZ]                      ;/*transfer buffer                */
char inchr                           ;/*received character             */
int n                                ;/*number of bytes received       */

main(argc,argv)
int argc                             ;
char *argv[]                         ;
{
/*
 *Check the number of input arguments.
 */
if(argc != 3){
      printf("Two arguments required\n") ;
      return                         ;
}
```

Figure 11.4. A Utility to Download S-Records. (*Continued on next page.*)

```
/*
 *Open the input file.
 */
if((f1 = open(argv[1],0)) == -1){
      printf("Can't open %s\n",argv[1]) ;
      return                            ;
}
/*
 *Open output device.
 */
if((f2 = open(argv[2],1)) == -1){
      printf("Can't open %s\n",argv[2]) ;
      return                            ;
}


/*
 * Get the characteristics of the output port and change them.
 */
if(ioctl(f2,TIOCGETP,&data) < 0){
      printf("Can't get characteristics of output port\n") ;

}                                         ;
else {
      data.sg_flags = 0                   ;/*clear flag bits            */
      ioctl(f2,TIOCSETP,&data)            ;/*set new characteristics    */


/*
 *Send the contents of the input file to the output port.
 */
while((n = read(f1,buf,BUFSZ)) > 0){
      write(f2,buf,n)                     ;
}
printf("Download completed\n")            ;

}                                 /*end of DWNLD.C file            */
```

Figure 11.4. *(continued)* A Utility to Download S-Records.

The function simply opens the input file and output device and then copies data from the file to the device. To accomplish this, the host's serial port must be configured properly for communication with the target system. For the Sun-3, this means that the port must be "configured out" of the system. That is, it must not be configured as a normal login port. This change is implemented by making the indicated adjustment to the system's **/etc/ttys** file and then rebooting the system (for SunOS 4.0 and more recent versions, edit file **/etc/ttytab**).

The host's port must also be compatible with the line discipline (i.e., baud rate, stop bits, parity, etc.) expected by the target system. For the case shown in Figure 11.4, the target of interest required that all flag bits in the port's characteristics data structure be cleared. A different choice may be needed to establish communications with an alternate target system.

Before the **dwnld** utility is activated and begins transferring records, the target system must be placed in the proper mode to accept the records. This is accomplished by entering an appropriate console command (e.g., **LO2**). The target system will then wait, and S-records may then be sent by running the **dwnld** utility. When the transfer is complete, both systems will display their respective prompts.

Note that **dwnld** does not wait for acknowledgements that may be sent after each record is transferred. As indicated earlier, this is usually acceptable, since the transmission link is very reliable. It should also be noted that the **srecs** and **dwnld** utilities could be combined into a single program. The resulting utility would convert binary image data to S-records and download them immediately to the target system as they are produced. This would eliminate the need for the intermediate S-record file. Of course, the disadvantage of this approach is that each time a file is downloaded, the S-records must be recreated. For a stable program it is more efficient to create the S-record file only once.

11.2.4 Loading Multiprocessor Systems

The S-record method may also be used to load programs into multiple processors. In fact, if the processors have dual ported memory that is mapped into the address space of the VMEbus, all programs may be loaded through the serial port of a single processor using the **srecs** and **dwnld** utilities described in the previous two sections. When the processor that is receiving S-records determines that the load address specified in a record is outside the address range of on-board memory, it will automatically attempt to write the data to memory on the VMEbus. A second processor's memory that is mapped into the appropriate address range will then accept the code. Thus, the programs for a multiple processor system may be loaded by simply downloading consecutive S-record files—each file specifying an appropriate starting address for the memory of a separate target processor.

This is all that needs to be said for processors that map their dual ported memory to the same physical address range for both on-board and off-board accesses. For example, if a processor board's memory is mapped into the VMEbus address space starting at 800000 hex and a program is linked to start at 801000, then the on-board processor may run it starting at this address and the program will generate memory references that are appropriate for the processor's view of memory. But this is not the case if the dual ported memory is mapped into different address ranges for on-board and off-board references. In this case, the program file must be modified to compensate for memory access offset.

We dealt with the memory access offset phenomenon earlier in Section 10.5 with reference to pointer queues defined in a common memory region. In that case pointers had to be adjusted to compensate for the different common memory starting addresses seen by on-board and off-board processors. A similar adjustment must be made when programs are loaded through a memory's VMEbus port and run by an on-board processor.

Consider a case in which a processor board's memory is mapped into the VMEbus starting at address 800000 hex but into the on-board processor's address space starting at zero. Then a program that is loaded over the VMEbus starting at address 801000 hex will be seen to start at address 1000 hex by the processor. In this case the program must be linked to start at 1000 if its memory references are to be correct for the on-board processor; but if we use the **srecs** utility to generate S-records for this program, they will start at address 1000 rather than 801000, as required. What is needed is another utility that can "fix" the program's binary image file such that S-records generated from it will start at address 801000 hex. Figure 11.5 shows a listing for a utility that can accomplish this.

The **fix** utility reads the header of a binary image file, checks to make sure it is an executable file, and then adds the hex offset value specified by the utility's second calling argument to the program-start address variable in the copied header. It then writes the revised header back to the file. This operation effectively changes the address at which the program will be loaded, since the **srecs** utility uses the file header's progam-start address to determine the load address for the S-records it generates.

```
/*
 *
 *      FILE: FIX.C
 *
 *      This file contains a program to change the program-start
 *      address in the header of an executable program file
 *      (i.e., the 'entry' variable in an executable file's a.out
 *      header). The 'fix' program has two arguments as follows:
 *
 *                      fix prog_name hex_offset
 *      where:
 *          'prog_name' is the name of the executable program
 *                      file.
 *          'hex_offset' is a hex number that will be added to
 *                      the existing entry point address.
 *      Example:
 *                      fix progfile 800000
 *
 *      If 'progfile' was linked to start at 1000 hex, its
 *      program-start address will be changed to 801000 hex.
 */
```

Figure 11.5. A Utility To Fix a Binary Image File.

```
int fd                      ;/*file descriptor             */

struct{                      /*a.out file header structure  */
      short mach            ;/*machine type                 */
      short fmagic          ;/*Unix "magic number"          */
      long tsize            ;/*text size (bytes, even)      */
      long dsize            ;/*data size (bytes, even)      */
      long bsize            ;/*bss size                     */
      long ssize            ;
      long entry            ;/*program-start address        */
      long rtsize           ;
      long rdsize           ;
}head                        ;

long offset                 ;/*converted input 'hex_offset'  */

main(argc,argv)
int argc                    ;
char *argv[]                ;
{

/*
 *Check the number of input arguments.
 */
if(argc != 3){
      printf("Two arguments required\n") ;
      return                ;
}

/*
 *Open the file for reading.
 */
if((fd = open(argv[1],0)) < 0){
      printf("Can't open %s for reading\n",argv[1]) ;
      return                ;
}

/*
 *Read the header (32 bytes).
 */
if(read(fd,&head,32) < 0){
      printf("Can't read file header\n") ;
      return                ;
}
```

(Continued on next page.)

```
/*
 *Close the file.
 */
close(fd)                       ;

/*
 *Test the magic number for a valid executable file type.
 */

if((head.fmagic != 0407) && (head.fmagic != 0413)){
      printf("File not executable\n") ;
      return                ;
}

/*
 *Convert 'hex_offset' ASCII string to a binary long.
 */
if((offset = strtol(argv[2],0,16)) < 0){
      printf("Can't convert %s to a long\n",argv[2]) ;
      return                ;
}

/*
 *Add the offset to the buffered header program-start address.
 */
head.entry += offset        ;

/*
 *Re-open the file - for writing this time.
 */
if((fd = open(argv[1],1)) < 0){
      printf("Can't open %s for writing\n",argv[1]) ;
      return                ;
}

/*
 *Write the revised header.
 */
if(write(fd,&head,32) < 0){
      printf("Can't write file header\n") ;
      return                ;
}

printf("Fix completed successfully\n") ;

}                              /*end of FIX.C file          */
```

Figure 11.5. (*continued*) A Utility To Fix a Binary Image File.

Thus, for our example case, the **fix** utility may be used to add 800000 to the 1000 hex starting address generated by the linker. The **srecs** utility will then produce records that start at address 801000 hex, and the program may be loaded across the VMEbus. Once loaded, it will run properly starting at 1000.

11.3 STARTING REAL-TIME PROGRAMS

A program that has been loaded into a target system must be initiated by some means. There are a variety of ways of accomplish this—either manually or automatically. We will explore some of the possibilities for both single and multiple processor systems in the next two sections.

11.3.1 Starting Single Processor Systems

In Section 11.2.1, we mentioned a method for automatically starting a program by means of a file-termination S-record. A target system's PROM monitor may obtain a program's starting address from this record and initiate its execution. In Section 11.2.2, we also indicated that the command to activate the monitor's download utility could be included at the start of an S-record file. Thus, by combining these two techniques it would be possible to automatically and remotely load and start a program in a target system. But we also noted that this method for starting a program is typically not implemented in most monitors. So another method must be found.

The most commonly used method for starting programs is to simply use the monitor's GO utility. The GO command is entered followed by the program's starting address. This is especially convenient during system testing and is not an unreasonable approach for systems that must be controlled and monitored via a terminal during normal operation. But, for systems that must start and operate without supervision, an automatic method is needed. This may be implemented by using the processor's nonmaskable interrupt (NMI) facility.

A monitor typically disables all interrupts—except the NMI—when power is turned on or the processor is reset. Typically, the NMI is controlled by an ABORT switch on the processor's front panel. When the switch is toggled, the monitor performs a so-called "soft-boot" operation, but it is possible to modify the monitor so that the NMI may perform a different operation. Specifically, it may be used to initiate program execution. We will first look at the operations that an NMI handler might perform to start a program and then discuss methods for modifying a PROM monitor to implement these operations.

Most processor boards have a preferred program start address. This may be the first location in the board's program memory or it may be a higher address if the monitor allocates the first locations for exception vectors and parameter storage. In any case, an NMI handler may be programmed to test the contents of this start location to see if a program is present.

Compilers typically start a program with an assembly language **link** instruction. The first word of this instruction is always 4e56 hex, so that the NMI handler may detect the presence of a program by testing for this value. If a program is found to be present, the handler may start it running. On the other hand, if the handler does not find the 4e56 value at the program start location, it can perform the normal monitor soft-boot operation. Thus, by implementing this technique, a program may be started manually by simply toggling the processor's ABORT switch or by causing an NMI by some other hardware means.

In the next section, we shall see that the NMI method will also provide us with a way to automatically start a multiprocessor system, but first we shall look at methods for changing the monitor program.

Clearly, the easiest way to modify a PROM monitor program is to simply change the source code. Some manufacturers make this code available at a reasonable price—and some don't. If the source code is not available, it is still possible to determine the contents of the program to the extent necessary to make the needed changes. One will need to apply some "reverse engineering" techniques to accomplish this. Obviously, one should make sure the legal agreement with the board manufacturer is not violated by these activities.

The contents of the monitor may be determined by disassembling it using the monitor's disassembler. In fact, if a hardcopy terminal is available, you can get a listing of the entire program. This listing will be somewhat difficult to read, since no symbolic variable names or comments will be present. On the other hand, only a few pieces of information are needed to make the necessary changes.

It will be necessary to find the point in the program where the NMI interrupt vector is set in the processor's exception vector table. The address that is stored must be changed to point to the new interrupt handler. One will also have to add the new interrupt handler to the program. The existing monitor typically will not completely fill the PROM, and additional space is usually available above it for the new handler. If the PROM does not contain sufficient free space, a larger PROM may sometimes be substituted.

Once all software changes have been determined, the monitor should be copied into the memory of a PROM burner and patched to change the address stored in the NMI exception vector. The modified program may then be burned into the new PROM. The new interrupt handler must then be loaded into the PROM burner and added to the PROM.

11.3.2 Starting Multiple Processor Programs

The technique of using a nonmaskable interrupt to start a program in a single processor system, as described in the last section, is also directly applicable to starting the programs in a multiprocessor system. With this approach, the programs may be started manually by simply toggling their ABORT switches. A procedure for synchronizing their operation after they start was discussed in Section 10.7. To review, each controlled processor performs its initialization operations, sets a **ready** flag in its common memory region and then polls its **go** flag. When the processors have all set their **ready** flags, a controlling processor sets their **go** flags in an order that is appropriate for the application program.

The NMI technique may also be used to start the programs automatically if it is possible to configure the processor boards such that an NMI may be initiated by the mailbox interrupt mechanism. We discussed the mailbox interrupt concept in Section 10.4.4 with reference to passing buffer pointers between processors. In that case the interrupt was used to signal the arrival of a pointer in a processor's input queue. Briefly, the technique allows a processor to cause an interrupt in another processor by simply writing to a location in a specified region of the target processor's VMEbus memory space.

If a controlling processor can cause an NMI in a controlled processor, the program in that processor may be started automatically by implementing the procedures described in the previous section. Thus, by using this approach, one processor may start the programs in the other processors of a multiprocessor system by simply writing to their respective mailbox interrupt spaces.

12

System Hardware Characteristics

As a result of our study of real-time system software requirements and possible solutions in the previous chapters, we are now in a position to identify some desirable characteristics for system hardware. Clearly, each project will require a unique collection of processor and interface components to satisfy its particular design requirements, but it is also true that most systems in this class have common characteristics that may be identified and supported by equipment designed specifically for embedded computer applications. Indeed, a very vigorous industry has emerged to supply hardware solutions for this category of computer systems. This is, of course, beneficial to those of us who must make equipment decisions, since a wide variety of choices reduces our design risk. On the other hand, we need to have some basis for choosing a particular set of components.

In this chapter, we shall identify hardware features that have been found to be generally useful in the design of real-time systems. We shall also discuss services that could be supplied by hardware but are not yet available. Our primary objective will be to provide some general principles that may be used as a basis for making equipment selection decisions, but we shall also be interested in suggesting hardware design areas that have yet to be adequately addressed by equipment suppliers. We hope that we may look forward to solutions in these remaining areas in the near future.

In general, real-time system hardware consists of processing elements, equipment interfaces, and possibly a backplane or bus. Again, we will limit our discussion to systems based on the VMEbus technology, for the reasons stated in Chapter 10. We will also concentrate on processing elements, both at the board and chip level, since general statements concerning these components will apply to a wide range of system designs. On the other hand, equipment interfaces are so diverse that it would not be meaningful to try to state general principles for their selection. However, it will be possible to draw some conclusions concerning the way these interfaces should be physically accessed by processing elements. We will therefore limit our discussion of interfaces to their accessibility.

It should be kept in mind that the equipment selection principles discussed in the following sections reflect the author's personal experience in building real-time systems that satisfy a particular set of design requirements. You may find that a modified or altogether different set of principles is appropriate. An important point that this chapter attempts to make is that it is possible to develop a basis for making equipment selection decisions and that both hardware and software considerations must be taken into account in arriving at that basis. The material in this chapter is offered as a starting point for beginning the process of developing one's own set of design rules.

12.1 PROCESSOR BOARD HARDWARE FEATURES

The VMEbus industry provides a wide spectrum of processor boards. Generally speaking, the selections are targeted at the needs of two distinct market segments. One segment is the general-purpose computer/workstation market. For this market the processor must be capable of supporting an operating system—often a version of UNIX. Boards for this market segment may usually be identified by the fact that they contain a memory management unit (MMU). This device supports the mapping of virtual addresses to physical memory addresses and also provides protection mechanisms needed by the operating system. Since real-time systems typically do not need these services, the MMU is of little value. As a consequence, if a board containing this device is to be used in an embedded system design, it must be possible to bypass the MMU. All other factors being equal, one should choose a processor board that does not contain an MMU, since the board space could better be used to provide some other service.

The second major market segment is embedded systems. Since this segment spans a wide range of applications, the processor boards designed to support it tend to be more versatile. For example, they generally contain several types of interface chips that support standard communication protocols. These ports are very important for real-time systems, since they provide direct access to equipment without having to transfer data across the bus. As noted earlier, bus bandwidth is a scarce resource that must be preserved. These devices remove some traffic from the bus.

Processor boards designed for embedded systems sometimes also contain a provision for attaching a so-called "daughter board." These small boards provide a way to customize the processor by adding an additional interface. Daughter boards containing standard interfaces may be purchased from the manufacturer or the user may construct his own. Again, this feature increases processor versatility and also improves system efficiency by removing traffic from the bus.

In the subsections that follow we shall examine several features of embedded system processor boards that facilitate the construction of real-time systems and aid in the testing and operation of the software that runs on them. We shall see that the features discussed support various aspects of the software architecture we studied in the earlier chapters of this book. The discussion will emphasize the relationship between hardware and software design decisions and the importance of considering both if one expects to extract the greatest possible performance from a system.

12.1.1 Support for System Monitoring

We saw in Chapters 5, 7, and 9 that it is very convenient to be able to monitor the performance of a system by toggling bits of a parallel port at various points in an operating program. Activity may then be viewed with the aid of a logic analyzer. This is an effective way to determine the operation of a program without substantially affecting its speed of operation. Sending single characters over a serial line to an idle terminal will also cause very little disruption of system timing. It is also very useful to be able to monitor program operation visually by means of a simple illuminated display.

Some processors include a seven-segment display or a set of light emitting diodes on the board's front panel. The display is driven by a software-accessible parallel port. A program may use this port to display status and/or error information. This "window" into the internal operating condition of a running program has proven to be invaluable for diagnosing system problems. It is especially useful in multiprocessor systems.

Consider a system that contains several processor boards. If one of the processors encounters an error, it is likely that the entire system will stall. The operator must then determine which processor experienced the error and then discover the nature of the error. Typically, a terminal is attached to one processor and is serviced by the application program in that processor. To get access to that processor's PROM monitor, the entire system must usually be reset, but this may disturb the system state that is needed to diagnose the problem.

Even if the monitor on one processor may be activated independently, there is no guarantee that it can be used to access another processor or equipment interface, since the error may have caused the bus to lock. What is needed is a way to display error information directly on each processor board. An illuminated display on each board satisfies this requirement. By scanning the displays on all processors, an operator may determine immediately which processor experienced the error and the nature of the error.

For processor boards that do not include an illuminated display but do provide a parallel port, it is possible to build a simple display and attach it to the port with a cable. The port's pins should also be brought out to a connector so that logic analyzer probes may be attached. This addition is functionally equivalent to an on-board display.

12.1.2 Support for System Communication

In Chapter 10 we discussed the importance of dual-ported memory for supporting inter-processor communications. We developed software methods for establishing common memory regions that contain data structures for passing parameters and messages between processors. We also extended the concept of buffer pointer queues to support inter-processor communication. To implement this technique, we noted that a processor board must support the test-and-set instruction. This instruction is needed to maintain a queue's semaphore flag. Thus, if the buffer pointer queue method is to be used, a candidate processor board must provide both dual-ported memory and support for the indivisible test-and-set instruction.

The queue method supplies a means for passing a pointer to a data block between processors, but it does not provide any support for actually moving the data, should that be necessary. Clearly, data may be moved using a standard program loop. The transfer rate for this method may be considerably increased if the processor includes an instruction cache that may be enabled and the instructions for the loop will fit entirely within the cache. But this technique is substantially slower than the bus is capable of supporting. Ideally, we would like to be able to move blocks of data over the bus at the fastest possible rate supported by the bus. In addition to interprocessor communication, we would also like to be able to move data between processor and interface boards at this maximum rate.

Data may be moved at a faster rate by using a Direct Memory Access (DMA) device. Briefly, this device is essentially a special-purpose processor chip that performs only the data transfer operation. A program initiates a transfer by sending it a source address, destination address, data block size, and a start command. The device then moves the data.

The principle reason why a DMA device can transfer data faster than a program loop is that it does not have to read and execute program instructions in addition to moving the data. Instead, it contains an internal "hard wired" program for performing its single operation. Conventional DMA chips transfer data across the VMEbus using the normal bus protocol for single data transfers. That is, an address is placed on the bus, followed by the data. Using this technique, a device, such as the Motorola 68450, can transfer data at rates up to 4 Mbytes/sec, but the VMEbus also supports a faster method.

In the block transfer mode, the VMEbus can support burst transfers of up to 256 bytes at its fastest transfer rate—40 Mbytes/sec. For this mode, the bus master device (the DMA chip) sends only one address to the bus slave. This is the starting address for the transfer. The slave then simply increments this address for each data item transferred. The resulting decrease in bus traffic is responsible for the increased data transfer rate.

At present, only a few VMEbus products support the block transfer protocol. We can expect to see more prevalent support for this mode in the near future when an industry-standard bus interface chip becomes more widely used. This chip supports the block transfer DMA mode between boards containing the chip. With this advancement, the effective bandwidth capabilities of VMEbus systems should be enhanced considerably.

12.1.3 Support for Program Loading and Initiation

The S-record method for loading programs was examined in Chapter 11. Although this procedure is reliable and is supported by the monitors in most available processor boards, it has two important limitations. As indicated in Chapter 11, it is relatively slow. In addition, it requires the host and target systems to be connected by a cable. Clearly, we would like to avoid the inconvenience of having to wait unreasonably long periods of time for programs to load into one or several processors of a target system. It is also possible that the target system will be located at a remote site or in a vehicle. In that case it may be either inconvenient or impossible to connect it to the host via a cable. We would therefore like to have an alternative method for loading programs that avoids the limitations of the S-record technique.

We are all familiar with the use of the floppy disk as a medium for transferring programs and data between computers. This technique has been very successful in the personal computer market. It is also reasonably successful in avoiding the limitations of the S-record method in that programs load relatively quickly and the medium is transportable.

The floppy disk owes much of its success to the fact that a standard has been established for the organization of data on the disk. As long as manufacturers adhere to the prevailing standard, programs and data may be transferred between computers without difficulty. It would also be very convenient for real-time system designers if a similar standard were available for the transfer of programs between host and target systems via a floppy disk. Since no such standard currently exists, we are left to our own resources if we wish to use this method.

In the subsections that follow we will discuss the characteristics of a floppy disk interface that has been developed and used successfully to transfer program image and data files between UNIX-based host computers and target VMEbus systems. Once again, it will be necessary to modify the target system's PROM monitor to include a floppy disk driver. Although this addition is not large (less than 8K bytes), it is beyond the scope of this book to present and discuss program listings for it. Instead, we will limit our discussion to a description of the interface design and to a review of its functional operation. Our primary objective will be to provide you with a design approach for establishing your own interface, should you decide to do so. Hopefully, the material presented will also stimulate interest in establishing an industry standard.

12.1.3.1 Accessing a Floppy Disk from a UNIX Host

Several UNIX-based host computers include a floppy disk drive as a standard peripheral or as an optional accessory. For example, the drive for a Sun-3 includes a SCSI controller that allows it to be configured into the system as a secondary disk. The drive is normally treated the same as any other disk on a system in that it may be mounted and unmounted using the UNIX **mount** and **umount** commands, respectively, and a UNIX file system may be created on it using the **mkfs** ("make file system") command. But before a file system can be installed, the disk must be formatted.

Disk formatting involves the partitioning of disk surfaces into tracks and sectors. Since the floppy disk owes much of its popularity to the personal computer market, it is not surprising to find that most UNIX-based hosts use the same disk parititioning arrangement as these machines. Thus, we begin to see the basis for a possible industry standard: a floppy disk with a standard personal computer format and a standard UNIX file system.

Once a disk has been formatted and a file system has been installed, it is possible to access it using the normal UNIX commands provided for manipulating files and directories on any other system disk. Specifically, files may be copied to the disk using the **cp** command in a sequence similar to the following:

```
# cd /                                    change to root directory
# mount /dev/sf0 /flop                    mount the floppy disk drive
# cp /usr/name/filename /flop             copy a file to the disk
# sync                                    flush file buffers to disk
# sync
# umount /dev/sf0                          unmount the floppy drive
```

The disk may then be removed from the drive and transported to a target system.

12.1.3.2 Accessing a Floppy Disk from a Target System

In the last section we discovered that it is relatively easy to access a floppy disk from a host system using standard UNIX utilities and a driver supplied by the manufacturer. But the interface becomes more difficult in the target system, since we must supply our own driver and add it to a target processor's PROM monitor.

As with most peripherals, a floppy disk interface design must be approached at two levels. One must first deal with the physical interface to the drive and to tracks and sectors on the disk, and then with the logical structure of the disk file system. At the physical level, manufacturers currently provide either a floppy disk interface chip or a SCSI interface for accessing a disk. In either case, the first step in writing a driver is to establish access to the data in any desired disk sector. This first level interface may then be used to investigate the structure of the disk's file system.

There are several sources of information on the basic structure of a UNIX file system (*see* Refs. 1–5). It essentially consists of a linked list of so-called "i-node" data structures that ultimately point to data blocks. A block consists physically of one or more disk sectors. The driver must "navigate" through the i-node linked list to determine the locations of data blocks belonging to a file. Since each manufacturer's implementation of this file structure is unique, one must perform some reverse engineering to determine the details of a particular design.

The content of specific disk sectors may be determined with the aid of the first level driver discussed earlier and the UNIX **dd** and **od** utilities. With some perseverance, this information may be used to discover the structure of the file system. It will then be possible to extend the driver to support accesses to directories and files placed on the disk by the host. Note that for our purposes it is not necessary for the driver to be able to create or delete files—we may rely on the host for these operations.

Once a working driver has been written, it must be added to the target processor's PROM monitor. As indicated in Chapter 11, this may be accomplished by modifying the monitor's source files, if they are available, or by patching the existing PROM program, if they are not.

Most monitor programs poll the processor's serial port for a command from the operator's console and then decode the command string by means of a jump table (or a **switch()** construct, in C). The first two characters in the command line determine which branch of the jump table will be taken. To add a floppy disk option to the monitor, one must either add another branch to the jump table or "take over" a currently existing branch. If the source code is available, a new branch may easily be added; otherwise an existing branch must be reassigned.

Typically, some feature of an existing monitor is of little use, and its branch location may be patched to transfer control to the floppy disk interface. Specifically, the two characters that select the branch when a command is decoded should be patched to a more appropriate command mnemonic for selection of the floppy disk interface. For example, they might be changed to **FL.** In addition, the branch address must be patched to the starting address of the driver. This will normally be a location in the PROM above the existing monitor program where the driver may be burned.

In operation, once the disk interface program is entered, all subsequent commands are processed internally. Control may be returned to the monitor by means of one of these commands—for example, **QU** (for "quit"). In the next section we will review other commands that might be implemented.

12.1.3.3 Floppy Disk File Access Commands

One can imagine a variety of commands that would be useful for accessing files on a floppy disk. We will examine a few in this section.

Since the file structure on the floppy disk is created by the UNIX **mkfs** ("make file system") utility and is therefore a standard UNIX file system, it is possible to create subdirectories on the disk using command **mkdir** ("make directory"). To be able to access these from the target system, we need a "change directory" command:

CD dirname

We would also like to be able to list the names of files in a directory. An **LS** command may be implemented for this purpose.

There are three types of files that are useful to a target system. They are: program, data, and command files. We indicated in Chapter 11 that UNIX program files begin with a standard a.out header structure. The header contains the program's starting address and size. Thus, a command to load a program file need only name the file:

LO progfile

By contrast, data files do not contain a header. As a result, it is necessary to specify the load address for these files:

CO datafile 100000

In this example, file **datafile** is copied to memory starting at address 100000 hex. Data files are useful for loading system configuration data that is needed during program initiation.

For systems that contain multiple processors, it is convenient to be able to load all program files automatically. This may be accomplished by implementing a command that reads the names of program files from a command file and sequentially loads the corresponding programs. As indicated in Chapter 11, if the processor that is reading the files from the disk encounters a program start address that is outside the range of memory on its board, it will automatically attempt to write the program to memory on the VMEbus. Thus, programs for the other processors may be loaded automatically across the bus (if processor memories are dual ported). An appropriate command to accomplish this is:

LI comfile

The command file for this "load-indirect" command is simply a data file that contains the names of programs to be loaded.

It is even more convenient to implement a command that will automatically load multiple program files and then start the program that was transferred to the loading processor's memory. This processor may then start the programs in the other processors using the mailbox and nonmaskable interrupt technique described in Chapter 11. An appropriate "load-indirect-and-go" command is

LIG comfile

Thus, a multiprocessor system may be loaded and started automatically by entering a single command.

It is useful to be able to visually monitor the file-loading process as it proceeds. Then, if the operation should stall for some reason, the nature of the problem may be more easily determined. To accomplish this, each load utility may be designed to display appropriate status information. For example, the **LO** command might display

progfile 100000 . . . .

Here, the program file name is followed by the load address and a series of dots. Each successive dot indicates that another block of file data has been loaded.

An example console display for an entire multiple processor load and start sequence is shown in Figure 12.1. Note that in this implementation the operator prompt is changed (to ">>") when the disk interface program is entered. After all files have been loaded and **progfile1** begins running, the console display shown in the figure would normally be replaced by an application program display.

It is also possible to add a feature to the disk interface that will allow running programs to access disk files. But since the files were created by the host system and are therefore of fixed size, a program must be written such that it does not attempt to write more data to a

```
>    FL
>>   LIG COMFILE

     progfile 1     1000 . . . . . . . .
     progfile 2     201000 . . . . . . . . .
     progfile 3     401000 . . . . .
     progfile 4     801000 . . . . . . . . . .

     (progfile 1 Starts—Redraws Screen)
```

Figure 12.1. Floppy Disk Load-Indirect-and-Go Command.

file than the file can hold. Direct access to files by a running program is most useful for reading and modifying system configuration data during system initiation. In the real-time mode, disk operations are often not practical, since disk access time is usually too slow.

12.1.3.4 Characteristics of a Floppy Disk Interface Standard

From our review of a specific disk interface implementation we may draw some conclusions concerning the general nature of a possible industry standard interface. We have seen that a disk that is formatted with a standard personal computer format and then configured with a UNIX file system may be accessed by a target system program that is less than 8K bytes in size. But the program had to be tailored to the host computer's particular implementation of the file system. Clearly, a standard would need to include a description of a specific file system implementation.

One problem with using the supplied UNIX **mkfs** command to build a file system on a floppy disk is that it normally partitions the disk into blocks that are large (e.g., 8K bytes). A large block size is appropriate for the file system on a host's main hard disk, but, for a floppy disk, the block size should be smaller so that disk space may be used more efficiently. Thus, a standard should also incorporate a block size that is more appropriate for floppy disks.

Perhaps an industry group could commission a software development firm to write host and target drivers and utilities for a floppy disk with a standard format and file system. This software could then be incorporated into the host and target systems provided by industry participants.

12.2 PROGRAM TESTING CONSIDERATIONS

Few veterans of real-time systems development would argue with the proposition that the most complex and time-consuming aspect of the software effort is program testing. The principle reasons why this is true are related to the inherent nature of real-time systems and to the tools that are available for testing them.

We have seen that real-time systems are generally concerned with servicing the needs of multiple devices that operate independently and therefore asynchronously. Thus, many of the "interesting" software problems are related to timing and/or data conflicts that occur as devices make simultaneous demands for service. To make matters more difficult, these instances of coincident demand may occur only occasionally and at apparently random times. Since these problems occur when the system is running at full speed, we need diagnostic tools that can monitor the system without obstructing its normal real-time activity. Unfortunately, we must usually make do with considerably less.

At present there are three basic types of tools available for testing real-time programs. They are the in-circuit emulator, the logic analyzer, and the PROM monitor.

The in-circuit emulator places logic between the processor chip and the remainder of the system. This inserted logic monitors and controls chip activity as the program runs at full speed. Specifically, it is possible to monitor the chip's address and data buses and its control and status lines by comparing them to prespecified values stored in "comparator" registers. The instrument may be instructed to halt processor operation when a match occurs, and instructions leading up to the condition may then be viewed. This is precisely the kind of information that is needed to test real-time systems. With this instrument, a program may be allowed to run at full speed until a fault occurs. Program instructions that were executed immediately before the fault may then be viewed to determine the source of the error. But the machine also has some drawbacks.

Generally speaking, in-circuit emulators are expensive—both initially and when it becomes necessary to upgrade them to support a new processor chip with a faster clock rate. They are also "intrusive" in the sense that the processor chip must be removed from the target system and replaced with a probe. Although some instruments provide support for testing at the source code level, software development tools must be chosen that are compatible with the instrument. In addition, no provision is generally made for testing multiprocessor systems. Later in this section, we will suggest that some of the features provided by these instruments could be more conveniently supported directly—as part of the processor chip. This would eliminate most of the limitations of the current approach.

In earlier chapters we saw that a logic analyzer may be used to monitor system activity. This instrument is invaluable for diagnosing hardware and software timing problems. It also has the advantage of not interfering substantially with the normal operation of a program, but it has limited utility in isolating software errors directly. Thus, if cost or other limitations prohibit the use of an in-circuit emulator, we are left with the processor's PROM monitor as our basic tool for diagnosing software problems.

The PROM monitor consists of a set of utilities that may be used to load, run, and test programs. Commands are available to read and change memory locations and processor registers, set breakpoints, start programs, and single-step through programs. The monitor is also capable of "disassembling" a program's binary memory image into readable assembly language statement syntax. Although it would be possible for a monitor to insert symbolic names for variables into the statements (by decoding a symbol table that could be included with the load module), this feature is not generally supported. As a result, it is necessary to make these translations manually—by referring to a program load map produced by the host.

Most current PROM monitors are, at best, crude tools for testing real-time programs. In addition to having to deal with a program at the assembly language level, the monitor does not offer any capability for viewing program activity as the program runs. That is, either the program or the monitor may run—not both at the same time. But, in spite of its limitations, the PROM monitor is the primary tool currently used to test programs. Clearly, some advances are needed in this area.

In the multitask program environment it is possible to provide some support for program monitoring in real time by including a diagnostic **debug()** task as part of the program. The task may be awakened by the interrupt handler for the system's application console serial port or by a handler for an additional test console port. In response to an operator-entered command, the **debug()** task may be run (perhaps preemptively) to execute a command.

A variety of useful commands may be implemented. For example, commands to read and write memory locations are possible. The **debug()** task may also be instructed to read and display one or more memory locations periodically. In this case the task might use the timing services provided by the **timer()** task discussed in Chapter 7. Obviously, the **debug()** task will require processor time to operate and will therefore modify normal program timing. But if its operations are kept relatively simple, the impact on program timing will not be substantial. Its primary benefit is that it provides a way to monitor activity as the program operates.

Program testing could also be facilitated by including some of the more useful services currently provided by an in-circuit emulator in the processor chip itself. For example, it would be very helpful to be able to determine the program instruction that changed a memory location. This might be implemented by including a "shadow" register that could be initialized with the address of the memory location of interest. The register contents would then be continuously compared to the processor's address bus as the program ran. If a match should occur, the processor would signal the event by generating an exception. The exception handler could then read the address of the instruction just after the one that caused the exception from the stack, since the processor automatically pushes this information onto the stack when an exception occurs.

It should also be possible to include support for tracing program flow backward from a fault. That is, we would like to be able to determine how a program arrived at a fault condition. Currently, program flow may be manually traced back only to the point of the first branch convergence. We would like to know which path the program took to arrive at that point. A chip feature that would save program counter values for the N instructions executed prior to the occurrence of an exception would provide this information. It might be implemented by establishing an N-deep FIFO of previous program counter values.

These two examples of possible chip support for program testing are typical of the kinds of in-circuit emulator features that could be provided. Indeed, now that it is possible to fabricate chips containing over a million transistors, it should be possible to include a comprehensive program monitor and a serial port to access it directly on the chip. For real-time system development this would be much more useful than, for example, an on-chip memory management unit.

Clearly, there is much room for improvement in the tools and methods available for testing real-time programs. Since a major component of current system development cost may be attributed to program testing, any significant advances in this area would be well received.

12.3 SYSTEM DEVELOPMENT SUPPORT

Anyone who has been a member of a team effort to build a complex electronic system has experienced the problem of gaining access to the equipment to perform tests. Often it is necessary to have control of the entire system to perform a single test. In the meantime, other team members must wait. This is an example of a classic scheduling problem: many people working in parallel on various aspects of a system and a system that must be operated serially to test each component. The situation is reminiscent of the processor scheduling phenomenon that we examined in Chapter 1. That is, an inherently serial processor must be scheduled to service several equipment sensors operating in parallel. Perhaps some of the techniques developed to deal with that problem could be applied here.

Our solutions to the processor scheduling problem were: (1) Schedule tasks efficiently on a single processor and (2) avoid the problem by using several processors. The first solution may work with program tasks, but people generally object to working odd hours and on weekends! A better solution is to provide multiple test sites for component testing.

One of the important byproducts of building a multiprocessor system based on standard components that interact via a bus is that much of the early testing may be done in parallel on separate test stands. Each processor board in a system and its associated sensor interface boards may be placed in a separate bus rack during initial hardware and software development. Since much early testing involves the establishment of equipment interfaces, this arrangement provides a way for people to work on these problems in parallel. Only when the hardware interfaces have been established will there be a need to merge system components into a single rack and deal with the issue of interprocessor communication.

Preliminary testing of communication interfaces may, in fact, be conducted independently at each test stand by running a simulation program on an additional processor board. This program should simply send and receive data and messages via the variables and queues defined in the system's common memory regions.

The multiprocessor approach also has several project management benefits. One important advantage is that it provides a clear basis for assigning functional responsibilities among personnel. The program for each processor may be assigned to one or a small group of people. With this arrangement, all interfaces to the other components of the system that each individual or group must deal with will by clearly defined—both logically and physically. Project management is also simplified by the fact that the system is divided naturally into functional and physical units that may be monitored independently.

At first glance, one may be tempted to conclude that the multiprocessor approach adds unnecessary complication to a system design. But, on further consideration, it becomes clear that this architecture simplifies both the construction and management aspects of a project. The individual processor programs are simpler and therefore easier to write and test, the equipment more closely matches the parallel nature of the real-time environment, and system components may be developed independently and concurrently.

1. Bach, Maurice J. 1986. *The Design of the UNIX Operating System.* Englewood Cliffs, New Jersey: Prentice-Hall Software Series.
2. Kernighan, Brian W., and Dennis M. Richie. 1978. *The C Programming Language.* Englewood Cliffs, New Jersey: Prentice-Hall.
3. McGilton, Henry, and Rachel Morgan. 1983. *Introducing the UNIX System.* New York: McGraw-Hill Book Company.
4. *Sun Operating System.* 1986. Documentation Sections on: File Formats, UNIX File System, Writing Device Drivers. Mountain View, California: Sun Microsystems, Inc.
5. McKusick, M., Joy, W., Leffler, S., and Fabry, R. *A Fast File System for UNIX,* University of California at Berkeley, ACM Transactions on Computer Systems 2, 3. pp. 181–197, August 1984.

Index